Change it UP

Transforming Ordinary Churches **INTO** Passionate Disciplemaking Communities

Dale H. Edwardson

xulon
PRESS

Copyright © 2013 by Dale H. Edwardson

Change It Up!
Transforming Ordinary Churches into Passionate Disciplemaking
Communities
by Dale H. Edwardson

Printed in the United States of America

ISBN 9781626974234

Unless otherwise indicated, Bible quotations are taken from The Holy Bible: New International Version. Copyright © 1973, 1978, 1984 by International Bible Society. Used by permission of Zondervan Publishing House. The author has added exclamations for emphasis.

www.xulonpress.com

Endorsements

Dale has written a very practical and useful tool in helping churches become more focused on disciple-making. Loaded with tools and resources, Dale has years of experience and a passion to see the Church alive and vibrant. Use this book as a way to move your ministry forward for greater effectiveness in fulfilling the Great Commission.

Dr. Dann Spader
President of Global Youth Initiative
and Founder of Sonlife Ministries

Of all that Jesus said, two promises have motivated The Christian and Missionary Alliance: "I will build my church" and "I will come again." With passion and energy, Dale Edwardson coaches church leaders and churches of all sizes to become disciple-making faith communities that impact their neighborhoods and the nations. Encouraging a thorough evaluation of both the obvious and the obscure aspects of the local church, this book is guaranteed to stir up questions and stimulate a fresh look at your church. Dale speaks with "hands on" experience as he has served both in C&MA pastoral ministry and denominational leadership/training.

Rev. Gary Benedict
President of the Christian and Missionary Alliance, U.S.

If you want a business as usual kind of read than this book is not for you. Dale does a masterful job in challenging his readers to think - really think. It is not enough to go through the motions in our church leadership. Too much is at stake and the need for more than cosmetic change is critical. Dale writes; "We are less adventurous with every decade and often live our lives around the security of established fixtures from our past." It is time to rethink, review and refocus the way we lead our churches. This book is both motivational and practical. It is written with piercing clarity and profound realism. It will carefully but unapologetically push into the places we feel most vulnerable and insecure but thankfully does not leave us hanging. Dale offers sound advice and innovative solutions that help us "change it up!" This is a must read.

Rev. David Hearn
President of the Christian and Missionary Alliance, Canada

Perhaps you have thought about how helpful it would be to hire a church growth consultant to walk beside you in ministry, to help assess the effectiveness of your church and make good suggestions about a way forward. Most of us would like a mentor that, but most of us can't afford it! Dale Edwardson is just that kind of person. He has read all the books you wish you could have read, and he has visited a thousand churches- some of them just like yours. If you can't hire a consultant, then the next best thing might be to read this book. It will give you new eyes on what your church is doing and how you can do it much more effectively.

Rev. John Soper
Lead pastor of Ridgeway Alliance Church and former
Vice-President of the C. & M.A., U.S.

The past couple of decades have been filled with talk about what it means to "do church." Too often lost in that conversation was what it means to "make disciples". This book brings those conversations together. At times provocative, always practical and unapologetically passionate for the church, the author challenges leadership to make the changes necessary to transform their church, whatever its style, into a disciplemaking community.

Rev. David C Freeman
Vice President, Strategic Interface for the C. & M.A., Canada

Dale Edwardson writes from a pastor's heart for the church in the 21st century. This work is full of practical "nuts and bolts" for a healthy congregation that Dale has learned from decades of effective ministry in the trenches. Anyone - pastors and laypeople alike - who wants to reproduce disciples can glean valuable nuggets here.

Dr. Rick Sessoms
President, Freedom to Lead International

The church must break free from the "consumer culture" that has been created over the past 30 years. Too many christians simply go to church expecting to "buy" a good sermon, a good worship experience or a good children's and youth ministry. This has created a generation of passive disciples who are not impacting their neighborhoods, their culture and ultimately their world. Dale Edwardson has written "Change it Up" to reverse this trend and lead us back to real discipleship. I strongly recommend this resource to pastors and leaders. It is part of the solution to help set us free.

Dr. Ron Walborn
Dean of Alliance Theological Seminary and Nyack College

For the pastor or church that has always wanted to hire a church consultant but didn't think they could afford one, "Change It Up!" is the next best thing to being there! The practical advice contained in these pages will help the newest pastor, the "stuck-in-the-middle-of-life" pastor and the pastor whose church can't see past the way they have "always done things around here." When you are done working through "Change It Up!", you will never look at your church the same again.

Dr. Rich Brown
Vice President for Student Development- Simpson University

With the desire to move the local church back to its' intended mandate, in "Change It Up", Dale Edwardson has provided for the church a comprehensive toolbox filled with about every tool imaginable for leaders in all the ministries of the local church for moving in a new and effective direction toward effective growth and disciple making. These are not theories with Dale. These tools have been proven as assets in his own ministry and the ministries of the hundreds of churches Dale has counseled toward change.

Rev. Bill Malick
National Director for Church Multiplication for the C. & M.A.
and founder of The Church Multiplication Training Center
and Boot Camps for Church Planters.

Dedicated to

My Dad and Mom, who raced before me,
Showing me how to never stop serving the Lord

My Wife, Gwen, who has walked beside me,
Riding the amazing waves of ministry

My Children and Grandchildren who follow,
Carrying the legacy to future generations

My wonderful co-laborers in the Kingdom,
Who share the privilege of changing the world

And

My Lord and King, who chose all of us,
Despite weakness and incompetence, to demonstrate
His Amazing Grace and Never-ending Power!

TABLE OF CONTENTS

INTRODUCTION

Change It UP!

This book is about discovering the things that will help your church become **more excellent** in accomplishing its Purpose and Mission.

It's about **uncovering** the details that really matter.
Because life is **simpler** when we take care of details.

Complexity can **cripple** us.
Simplicity of vision and purpose can **set us free**!

It's about **being attractive** to visitors and regulars alike.

It's **not** about
compromising your standards
to **grow** your church to be big and self-rewarding.

But it **is** about **changing** the things
that **Stand** in the way of people
Coming to Jesus in a new century.

It's about **helping** you Assess and Identify the areas
that you are **Doing Well** and the areas
that you **can Improve**
for Greater Effectiveness.

Now, that's what you're here for, isn't it?

So let's **CHANGE IT UP!**

We want that change to be an upward movement, a clear and calculated improvement. God calls us to excellence in everything we do. Everything drifts away from excellence, whether we like it or not. That creates a need for constant change.

However, we don't change simply for the sake of change. That would be ridiculous. It's critical that we systematically take the time to evaluate, refocus and then change for the sake of the Kingdom. This is about the Kingdom! We don't want to stand in God's way. We don't want to be The Obstacle!

God also wants you and your church to succeed in the tasks that He's given to you. So the purpose of this book is to

1) challenge you to **Rethink** the way you are doing church,
2) help you **Review** the form and functions of your church and
3) provide you with the tools to **Refocus** so you can achieve your goals for God.

If you're planting a church, this will help you establish a great plan. If you've landed in an established church, or if you've been serving in your church for years, use this moment as a great opportunity to stand back and evaluate what's really happening. I pray that this book will stir up a thousand "what if's" in your heart and mind.

Details matter, and they matter a lot! Nations rise and fall because of details and so do churches. As pastors and leaders, we can have grand ideas of what we want to accomplish. If we don't have the discipline and diligence to uncover the details that will help us succeed, we won't! I've watched too many pastors with grand ideas fall on their faces over and over again because they didn't pay attention to detail.

It's been said that the devil is in the details. It may be true. Details ignored can become the death of us! That's why **God cares about details**. From beginning to end, God fills His Word with detailed instructions on plans and programs and buildings and beliefs. He commands His children to do the details for their own best interest.

God says to Joshua, "Be strong and very courageous. Be careful to obey all the instructions my servant Moses gave you; do not turn from it to the right or to the left, that you may be successful wherever you go. Keep this Book of the Law always on your lips; meditate on it day and night, so that you may be careful to do everything written in it. Then you will be prosperous and successful." (1:7-8)

God gets even more personal with shepherds. In Proverbs 27:23, Solomon says, "Be sure you know the condition of your flocks, and give careful attention to your herds." Here's a chapter about character and humility and righteous action. The writer of this passage goes on to talk about personal well-being, success and having a future. What he's saying is: the shepherd who wants a future must pay attention to details and care for his sheep! Think about the shepherd who daydreamed or slept a lot, or who was focused more on better pastures or bigger profits than on the actual condition of the sheep. If he missed out on those little details of caring for, protecting and strengthening his flock, I'm sure that he didn't have much of a future in shepherding.

I personally was challenged every time I read this passage through my first thirty years of pastoring. I began ministry with a strong commitment to the care of all the sheep and whatever that entailed. As the sheep multiplied and as the responsibilities to oversee the pasture grew, I found myself slipping on details of care. I often found it easier focusing on big picture issues than small sheep compassion and attention. Then I would be reading in my devotions and Solomon would nail me once again! "If you don't care for your sheep, you won't have any sheep!"

This is just one example of details that matter. This book is about those details. Taking care of details is being "faithful in little things." See the big picture and overlook the depressed, suffering, immature or sensitive sheep and watch them slowly disappear. And watch how quickly loyalties can shift when you're not paying attention to details! Not all of the details are as important as the care of the sheep. But they are all important- especially if you want your sheep to multiply. Let me say one more time that **details matter to God!**

God wants us to take care of the details so the details don't take care of us. God want us to excelerate! **Excelerate** comes from the Greek words: excel and accelerate. Just kidding. But go ahead. You can use it. God wants us to excel and He wants us to accelerate. God want us to aggressively move forward with the purpose of making and multiplying as many disciples as we can.

And, again, from cover to cover, God calls us to be excellent in everything we do. He cares about quality, He cares about purpose and He cares about the detail. If you have any doubts, take another walk through Leviticus or Ezekiel. God understands the importance of looking carefully at what we are doing and making sure that what we are doing will in fact succeed. He even wants our end goal to be His very own glory. So His name and His reputation are at stake in everything we do! If that's true, then we need to step back and thoroughly assess our ministries.

So here's my question: Why would we want to do an average job of leading our churches when we can lead with excellence? Why would we? I hate doing details- always have and always will. But I see them and I know they have to be done. When I don't make sure the details are done, I always suffer. Always! That past experience drives me to find the details and get them done. I believe that most of us, given the opportunity, would rather change and excel than continue on doing the same old, ineffective things. I'm sure that's why you are reading this book and are beginning this adventure in assessment and change.

Get ready for thirteen chapters filled with loads of details about your church. In our first two chapters, we'll wrestle with change and why it's so necessary in order for us to be effective. Then we'll begin looking at your church, especially through the eyes of people when they actually come to visit you. We all know that the church is not a building; it's a family in community together. But to the watching world, church is a group of people, their building and services on the weekend. We'll approach our conversation from that point of view. We can correct their ecclesiology as they begin to enter into a deeper walk with God. So we'll begin our journey together in your neighborhood, evaluating your community image through the eyes of your neighbors. If we truly want to become the missional people that God has called us to be, we've got to see ourselves through the eyes of those who don't yet know Jesus! What does our church family look like to the watching world? Why would anyone ever come to our church gathering? What would we do with them if they did come? Are we ready? Most churches aren't! And what do we do with them if they come back? What do we do with people when they get saved? Do we have a plan? As we move through the book, chapter by chapter, we'll look at every detail of our ministries. And we'll look specifically at the process that we are taking new attenders, new believers and our people through on that road to maturity and multiplication. We'll affirm that God has literally commanded us to help turn self-serving non-believers and believers into fully devoted disciples who go and make more disciples. He's serious about that! I'll shout over and over again that **that is** the Main Thing! What's our strategy? Do we have one? And is it working? How do we measure that it's working? Do we see our church filled with authentic disciples who are going? If you don't have a plan, or if you have one that's not working, let's wrestle through to find God's plan for your church!

This book is meant for young pastors and leaders, older pastors and leaders, church planters, church rebuilders, cell birthers, pastors and leaders from every race and nation, in denominational and non-denominational churches, in churches under 200, over 5000, and all of the churches in between! Have I left anyone out? In other words, this book was written for you! It's meant to stimulate you and really make you think. It's **not** meant to be brilliant. That would be tough for me. It **is** meant to stretch you! You'll find that I will restate the same ideas in many different ways to get you to truly assess and evaluate your own ministries. For some of you, it will affirm what you know and have already applied.

Some of you will discover that you have drifted away from where you intended to go. Others of you will find yourselves swimming or perhaps drowning in a sea of information. Keep it simple. Start with one or two key areas that you need to change, and begin to work on them. Some of you will agree with most of what I share in this book. Some of you will be sad and others will be mad. Get mad! Argue with me! That's part of the process!

Dig deep into the foundations of your own beliefs and reasons for your actions and practices. I don't want you to agree. I want you to think! I want you to wrestle with God on issues and structures and forms that will make or break the future of your church. Some of you are stuck and you don't even know it! You were on course several years ago, but you've drifted. Or you're doing what you've always done and what you've always seen done. Maybe you're trying to do what someone else is doing, but it doesn't work for you! This isn't your Daddy's millennium! What worked yesterday isn't necessarily working today! And what works for Rick, Andy, Bill, Ed and Joel just may not work for you! Some of you have been doing the same things over and over again, and you're still wondering why you're getting the same lousy results! Wake up! Get uncomfortable. Measure the fruit of your labor! What should you be changing to become more effective for the Kingdom? Do you know where you are going? Do you have a plan?

I don't want you to read this book and do things my way. Come on! I want you to do things God's way, in your own uniqueness and creativity. Please don't miss this opportunity to look at every detail of your church ministry, with God. There is no doubt that all of us will find areas that we need to rethink, review and refocus, if we're open to Him and are willing to listen. So listen! Let this journey move you closer and closer to the standard of excellence that God deserves. Let the journey itself be an offering.

The Assessment

So Where Do We Begin?

I've written this book with the plan that you will aggressively walk through a process of assessment and change. I've also written an assessment that will help you in that process. Here's the way to move forward.

1) **Read the book first.** Read it through and underline or circle key areas of concern. This book will open up questions and insights on hundreds of issues that you will not get using the assessment alone. This book isn't an easy day or two read. In fact, it would better serve you to take a chapter or two at a time, so you're able to process, really look at yourself and begin to uncover areas of concern. I would encourage you as key leaders to read the book through individually before you do the assessment. Come up with your own list of issues and ideas that you can bring to the table. You can then pool them together, sort them out and set priorities when you come together as a team. It would be good to process this together by working through one or two chapters at a time. If you move through too quickly, you'll most likely miss out on this important opportunity to deal with details that matter. Your goal to reach your full potential needs to include all of your leaders asking hard questions and working through these important issues. The more people you involve in this process, the more ownership you will gain. "Plans fail for lack of counsel, but with many advisers they succeed." (Proverbs 15:22) And the more likely change will actually take place!

2) **Do the Assessment.** The assessment, sampled in the last few pages of this book, is found online at changeitup.com It's purpose is to help you think together as a team. It will aid you as you look at yourself in relationship to the details of your ministry. It's best done by a broad group of leaders from the church. Try to pull together enough representation from the body that you aren't reinforcing common areas of blindness. Birds of a feather will miss the same points together. In larger church settings, you will also want segment

groups working through the assessment and evaluating their own areas of ministry along with the broader vision and character of the church.

Let's have our first transparent moment here together. Many of us hate assessment. We have no problem assessing someone else, but many of us will work quite hard to avoid any kind of genuine assessment of ourselves. The reasons are obvious. Underneath whatever exterior we are wearing, most of us carry varying degrees of insecurity. Isn't it true? Our natural instinct is to protect ourselves from loss- loss of credibility, loss of dignity, loss of authority, and perhaps, a fear of the loss of our job. Now, let's face it. All of us have weaknesses that we have to compensate for. And assessment can provide the opportunity for our critics to try to hurt us or to expose those weaknesses. It can and it sometimes does! But a lack of assessment can leave us swimming in mediocrity. And it can hold us back from ever reaching our full capacity in Christ. We don't really want that, do we? Don't we want to reach our full potential as a church and as leaders? Let's not sacrifice all that God has intended for us by hiding from that potential exposure of weakness. Come on! Let's face our weaknesses and get on with it! If we can fix them and we haven't, then let's fix them. And if we can't, let's figure out how to surround ourselves with leaders who can help us and compensate for us. Many of us are already doing that. A healthy assessment process will only make us stronger and better for it. And God will use the process to deepen us and give us more clarity on where He wants to take us as leaders and as His church.

3) Take one section of the assessment at a time. Take as long on each section as you need to thoroughly discuss the issues.

Remember, you want to

    a) **Rethink** the details of that particular subject,
    b) **Review** the way you are doing what you are doing and
    c) **Refocus** in those areas that you discover you need to change!

I've sat through so many meetings where the agendas were rushed and few were satisfied in the end. I'm sure that I've lead some like that myself. Don't simply do a token assessment so you can move on! Scratching the surface only prolongs and increases the pain that will inevitably come. Don't mine for your own agenda. Let this process truly expose the issues that need to be addressed.

4) Make realistic plans. Set realistic goals. Make sure someone is responsible for each goal. Set deadlines. By the way, it always helps to have a coach. We're all blind to our own subjectivity on areas that really count and make a difference. We are!! So here's the question: why would we **not** want to become our very best? The right coaching can help us see and face our areas of weakness, bring about appropriate change and help us become the leaders and churches that God intends for us to be! Sometimes we can find that objective man or woman in our own church family who will help us and will speak the truth in love. But we will often need to look outside ourselves to find some excellent, non-biased coaching. Do what you need to do!

Some of you will read this book and will discover so many areas that need change that you will end up doing nothing. It's true! Don't do it! What a waste of time and energy! This journey is about the Kingdom and serving Him to the best of our ability. Let God help you accomplish His will as you go through this process. Don't get overwhelmed. Mark the book up. Take notes. Start making a list of priorities. Work together as a team. Do one thing at a time. And watch God begin to work with those changes!

Change it UP

PART ONE

Just Change It!

THOUGHTS ON CHANGE

For the past 33 years, I have looked in the mirror every morning and asked myself: 'If today were the last day of my life, would I want to do what I am about to do today?' And whenever the answer has been 'No' for too many days in a row, I know I need to change something.
Steve Jobs

All I want to do is change the world.
W. Clement Stone

A year from now you will wish you had started today.
Karen Lamb

1. CHANGE - TO BECOME OR MAKE DIFFERENT
"What the Church, Needs Now, is. . ."

Change is the beginning of revolution. Change is the start of transformation. Without change, the end draws near. That's a fact of life. Businesses die everyday, simply because they won't change. We see it everywhere. And churches lie empty and dormant across this land for the very same reason. Now, there are plenty of other reasons why businesses fail. Business cycles, recessions, over-saturation, poor leadership, poor management and poor planning are a few of many reasons why stores and companies all around us close their doors. But, in every case, they either can't attract customers or stop attracting customers with their products. And they die. In the same way, enough change takes place over time that churches that were once full and vibrant and attractive now sit empty and cold. Or they remain open with a declining number of people, focused on God but irrelevant to man. I remember as a teenager moving with my family to Fort Wayne, Indiana. My dad was called to pastor the Fort Wayne Gospel Temple. It had once seated over 3000 people and had been led by some of the greatest pastors in America. But when my dad accepted the challenge to pastor there, he arrived to less than 100 people. Amazing!

The world is constantly changing. That's one of the harsh realities of life. Look at the radical cultural changes of our new century. The world is getting smaller and is so interdependent and interconnected. The economy of one impacts us all. The revolution in one could change the course of history. Geopolitical change is ever before us, but the re-forming of our world with growing Islamic cohesiveness is eye-opening. Our own racial and generational cultures are shifting all around us. We've entered this new season with a perpetual theme of terrorism, economic uncertainly across the globe, dream-defying debt, political and employment upheaval and growing unrest. Things are constantly changing, aren't they? Now, it's exciting to those of us who are young and challenging to those of us who are middle-aged. But as we grow older, we tend to settle in and establish comfort zones. We mark our boundaries and ever-increasingly stay within them. We are less adventurous with every decade and often live our lives around the security of established fixtures from our past. And so it is with music. And so it is with where we shop or eat or buy our gas or vacation or worship. And so it is with most of the patterns of our lives. Isn't that true? We become less and less comfortable with change. But, again, the world is constantly changing, and if we aren't, we are left behind!

> We are less adventurous with every decade and often live our lives around the security of established fixtures from our past.

Let's take music for example. Most of us love the songs surrounding our youth. And some of us have stayed there! Don't you just love "Chicago?" You don't like "Chicago?" Are you kidding? Many of us spend our lives listening to the music of our past while the rest of the world keeps creating and inventing new styles and forms of musical expression. Some of us have embraced the full scope of decades of songs, while others of us have burrowed in, largely rejecting the constant changes of society. Picture a business, always catering to the music and expressions of the past. Apart from the rare exception, it would attract an aging and declining audience and eventually would place a closed sign on its door. There's no doubt about it. But here's the question- how many of our churches, living in the past, have religiously rejected the musical styles of today? Is the music of yesterday so much more righteous? Or do we just like it, because it was "our" music? And we wonder why we're declining and can't attract any visitors. Some of us have actually become comfortable with our shrinking size, perhaps subconsciously, knowing that at least we ourselves are happy and will be taken care of until the end. How sad. How un-Christlike. God hasn't called us to be comfortable. He's called us to change the world! And if we **are** to change the world, we'll often become uncomfortable, for the sake of the Kingdom!

How Fast are we Changing?

The world we live in is changing at lightning speeds. John Kotter, in his book, Leading Change, says: "The rate of change is not going to slow down anytime soon. If anything, competition in most industries will probably speed up even more in the next few decades." [1] It's true! And the church must pay attention! We must! Let's look at the vast changes happening all around us. Just look back at what's happened over the past 100 years. And then think about the past ten to twenty years. Everything is changing around us. Everything! Older generations struggle with new innovations and younger generations complain because change isn't fast enough. Isn't that also true? When will high-speed Internet really be high-speed? Twenty years ago, the world had barely heard of a personal computer. Today, we can barely live without one! Over thirty years ago, Xerox, IBM and, ultimately Apple, with a young Steven Jobs, introduced the world to the personal computer and then the Newton, the original iPad. The Newton flopped, Bill Gates grabbed a world monopoly with Windows, and Jobs was fired. Jobs returned ten years later to build Apple into one of the most celebrated companies in the world, and his iMac, iPod, iPhone, and iPad monopoly has changed everything again. Fifteen years ago, we were shifting to laptops. Today, we're shifting to pads. Most experts are predicting the death of the P.C. Paper was once the greatest invention. Now, we're celebrated when we go paperless! Tomorrow will bring new innovations and elements of change that we haven't even dreamed of! It's amazing! I love it!

Disruptive innovation is a concept that first appeared in the 1997 bestseller *Innovators Dilemma*. [2] The author analyzed why some innovations are so radical in nature that they change everything. Sustaining innovation improves the performance of existing products, but disruptive innovation brings new solutions to us that leap over and run past the products and lifestyle that we are used to. They disrupt companies and entire countries, which then have to change to compete, or they will wither up and go away! Digital everything has eliminated past products that we thought we couldn't live without. Where did the typewriters, dial-up phones, telegraphs, incandescent light bulbs and vinyl records go? Flash drives are replacing hard drives, which replaced discs, which replaced cassettes, which replaced eight tracks, which seemed so cool! Every change is hard at first. We're replacing lots of stuff at significant cost, but, personally, I can hardly wait to see what comes next. We're already doing amazing things with brain implants. We're making significant strides with hearing and seeing and limb technology. We're rapidly changing the speed and quickness of communications, soon moving from personal smartphones to access devices like wristbands, watches, rings, digital cell-glasses, and digitally-coated contact lenses. Think about that for a minute! Now we find the information we want. Soon it will find us, intuitively. Voice recognition, gesture and eye-tracking will make touch obsolete. Eye-tracking! Are you kidding?

Accredited degrees through free online education is a rapidly growing solution as inflating costs move our schools further and further out of reach for our students. Screen technology now is paper-thin and will be bent and applied everywhere to everything- watches, walls, desks, cars and we can only guess on what else! Wireless power will soon be built in to all of our counters and desks for appliances and our electronics. I've seen light bulbs glowing with no visible power source! What about apps? There seems to be an app for everything. But we ain't seen nothing yet! Apps (and the internet) will create the revolution of tomorrow. As apps are built into our homes and cars and lives, everything will be one second away- from monitoring, media and coaching to education, connecting and work! Imagine Siri on steroids! How about 3D printing? Instantly creating dimensional products, like equipment and weapons? And listen to this- we actually have amazing vehicles programmed to drive themselves! The science has been perfected and "safe" vehicles are on the road, right now, without drivers! These computer-driven cars and transport vehicles are safer than those driven by people like you and me! Jetsons, here we come! What? You haven't heard of the Jetsons? And where's the disruption? Add taxi, bus and truck drivers to the unemployment list for starters!

Of course, the Internet is one of the greatest disruptive innovations of our time. Think about all of the products that have landed on the Internet and talk about disruption! Several years ago, I read an article lamenting the demise of bookstores, accusing the Internet of destroying everything! And it's true that the impact is revolutionary! Now, some will quickly point at wars, recessions, politics or the economy as causes of these great changes all around us. While they certainly influence our circumstances, technology has been a far greater agent of change, actually shaping the way we live. Disruptive technology has produced cell phones, digital cameras, gaming systems, Skype, online education, healthcare competition, social networks and so much more. Consumer electronics, healthcare, telecommunications and education are but a few of the many industries that have been significantly impacted. Just think about all the changes that have taken place because of companies like Wal-Mart, Microsoft, Apple, Amazon, and Best Buy. Great companies like these still must find a balance between sustainable innovation and disruptive innovation, or they will die!

The world is changing so rapidly. In my first visit to Cambodia, it seemed like all the children, young people and adults were texting each other, in villages and cities alike. Here's a poorer third world country, highly impacted by simple, transferable technology. It's amazing! Seventy-two percent of American adults use the Internet, at least once a month. [3] The Internet has truly influenced the demise of retail America, considering the fact that so many of us flock to centers of e-commerce like Amazon, eBay and other .coms to buy our products. Remember Comp USA, Circuit City, Christian bookstores and Tower Records? Borders has died, Blockbuster stores are almost gone. Newsweek, perhaps as a last hooray, said goodbye to print and surrendered to a digital future. Apple, Netflix, Redbox,

Google and Amazon are all battling for categorical leads in the online marketplace.

True innovation comes as needs are identified that past products haven't totally satisfied. The cell phone was an entirely new innovation, like the laptop, and now, the pad. Everything will change again, as storage, speed, memory and clouds merge into consistent and reliable systems. Name an innovation or product, give it ten years, and it will already be disappearing, whether we see it or not! Sony, IBM and Microsoft had their day. Apple, Google Samsung and Amazon are having their day. As these great companies lose their innovative and disruptive edge, they will fade and new names and leaders will show up. Companies have their season in the sun, time passes by and the world moves on. Sounds rather Biblical, doesn't it?

Along with the changes of technology come the radical cultural changes of a new century. We see it happening everywhere. In the midst of things that would divide us, there has also been an increased drive to resource our desire for greater social contact. And, of course, technology has again come to the rescue. Social networking is also one of the greatest disruptive innovations of the new millennium. Arriving to a generation hungry for connection, companies have come and gone, competing to be the mother of friendship. Remember when Facebook seemed like it was gaining world domination. And then, suddenly, it began to fade. Remember the great "Timeline" transition, and then there was the IPO. It all spelled the beginning of the end! And Google+ slowly took its place. Now, I'm just kidding. But by the time you read this, everything will have changed! The concept of people connecting with each other has been around for a long time. Companies have created, marketed, grown, led and then lost their edge. Remember AOL and chat rooms, Prodigy, MySpace, and Buzz? These and so many more have been left behind for Facebook, LinkedIn, Twitter, Yelp, Tumblr, Foursquare, Yammer, Path, and hundreds of other companies and apps. Innovators will keep looking at the needs of socializing Earth Dwellers and will continue to leap–frog over each other to try to gain the largest market share. Isn't that way it's always worked?

Here's the big question you've wanted to ask: What in the world does all this have to do with the church? Everything! It has to do with relevance. It has to do with being truly missional in the twenty-first century. It has to do with actually impacting our world! We're surrounded by rapidly changing cultures, generations, and ethnic diversities. Everything's swirling all around us. As we stand still, we drift further and further behind! For example, we're all surrounded by innovative change. We can be part of it or we can be left behind. Think with me. Why in the world would we use an overhead projector when we can project in high definition or 3D? Let's go back a few years. Why shout when we can use a mike? Why use candles when we can use lights? Why use bulletins when we can use smart phones and pads? Why ask for questions when they can tweet or message their answers? Why call when we can e-mail, text or video chat? And it goes on and on.

Everything keeps changing. We need to change with it, and we need to take advantage of it! Why should the church be the last to change? Shift is happening. Why can't we actually lead appropriate change? Many Christian leaders and churches are bringing their own disruptive and sustaining innovations to the table that will better serve the cause of Christ. Why not learn from each other and reach new generations for Christ with tried and tested formulas as well as great, new innovations? Is your neighborhood changing? Why not diversify? Are you maximizing the potential that God has given you as a church community? Are you thinking about things like that? Here's one great, big innovative idea we'll focus on–why not make disciples? No–I mean real disciples who reflect Christ's mind, character and priorities, and they multiply it! Now, that would be disruptive. That would truly change everything!

Listen to this quote by Tim Cook, CEO of Apple in an NBC interview by Brian Williams near the end of 2012:

> Our whole role in life is to give you something you
> didn't know you wanted. And then once you get it,
> you can't imagine your life without it. And you can
> count on Apple doing that. [4]

Now, that actually sounds a lot like Steve Jobs. But doesn't that also sound like what our role in life should be? Isn't that what the life of Christ is all about? Isn't that what we're supposed to be doing? Shouldn't we be dreaming up ways to be so relevant, so practical, so revolutionary that the world stands back with amazement? That's what Jesus did. And that's what God wants now. That's what will happen if the church wakes up to the opportunities before us!

Social Networking

Let's talk about social networking and your church as one example of our changing culture. So many of our people have joined some kind of network online. Numbers are growing rapidly. People find their friends and then encourage more friends to join. It's embarrassing and alienating to those on the outside who haven't yet joined "the network." Being on the network continues to be the "in" thing, for now. So everyone joins. For different reasons! Some join for friends and dates and any sort of social action. Others use it as an escape from the real world. Why watch TV or go out when you can play Farmville? Many use the network to communicate their message or to market their product. Lonely people join. Social people join. Companies join. Business people join. Bored people join. They join for many reasons, but one purpose–connecting on some level with a select group of people in ways that would never happen in real life.

Think about that! In a circle of friends, communicating about the details of their lives becomes normal in the average social

network. Shy people with limited social skills who rarely communicate with more than a handful of people now feel the confidence to be a part of a larger group of friends. Those friendships may never go deeper than reading and writing on the Internet, but something's changed- forever! We now have the opportunity to have closer relationships with family, current and past friends, acquaintances, leaders across the land, missionaries around the world and perhaps our entire church! Amazing! Let's look at the possibilities in all of this! Why ignore it when we can encourage it and use it for the kingdom? Here are just a few ways that churches are using social networking:

1) Picture everyone in a small group or a specific ministry sharing together on the same network and the leader using that as a leadership and disciple-making tool.

2) Imagine everyone in the church on the network and the pastors and leaders use that as a way to encourage their people, promote events, celebrate wins, and build kingdom thinking. It's happening everywhere!

3) Think about everyone in the church purposefully connecting with their lost friends on the network and how much more quickly that will generate deeper friendships. Think about what happens as others from the church friend them and begin to interact with them!

We'll talk more about ideas like these as we move through the book. Again, you need to know that this is already happening everywhere! So many churches are taking advantage of the opportunity to better connect the body with each other, with their leaders and with the lost! But here's one more question that some of you are asking. What about the evils of Facebook and other social inventions? Here's the truth- there's always evil lurking around every corner. Bad people use the Internet for evil purposes. Social networks are filled with opportunities that can destroy lives. We all know that the Devil can and has used the TV, the telephone, movies, music, bowling alleys and so many other things to destroy lives. But God has used those same tools to breathe life, strength and missional vision into so many, including you and me. Bored and addicted people can waste hours on Facebook and Farmville. Wrong relationships can happen, pornography can be hacked into an account, and immature people can blame, stab, swear and slander others. An article in *Wired Magazine* recently pointed out, somewhat in jest, that one of the most damaging side effects of social networking is the narcissism that it creates in so many of us. [5] I think it's true. Life truly becomes all about us! Think about it for a moment. Well, the list goes on. Social networking can certainly lead to sin, but it can also lead to salvation and so many good things. So let's seize the moment! We certainly need to watch out and warn others against potential issues, but we can't be afraid to use the best of today's innovations for God and the advancement of the Kingdom.

This too will Change. Every action causes some sort of reaction! You can count on it. Networks like Facebook will miss the mark as they try to anticipate needs. Fans will react and move on to new companies like Path that are more in tune with changing cultures. I predict that as many of us tire of a constant stream of gibberish, we'll establish ourselves with smaller, more private circles of friendship. Technology will get faster, and instant group "FaceTime" features will thrive. I do believe that we are simply getting a taste of things to come. The world will get smaller with instant communication. Our hunger for relationships balanced by our desire for privacy will drive innovation. All of this will significantly impact our life as a church community, at home and around the world. We'll capitalize on it and it will help us be even more missional! Training, conversations, telling the Story, care, prayer and accountability will be as close as the source of our wireless access- our smartphone or earpiece or glasses or ring or. . . . Imagine how this will accelerate our ability to have tens of thousands of preaching and training points in homes and villages all around the world! I can only begin to imagine the potential before us to change the world for Christ! Innovators will keep dreaming and we will keep on benefiting from the latest and greatest. But, for today, we live with our current tools of communication and the opportunities that surround us. So let's use them.

Back on the topic- this book is far more about change than it is about innovation. My goal isn't to help us become the most innovative and creative churches on the block. That just isn't possible nor is it intelligent for most of us. In fact, Jim Collins, whom I'll soon talk about, is quick to point out:

> Technology and technology-driven change has virtually nothing to do with igniting the transformation from good to great. Technology can accelerate a transformation, but technology cannot cause a transformation. [6]

What we need, more than anything else, are churches transformed into healthy, vibrant communities of believers significantly impacting our world for Christ. As technology supports that, great! But my goal is to help us become relevant and get on track! Just remember, there's our track and then there's God's track. Elmer Towns, Ed Stetzer and Warren Bird join in writing a great book summarizing the many styles of churches and movements that God is using across our nation. *11 Innovations in the Local Church* is a thoughtful work, challenging us to find unity as we look at the challenges of a changing culture instead of competing in the area of new ideas. They press us on the need to change- appropriately. And they challenge the premise that we need to be innovative, without a God-guided reason and End-Product in mind. In a section entitled Too Much Innovation, they say, "The point is this: We need to constantly ask, 'Will God be pleased with our innovations?' Life isn't about what we can do- it's about obeying what Gods wants us to do. We must make sure our actions are right in His eyes!" [7] In the next chapter, we'll talk about why so many of our churches are derailing, whether we know it or not. The purpose of this book is to challenge us and to show us how to aggressively change the things in our own church culture that will then allow us to influence and impact our surrounding communities. We want to be followers of

Christ, bringing radical transformation to a world that's desperately lost. That disruption will be so massive to your people and your community that God only knows the outcome that it could bring. Now, that's innovation to the max! Let it come!

How Essential is Change?

Change is critical. Change is hard. Change opens doors of great opportunity. Change can take away our comfort. Change makes life better for some people, but it's often at the expense of other people. That's the difficulty with change. You just can't please all of the people, ever. Never! So if you want to die with your church, don't change anything. But if you want God's great future for your church, you'll have to take risks and accept the pain that comes with change. Hundreds of books have been and will continue to be written on the important subject of change. They constantly move to the top of the best seller's lists, both in the marketplace and in the church. Go to Barnes and Noble or Amazon and check it out! For example, Peter Drucker, one of our brilliant leaders in business and management shares these thoughts in *Management Challenges of the 21st Century*:

> Everybody has accepted by now that change is unavoidable. But that still implies that change is like death and taxes—it should be postponed as long as possible and no change would be vastly preferable. But in a period of upheaval, such as the one we are living in, change is the norm. [8]

One of those classic best sellers of recent years dealing with the subject of change and excellence is Jim Collin's book, "Good to Great." Collins shares the research of almost 1500 companies in search of those that had truly transformed from good to great. Only eleven companies demonstrate the same, consistent seven qualities that helped them become truly excellent businesses in the marketplace. And can you guess the central theme that quietly moves beneath the fiber of every action? It's change! Changing a leader or leadership style. Changing the leadership paradigm. Facing the inevitable changes that must come, no matter how difficult they are. These represent a few of the insightful concepts that Collins presents so clearly. Change! The company that focuses on the need for continual, appropriate change has the potential to succeed, but the company that doesn't begins to fade away. There's got to be something there that we can learn from as we look at excellence and viability in the church. By the way, Collins begins his book with this massive thought- "Good is the enemy of great!" [9] Good is the enemy of great! "This is good enough." "This will be O.K." How many of us have been satisfied with a good past that's diminishing into a not-as-good future? That's not O.K!

Why is it such a critical subject and why are so many writers addressing this issue? It's because of our blindness! We don't see! It's amazing! We start or enter our ministries and churches with our very best efforts, eager to serve and succeed. But we're all blind, great and small. I'm talking about you and me. We just can't see what we can't see. There are so many factors at play all around us and they are always changing. So we all make mistakes and mis-calculations, even at our very best. Changes have to be made. They have to! And they have to be made- again and again and again. What are some of the keys to appropriate change?

1) **Be flexible- Flexibility is key to succeeding in an ever-changing world.** Some of us can do change quickly and repeatedly. In fact, some of us thrive on change, to the horror of many who are spinning around us. Others of us can't- or won't and don't want to! Some of us will cling to a method or policy of the past or our latest bright idea, if it kills us. Pride and stubbornness often keep us from being flexible. It's hard to admit that we are wrong and move on. But we have to, if we what to succeed!

39

Listen to this great example of appropriate flexibility. A woman living on a fixed income saved up over time to get her first computing device. She walked into an Apple store with great excitement and a wad of cash to buy her iPad. Can you imagine her shock and pain when an employee told her that Apple could only work with credit? It was the nationwide policy! The woman left with her dream shattered! But word of this situation leaked to management and, can you believe it- change happened! Not only was the policy rewritten, but two Apple employees delivered a new iPad to this woman, at her home, free of charge! Talk about quick flexibility. Now, we could excuse and write off this action all because of the company's need for good press. But the point is, they did the right thing! Apple could have stubbornly clung to the carefully crafted policies of the past and missed the opportunities for today. Instead, they seized the moment and brought about the right change! How many companies and churches and leaders won't flex even when everybody else sees that change is called for?

Here's a novel idea: Have you ever thought that you actually might be the problem person in the room instead of the other people you're identifying and pointing at? Hopefully most of us realize that we are our own worst enemy! As the famous sage Pogo once said, "We have met the enemy, and he is us!" Listen to these thoughts from Robert E. Quinn:

When we see the need for deep change, we usually see it as something that needs to take place in someone else. In our roles of authority, such as parent, teacher, or boss, we are particularly quick to direct others to change. Such directives often fail, and we respond to the resistance by increasing our efforts. The power struggle that follows seldom results in change or brings about excellence. One of the most important insights about the need to bring about deep change in others has to do with where deep change actually starts.[10]

We all carry enough baggage in our own personalities and subjective worldviews to make _us_ God's first priority when it comes to change. Let me share a bit from my own journey. Through the years, I've had to really work hard to listen first to the Lord and then to people around me. My mind is always full of ideas, so it's easier to talk than to listen. Do I hear an "Amen" out there from people close to me? I have always known and taught that we all have invisible weaknesses, waiting to bust out at inappropriate moments. Whenever my weaknesses have been exposed, I've always been embarrassed. I've hated it! I still do! But my drive to do well usually has been strong enough to motivate me to work on change. In all honesty, there have been many times, more than I will ever know, that I didn't listen, blinded by my own stubbornness or forgetfulness or laziness! And I've lost out! I know that there have been many friends along my path who knew that I didn't want to hear their insight on my deficiencies. It can be so tiring to hear, think about and work on change, especially when it's personal! This whole issue of blindness leads us to our second key.

2) **Listen to others- it's so necessary!** Listen to me! I'm talking to you now! Don't protect yourself and your emotional frailty. Be bold! Others can see what we cannot. Zig Ziglar says: "Little men with little minds and little imaginations go through life in little ruts, smugly resisting all changes which will jar their little worlds!" I don't want to be one of them. Do you? Now, we can eliminate the seers by surrounding ourselves with yes-men, and we can subtly create an atmosphere of fear and intimidation. But let's see how

far that will get you! I've watched leaders, board members, secret power brokers and/or pastors, fearful of opposition and freethinking, work so hard to establish rules of silence, uniformity and conformity. It's so sad. They lose- every time! Just give it time and it will blow up or die, and they will be gone. Or the Holy Spirit will be gone. In fact, He may already have been long gone! That reminds me of a story I once heard when I was working decades ago in the South. A black man tried to visit a white church back in the days of segregation. He arrived late and planned to leave early. His heart's desire was to simply slip in to worship the Lord and hear His word. Three weeks in a row, as soon as the pastor stood up to preach and saw the visitor, he asked him to leave. When the black man died and went to heaven, he asked the Lord about it. And the Lord said, "Don't worry about it. I couldn't get past the front door either!" Think about how often we've protected our presumptions and prejudices and missed out on God!!!

> I've watched leaders, board members, secret power brokers and/or pastors, fearful of opposition and freethinking, work so hard to establish rules of silence and uniformity. It's so sad. They lose- every time!

Here's a great word to ponder- The Truth will set you Free! Let's not be afraid of the truth. No matter how hard it is to hear, it will lead us to the changes that we really need to make, for everyone's sake. Seek the wisdom and advise of others. Learn to hunger for it, to depend on it. I've already said that Solomon, in Proverbs 15:22, shares this critical insight: "Plans fail for lack of counsel, but with many advisers they succeed." That sounds like decent advice, doesn't it? Humble servant leadership ranks at the top of every list of truly great leaders. In fact, Jesus even says a few things about it. In Matthew 23, Jesus warns us not to be like the religious leaders of His day, imposing self-serving rules and regulations on their people, protecting themselves from exposure. He attacks their blindness and unwillingness to see the Truth! And in the midst of it, He says, "The greatest among you must be a servant. But those who exalt themselves will be humbled, and those who humble themselves will be exalted!" Humbling ourselves has to include our willingness to give up control and to look honestly at areas in our own lives and ministries that need to change. How sad that there are pastors everywhere who are failing simply because they've isolated themselves! Charles Snow writes an amazing and practical book for all pastors and ministry leaders, describing the very things that bring us down. In *5 Ministry Killers and How to Defeat Them*, Snow unpacks these issues and more: 1) head-in-the–sand mentality, 2) misdirected emotional investment, 3) unhealthy response to ministry killers, 4) an attitude that "God and I can handle this," and 5) lonely, hurting wives. [11] What a powerful and insightful list of the killers we face! Can you see some connections that each of these areas has in common? They all point to leadership in isolation, disconnected from the input that God intended for us to have.

Many of us as pastors and leaders actually fear assessment and outside consultation. We might not admit it, but it's true! We'd have no problem if the assessment didn't include our own performance. But it usually does, and that often scares us to death. Some of us have had bad experiences with assessments and consultants and the rest of us have heard the stories. I know I have. And there are bad ones! Our egos are often more fragile than we'd like to admit. And we don't need one more person taking shots at us! Isn't that right? I know I didn't! But here's the sad reality. Instead of having that young and fresh appetite and eagerness for excellence and effectiveness, no matter what the cost, we end up virtually hiding so our weaknesses don't get exposed and things don't get out of control. Come on! We've got to get past our own insecurities and fear of exposure. What are we trying to hide? Whether we are leaders in churches of 50 or 50,000, we're all messed up! We all have blazing weaknesses! Paul tells us in Romans that God picked us as believers to confound the world- His power manifested in frail beings! And I'm convinced that he picked us as leaders with the same goal in mind. As everyone sees us with all of our weaknesses and inadequacies, even at our very best, and as they watch the transforming and enabling power of the Holy Spirit in us, they will be amazed. That's the story He wants us to tell, not the one about having to cover up and control everything so our weaknesses don't get exposed!

How in the world do we learn to trust others in this difficult arena of assessment and change? There is no easy formula, but there is a place to start. A wise man once said: "Trust in the Lord with all your heart. Don't lean on your own understanding. In all your ways acknowledge Him, and He will make your path straight!" He will straighten things out in front of us, if we trust Him first. As we trust Him, as we humble ourselves before Him, He will make our hearts tender, He will help us listen better, and He will help us change! It always starts with Him, doesn't it? As we trust the Lord and draw close to Him, He will give us the wisdom of who to trust and how to work with change. We clearly can't trust everyone around us. That's life! Remember Judas, the treasurer? But we can learn to let go of our control and move forward as we listen to Him and walk in His Spirit. That is the secret.

3) **Don't be afraid to change.** Many of us could never be the President. We'd just stare at that suitcase and the nuclear button- forever, frozen, unable to push it, no matter how grave the crisis! But there are so many times, in ministry and in the church, when we just have to push the button, whatever the cost. We may lose people. We may lose leaders. We may lose resources and salary. We may lose our job. We may get an endless sludge of nasty emails or phone calls. But that's life! "That's what you signed up for, Sonny, when you took this here job, whether you realized it or not." Ed Stetzer wrote this in an *Outreach Magazine* article: "The most common factor for successful transitioning is leadership- specifically, equipping and preparing leaders. Painfully, the issue is too often ignored by those who would rather wag a finger at unruly congregations and congregants."[12] Collins, in "Good to Great," addresses the critical need to confront

the brutal facts of our current reality, whatever they may be. That concept has to include looking at ourselves and our leaders, as well as the systems and structures that we have created. Collins writes his entire book on the greatness that comes as we resolve to change and determine to prevail to the end. [13] Picture that soldier facing his first battle and the decision to pull the trigger- or not. Some of us are afraid to start pulling or to keep pulling the trigger on change. But if we don't, we'll never see the light of our dawning potential that God has created for us. Come on! Pull the trigger!

> The time it takes to build a unified leadership working together to bring about critical change is negligible in comparison to the future that can be reached!

4) **Get your leaders on board first.** Change has to be modeled and led by your entire team of leaders if you want significant, long-lasting results. Senior pastors must have the hearts and minds of their staff and wives or husbands to bring about church-wide change. And the board has to be on board! Church families are blessed and are significantly impacted as they experience a completely united leadership moving forward to accomplish God's will, no matter how hard the changes are. The time it takes to build a unified leadership working together to bring about critical change is negligible in comparison to the future that can be reached! So take the time to win those hearts and minds! Change is a team sport! We have to have everyone on board- on the bus, in the right seats, all eyes forward and minds focused, working together to influence appropriate change. If anyone, over time, can't get onboard, there are plenty of other buses a 'coming. Unity and teamwork is critical!

But what if..? What if I'm new? What if this is a new church plant and my core group isn't solid? What if half of my board members won't get on board? What if I can't see eye to eye with a very influential staff member? What if I've tried and tried to lead this charge and I'm tired and ready to give up? Now we meet the tough realities of life. These difficulties represent a few of the reasons why so many leaders give up and never do bring about the changes that are needed. Here's the truth. Some churches will die! It's inevitable. There are enough entrenched obstacles in the way that no one could ever break through them. No one! Not even you! Secondly, some of us will lead change better than others of us. Actually moving to another church may be the key for the future, both for the pastor and the current church. But thirdly, for most of us, we need to outsmart our circumstances! We have to pray and seek counsel, followed by more praying and seeking counsel. And then we have to either overcome or find a way around our obstacles.

A greater part of our solution is patiently working with people. Some of us want quicker remedies than God has in mind. The process of winning hearts and minds and growing through that process is often far more important to God than the next step that we have planned! Years ago, Robert Logan, in his book, *Beyond Church Growth*, envisioned the key ingredients needed in today's church.

> The successful church of the twenty-first century and beyond will be one that learns how to listen to people, establishes a culturally relevant philosophy of ministry, and adapts its ministry strategies to their ever-changing needs. [14]

If we want to be relevant and meet real needs, we've got to start by listening to people! We have to! If you are new to your church or you're a church planter, it will take time to earn trust and the rights of leading. Most of us want to bypass some of these early steps because the need for action is so great. We forget that in the foundational stages of development in our churches, God is more concerned about growing and deepening people than raising buildings and programs. I was so frustrated as a young pastor when our numerical growth suddenly plateaued for four whole years! We had experienced significant growth and would experience it again. But what were we doing wrong? I didn't realize until years later that God was unifying us, deepening our roots and raising up leaders for decades to come. It was all part of His plan! Jesus spent half of His ministry developing relationships and building an atmosphere of trust and love. All of this was done before He began to do His broader national ministry and more demonstrative events. Most of these men that He was hanging out with became the leaders of our movement! We probably could learn something from Him!

I don't want to ignore the fact that people who won't work with us have to move on. There have been many times when I've prayed and prayed and prayed, and some leaders have changed while others have exited. In a few cases, I've had a series of those difficult talks, and then I've had to help them move on. And, at the same time, in situations like this, God is always preparing leaders, perhaps hidden in our midst, who will choose to live the Kingdom with us today in order to have a great future tomorrow. We'll spend more time throughout this book looking in detail at ways of working with difficult people and circumstances.

5) **Be clear. There are times when we see the changes that are necessary for the next step in our church or ministry, but we don't make them clear to our people.** And we don't even know it! We think it's their problem, but it's ours! I've done this myself. We see the issues clearly, and we see the reasons for change and what the solutions will bring. But we have a difficult time convincing others of the need for that change. We're passionate, we're determined and we feel deterred! What we need to do is slow down, take a breath, step back and start over. Write it down. Weave your way through your logic. What's the problem, why is it a problem, and what are the steps of change that we need to walk through? Sit down with several friends who think clearly and honestly. Walk each of them through your process of thought and see if they get it. Ask them for help. What isn't clear? What pieces

47

of information have you left out? What needs to be added or stated in a better way?

We'll talk a lot about clarifying our purpose to our people. That's what we have to be clear about. Our people need to see that the changes that we are making are purposeful and critical to the future of our church, or they won't agree. Rick Warren, pastor of Saddleback Church in Southern California, says this:

> . . .your most important task is to redefine your purpose. Forget everything else until you have established it in the minds of your members. Recapture a clear vision of what God wants to do in and though your church family. Absolutely nothing will revitalize a discouraged church faster than rediscovering its purpose. [15]

Sometimes our very presentation and personal body language turns our audience off. Some of us don't realize how strong and unwavering we come across. We lose our listeners before we have barely begun to speak with them. By the way, there are several fruit of the Spirit to help us with that. If this is your problem, you probably won't believe it and won't want to hear it. And people may not tell you what they know you don't want to hear. Listen up! If you want that great future that you've been dreaming of, you've got to learn and listen, whether you like it or not. Change begins with you and me! This again comes back to slowing down and learning how to truly win hearts and minds. Jesus demonstrated that strategy and lifestyle everywhere He went and look where that's brought us today! That leads us to the next key.

> People want to be brought along. They want to be respected. They want to know that their opinion counts. They want to be walked through the same process and logic that you had to walk through.

6) **Implement change with the blessing of your people- as best you can!** Some of us are impulsive or impatient- we just can't wait to bring our people along. You lose! Always! You may call it decisive leadership, but it's not. There are fewer and fewer tribes left on the planet that don't mind a dictatorial pastor and leadership. Fortunately, there are many changes that can be made in the life and programming of ministry and the church that don't involve the majority of our people. They wouldn't know the changes that we're making and they wouldn't care. But my observation is that, far too often, we will make decisions impacting the people without ever conferring with the people. We certainly don't like that in government, do we? By the people, for the people! And they don't like it in their churches either. People want to be brought along. They want to be respected. They want to know that their opinion counts. They want to be walked through the same process and logic that you had to walk through. Sometimes we take months of endless interaction and dialogue behind the scenes and then expect our people to accept our quick and brief mandate- without question. How unkind and unthoughtful! Now, we can't be looking for their unanimous approval. They won't all agree. But there's got be a process to help bring people along on change, no matter how big the church or ministry. There just has to be!

Others of us want everyone on board before we implement change. You lose too! You'll never do it! You just can't get everyone on board. It would take forever trying and you'll miss months and years of opportunity. Introduce the plan, walk them through the logic and help them understand, give them time to process, listen to their input, keep asking God for wisdom, and then, pull the trigger! Decide to do the change, or decide not to do the change. There will always be a price, either way. Don't go on forever. If the leadership is leading, God is leading and the vast majority seems to be on board, go for it! The rest will come along, or not. It doesn't matter. You've done what's needed to be done! But, if the people aren't with you, you'd be so foolish to move forward. There may be a better time in the future. There may be a better change to work on first. Perhaps you need to go back to building relationships and maturity in the body. But here's the fact- you can't lead if no one follows! I've watched pastors lead that charge, and it's just a matter of time that they've learned the hard way or they're out the door! On very rare occasions, God will give a clear indication that He has called you to move against the majority, regardless of the cost! He's the only One who knows what will happen next. He may want to break hearts or He may be done playing church. He's made that call throughout history to faithful men and women, like Stephen, for example. But you better be sure that you are hearing from God and not making it up as you go! Too many pastors have thought that it was God speaking when the evidence ultimately proved that it was only their egos.

7) **Never stop changing!** Change can be tiring and frustrating and endless, if we are determined to be relevant and missional, both as leaders and as the people of God. It can be tiring if we are always in the middle of it. It can be frustrating, especially if the change jeopardizes something that we love and have invested in. And it's endless! It just never ends. Some people quit their jobs, or their church, just to stop the change. They can't take it anymore! We've already said that many people prefer less and less change as they age. Some long for retirement so they can get out of the race and stop the change. But it doesn't stop! We either stay a part of it, or it passes us by. So jump in! The water's refreshing. Don't be afraid. Open your eyes. Look at all of the potential that we have! Let's learn to swim, carefully focused, one day at a time, one change at a time. Let's pace ourselves- let's not spend our energy all at once. If we want to endure and last until the end, we need to be careful not to move too fast or too slow. And remember, this is God's Church- it's His Kingdom! We're just along for the ride! We've got to continually rely on His guidance and strength or we will not survive!

Here's one of my own stories of resistance to change and what it cost me. God allowed me to pastor a church that grew significantly over several decades. We multiplied people and services and developed a healthy blend of attenders crossing both socio-economic and generational divides. I loved having everyone in every service- the young, the old and everyone in-between! I felt that cross-pollenization would help us best achieve our ultimate goals of growing healthy disciples of all ages. I even wrote a grad-school paper on the value of unity and staying together generationally as a people. Listen to this! I wanted to reach and inspire each generation, so we would sing three styles of worship songs in every service. I'd joke about making everyone happy a little and mad a little, for the sake of being together. And it worked! We grew and grew over 24 years of ministry. There's no doubt that we accomplished many good things with this strategy. But there's more to the story.

Near the end of my time serving in this ministry, my college pastor and my oldest son decided to begin a weekly Sunday night worship event, tar-geting young people and young adults, beginning at 9 p.m. They started with 40 in attendance on the first night and it grew to 6-700 young adults in less than a year! Can you believe it? Hundreds of young people showing up late in the evening, every Sunday night, right before a new school day, seeking after God, with so many of them passionately worshipping with all their hearts! It clearly was a powerful movement of God, in His time, for His purposes! Vibrant testimonies were being shared each week, with a constant flow of non-believers attending and getting saved and dozens upon dozens being baptized. Wow!

As I stood in the shadows and watched this event take place week after week, I realized that most of these young adults would never have set foot in our other worship services. They just wouldn't have! Call it prejudice, immaturity, or anything you want. The fact is that they would never have tolerated the three music styles and other things that we presented in our Sunday morning culture. And we would never have been able to reach them for Christ! But, attracted by their own style of music, by younger leaders and a younger room of attenders, they came! They came to the same room, to the same Jesus, and then moved into small groups for deepening discipleship! And personally, I would never be the same!

In hindsight, I think of all the young adults that we could have reached down through the years if we had made some modifications to one of our services! Or if we had added another generation-ally-focused service years earlier! But, someone might say, isn't this compromise? Are you kidding? That change would only have compromised my personal wish to keep us all together.

That's the same reason why so many people didn't want us to move from one service to two and then three services. Our auditorium was packed out. We had to do something. But our people loved each other and liked being together. It wasn't a bad value- it just didn't take into consideration our need to reach more people for Christ! We simply had to move to multiple services! In the same way, I had good reasons for my stance, but I didn't realize that I was compromising my biblical call to reach as many people as possible! Can you see how easy it can be to fortify our values and build our structures and programs in such a way that we miss the changes that will transform everything? I'm afraid that many of us are doing that today.

Change without Compromise

One of the great concerns expressed about keeping up with a changing world is the fear of compromising our spiritual values. And we should be afraid of compromise! It's been the ruin of God's people since the beginning of time. It's one thing to keep up with a changing world. It's another thing to go down with it! Counting on the pull of the flesh, the world and the devil, it's inevitable that the church will continue to be pressured and seduced to slowly succumb to compromise! **We must never, never, never give in to the changes and compromises that will move us away from being centered in the Word and will of God! Never!** We see example after example in God's Word of believers and churches compromising the truth and suffering the consequences. And we are reminded throughout the Word **not to be** conformed to this world but to be transformed by the renewing of our minds. By the way, being transformed takes significant change as well. The one thing that is as bad as being conformed to this world is staying conformed to our own will instead of the will of God. Many believers and churches find **that** change even more difficult than keeping up with cultural change! In fact, most of the change that we will talk about in this book will focus on returning to a more Biblical way of living and doing church than many of us have been accustomed to.

> We've got to be so careful not to deify our likes and dislikes at the expense of God's own desire to keep His church and His gospel relevant and contagious to the average man or woman!

We need to remember that not all compromise is evil! In fact, compromise is a critical part of bringing balance to life! Wikipedia says "to compromise is to make a deal where someone gives up part of, or all of its demand. In arguments, compromise is a concept of finding agreement through communication, through a mutual acceptance of terms—often involving variations from an original goal or desire. . .In the negative connotation, compromise may be referred to as capitulation, referring to a "surrender" of objectives, principles; it's frequently said to be an agreement that no party is happy with. . .because the parties involved often feel that they either gave away too much or that they received too little." [16] Isn't that the truth! Wiki says it all.

There is a healthy compromise where we reach a mutual agreement, laying down some of our individual preferences to reach a common good. It usually doesn't feel good, because we surrender something that we like- something that we are comfortable with. But if our surrender achieves God's purposes, it will be worth it and hopefully we'll grow to actually enjoy the change. Let's look at several of the problems we have with compromise.

Sometimes we spiritualize and thus fortify our preferences, and it makes it so much harder to let go of them. It feels so wrong, like an ungodly compromise for the sake of a changing culture. Listen! There are God's mandates and our preferences, they are distinctly different and must not be merged. We've got to be so careful **not** to deify our likes and dislikes at the expense of God's own desire to keep His church and His gospel relevant and contagious to the average man or woman! Here's an example: Imagine the church forcing people to get excited about a Bible that's still using terms and language that's incomprehensible and hundreds of years old. Yet, for centuries, those who understood English were forced to either learn or sit through Latin as God's language of preference! How sad for us to do the same thing today, clinging so tightly and so spiritually to our own preferences at the expense of the furthering of the work of God! God help us to be clear-minded and spiritually in tune enough to see the difference between what we prefer and what we need to do to make disciples in this 21st century.

There was a man named John. He had been part of our church for ages. He had weathered many storms and pastors, but he had never been a part of a growing church. Now, John had grown accustom to a small church where everyone knew your name. As the church began to grow larger and larger, it became less and less comfortable for John. Things were changing so fast. It just wasn't the same! But John also had a heart for the Kingdom. He couldn't escape seeing the hand of God working in our midst. So every year, during a sharing time in one of our services, John would invariably stand up and speak. I'd hold my breath at the beginning. "Well, many of you know that there are so many changes going on around here! Sometimes I'm not very happy and I don't know what to think." Then John would always start to cry and he'd say, "But I see so many new faces and people coming to church and to the Lord. I know God has to be in it! And so I support it!" Now, there was a man who knew how to compromise for the Kingdom!

As I've journeyed through a number of decades of change, I've wandered into settings of older generations holding forms and cultures from the past over the heads of younger generations like an oppressive force! And I've seen spirits broken and thousands upon thousands exiting the Kingdom, over nothing of heavenly value!!! How tragic! Thank God that, in the same lifetime, I've also witnessed countless believers and leaders celebrating younger generations, encouraging them, empowering them and treating them as co-laborers in the great work of the Kingdom!

While I've described those of us who sometimes use preferences to oppress, others of us love to shed the preferences of the past and bring on change, as quickly as possible. In an attempt to be culturally relevant and amazingly different from the old guard of the past, I see a slew of pastors and writers today challenging and changing everything! So much of it comes with an in-your-face attitude and a subtle hunger to be out on the edge of truth, discovery and, at times, personal glory.

> Jesus carefully articulated a forgotten but accurate truth- they will know we are Christians, not by our doctrinal purity, our agreement, nor our revolutionary change, but by our love for each other!

Listen to this critical word: change has to come with a love and respect for past generations, especially when we're changing the things they hold dear! We live in a culture of rebellion, disrespect and dishonor. We see it everywhere, in what we watch and listen to, in our politics and even in our conversations. But it flies in the face of God's Word. From the beginning to the end, God mandates us to demonstrate humility and honor, for all. In the Old Testament, God tells young new leaders to learn from the past and to not simply move on and do their own thing. In Deuteronomy 32:7, God says: "Remember the days of old, think about the generations long past. Ask your father and he will tell you, your elders, and they will explain to you." The impression is that leaders weren't doing any of this, or God wouldn't have said it. A culture had developed that ignored the past, with it's priorities, values, experiences and lessons learned! In 1st Kings 12, Rehoboam is the epitome of an arrogant young leader who ignored the advice and experience of his elders and went with the ideals of his own generation. In the end, he lost half of his followers and almost lost his life!

In the New Testament, Jesus, Paul and our other writers press us even further in a life of love, in everything we think, say or do! And this is a word for all generations! In Romans 12: 9-10, Paul says: "Don't just pretend to love others. Really love them! Hate what is wrong. Hold tight to what is good. Love each other with genuine affections and take delight in honoring each other."[17] When this is clearly modeled, it includes the younger believers, the older believers and everyone in between! Listening to and appreciating the heritage from past generations of faithful stewards is God's plan for our lives. It provides us with context, with struggles past and present and a broader look at intentions of both heart and mind. It deepens our insight and ability to appropriately and carefully change things for a better tomorrow!

God clearly commands us to never compromise the law of love! We love first! Then we can make disciples. Jesus carefully articulated a forgotten but accurate truth- they will know we are Christians, not by our doctrinal purity, our agreement, nor our revolutionary change, but by our love for each other! Change must be done in an atmosphere of demonstrated love, to the very best of our ability. We challenge and we change, but we do it all with tender, humble hearts, filled with His love and His patience. Doesn't that sound right?

Many Christian leaders and authors have written about and have reacted to the incredible effort that some churches have made to become attractive to the world. One camp calls it relevance and the other calls it compromise. And both camps can be so self-righteous. I've watched churches cling to forms of the past, moving further and further away from any influence on the world, with guns a 'blazing at any and every church with a different set of values. And I've seen other churches doing almost everything to attract a crowd, all in the name of saving souls. Bring on the dancing girls! Hollywood, here we come! Look out, American Idol! You get the picture. So do I believe that some evangelical churches and ministries clearly compromise the principles of godliness and Biblical truth to be more attractive to the world? Absolutely! But I also believe that many of the attractional lines that are being crossed today are preferences and are not un-Biblical. For example, we've watched the battle of drums and guitars in the church over the past fifty-plus years. You can't tell me that that battle has been as important to God as it has been to man! In fact, millions have fought over their musical preferences in the church while tens of millions have gone to hell! What do you think God thinks about that?

I still remember visiting a church as a young man while I was working in a new community for the summer. This was my only visit to that church and I'll tell you why. The music was good, the people were friendly and the pastor was a good communicator. But, in his sermon, he began to talk about compromise. One of his examples was longer hair on men. I looked around the auditorium at the younger men with longer hair. And I wondered how many of them would walk away from church that day. Over the length of hair! What a sad commentary on how easily we can lose our opportunity to influence generations! Why do we major on minors instead of focusing on the matters of the heart? As Samson might have said, "Hair today, gone tomorrow! There are more important things to worry about!"

I believe we can change without compromise! I'm sure of it! The Bible is filled with examples of radical, Spirit-led change, in the face of compromised, declining spirituality. And our history, even in the last one hundred years, also gives countless examples of mighty men and women of God introducing revolutionary change to move the church back to a place of impact and influence on society. Isn't that what we want? Don't we want to change the lives of as many people as possible? I know that's what God wants!

Notes

THOUGHTS ON CHANGE

It may be hard for an egg to turn into a bird: it would be a jolly sight harder for it to learn to fly while remaining an egg. We are like eggs at present. And you cannot go on indefinitely being just an ordinary decent egg. We must be hatched or go bad.
C. S. Lewis

Everyone thinks of changing the world, but no one thinks of changing himself.
Leo Tolstoy

Change will never happen when people lack the ability and courage to see themselves for who they are.
Bryant H. McGill

2. WHY CHANGE? - THE COST OF NOT CHANGING!
Without Change, our Churches will Perish!

"Houston- we have a problem!" The year was 1970. Those were the last words the crew on Apollo 13 wanted to say back to their base. These men were on a glorious mission to the moon. They certainly didn't want to report a major failure in the electrical system after the oxygen tanks exploded. But it was what it was! Assessing the damage, the crew used their resources to survive great hardship and returned to earth. Their determination to think clearly, assess carefully and make appropriate changes saved their lives! Now, it was obvious that they had a problem, and changes needed to be made. I think most of us today know that we have a problem in our churches, but many of us don't really know what to do next. We don't know where to begin and what changes will really make a difference.

Reasons for Change

Change is critical, but it has to have purpose and it needs to be God's purpose! Appropriate change has to be the product of holistic thinking, dialogue, prayer and planning. We've got to see the big picture as we plan for changes. We have to rest in God's guidance and wisdom as we bring changes to His church. We don't change impulsively. We don't change thoughtlessly. And we don't just change for the sake of change. That would be foolish and irresponsible, wouldn't it? "Things have become boring. Let's change the carpet. I have an idea. Let's add another service. It sounds so exciting! How about a building addition? Let's get started!" Watch out. Time and money spent without real purpose may gain short-term enthusiasm, but it will do nothing in the long run. Trust me.

We may even lose people over it. But I see churches and leaders doing it all the time!

> Unless we bring about appropriate changes in a large percentage of our churches in North America, we will disappear into cultural irrelevance.

We'll jump in and change something, and it looks a lot like it's simply for the sake of change, like buying a new car. Or we'll act on a new conference or copy that church in California just because everyone else is doing it. But it's not on purpose, or not the right purpose! Not really. That change hasn't clearly come out of a genuine need rising from our church or community. Or it hasn't been carefully developed, constructed, thought through and prayed over. No wonder so many of the changes that we make in our churches don't have lasting results!

So what are some basic reasons why we should bring change to what we are doing right now? Let's look at four of them.

1) **The North American church is undergoing the greatest crisis in recent history.** We're in Big trouble! Our iceberg is melting! John Kotter writes a compelling parable about a family of penguins happily drifting to their doom on a familiar iceberg. [18] The story unfolds as the discovery of imminent danger leads to a series of difficult discussions over the need for change. Working through stages of disbelief, apathy and indecision, the entire tribe finally arrives at the radical changes needed to live! **We are that tribe!** Unless we bring about appropriate changes in a large percentage of our churches in North America, we will disappear into cultural irrelevance. In fact, we are way down that road! Time is passing and opportunities are passing us by. We can let aging churches with irrelevant structures die away, and they will and are. But if we're not replacing them with something

that's redefined, relevant, contagious, transformational and impacting our communities, we're done! It's over! Adios Amigos!

Barna and other pollsters keep us well-informed on the rapidly changing cultures that we are a part of. [19] There is clearly a decline in the religious impact and significance in America today. For one thing, church attendance has been and continues to drop every decade. We have very little room to go. We've dropped from fifty percent to forty percent to thirty percent all the way down to less than twenty percent of our continent attending church on a regular basis. Mainline churches have suffered the greatest loss. And why not? Without the truth of the Good News about Jesus, why would anyone go to church? Catholic churches have lost a fair percentage of their attenders. And evangelical attenders have barely changed. We often change churches, but our totals remain the same! That means that as mega-churches thrive, other churches revive, many churches die, new churches are planted, new converts enter in and the disillusioned leave, the numbers stay the same. So sad! Heartbreaking, actually. Something's terribly wrong!

David Kinnaman and Gabe Lyons, in their book, *UnChristian,* **unpack some of Barna's findings as they relate to the growing generation of lost young adults.** Two out of five young non-believers have a bad impression of present-day Christianity. The number has tripled in just ten years. Their reaction isn't to our theology- it's to our arrogance, our character and our actions. They see us as "aggressive, pushy know-it-alls, anti-homosexual, judgmental, and hypocritical!" We are ". . .old-fashioned, too involved with politics, out of touch with reality, insensitive to others, boring, not accepting of other faiths and confusing." [20] Now, we can react to their perception, defending and defining ourselves, but this is clearly how a growing percentage of our nation feels! Perception is everything!

David Olson, in his book, *The American Church in Crisis,* **clarifies that poll numbers are skewed and that we're often in worse**

shape that the numbers show. [21] As our population continues to grow, the percentage of believers in North America is declining! There's an attendance shift. There's a religious shift. There's a theological shift. There's a great social shift. There's a decline in convictions about the authenticity and the inerrancy of the Word. There's a decline in our convictions on divorce and marriage and morality. In fact, the majority of adults simply don't believe in absolute moral or spiritual truth. And they will no longer tolerate powerless platitudes about God and religion. If we truly want to influence our nation toward Jesus, we're going to have to start living like He actually is our Lord and Savior!

Ed Stetzer, President of Lifeway Research, puts some insightful analysis behind the latest research on the North American attendance decline. In a USA Today article entitled *Christianity isn't Dying,* Ed assesses the declining numbers of church attenders in the last fifty years. He divides attenders into three camps- Cultural Christians, Church-Going Christians and Born-Again Christians. Cultural Christians don't really practice the faith. They've been Christians in name only. Church-Going Christians occasionally attend church, but it's also not a real part of their life. Born-Again Christians have made that deeper commitment to Christ that sets them apart. The decline of the past fifty years of attendance has simply been a weeding out. It's no longer critical to go to church as an American. Cultural Christianity is dying. Many mainstream denominations are emptying out, along with churches filled with nominal believers in name alone. "Those with only a loose religious affiliation are finally admitting that they don't really have one at all. . .Christianity is not collapsing, but it is being clarified." [22]

Stetzer affirms that the numbers of real believers aren't shifting. They've actually remained about the same for the past twenty years. That means there's good news and there's bad news. The good news is, when someone tells you that she is a Christian, she may actually be one! There will be fewer people giving Jesus a bad name. The world will have a clearer picture of what it really means to be a Christian. And we'll have more clarity about how big our mission field is here in North America. Again, the bad news: We, as believers, haven't grown our numbers in twenty-plus years! So much of our activity has been shifting from little, dying churches to bigger thriving churches. I call that the Church Hop! In fact, the numbers show us that about 97.8 % of our church growth has been transfer growth and about 2.2% is conversion growth. [23] As much as it looks good in the churches where people are getting saved, the real numbers are heartbreaking! We're barely moving! We may be passionately in love with Jesus, we may love our church and church family, but we're barely impacting our world. It's slipping away! How much longer can we hug in our holy huddles, as the lost die all around us? And how much longer will they allow us to meet, if we continue to ignore them and lose our influence? Slipping away! We've got to examine ourselves, critically, honestly and spiritually to see clearly what needs to change. Here's another reason why.

2) **Many of our structures and a lot of our programs will not work the way we've been doing them.** A large percentage of our churches are still functioning under the forms and structures that worked well three to four decades ago. Although there are models everywhere of churches that have tried to pioneer a culture that's relevant in today's society, many churches, I'm afraid, haven't figured out how to move forward. There are churches everywhere still living in the twentieth century. And they don't even know it! I can still remember when churches would buy a fleet of buses to pick up children from everywhere in a community. Over time, that method somehow died away and I can still picture parking lots filled with unused, rusting buses. Everything keeps changing, but some of us won't stop trying the things that worked thirty years ago!

Alan Hirsch and Dave Ferguson talk about how 90% of today's evangelical church is stuck in a common model that makes them compete over the same 40% of the North American population. [24] What about the other 60%? Are we so uncreative and single-minded that we won't reach the rest of our nation? In their book,

On the Verge, these writers go on to talk about opposing models in our country that fail because we as leaders can't or won't learn from each other. We're more determined to defend our way of doing church than to perhaps find God's solution. Alan and Dave say, "Part of the problem with this is because, to use business consultant Jim Collins' terms, they fail to embrace the genius of the 'and.' Both groups are locked into the trap of either/or thinking. Seen from the perspective of either/or, these forms of church are irreconcilable, but reconceived from the perspective of the both/and, the supposed clash of imaginations begins to fade away. Collins rightly says that a truly visionary organization embraces continuity and change, conservatism and progressiveness, stability and revolution, predictability and chaos, heritage and renewal, fundamentals and craziness." [25]

Because we often are locked into the patterns of the past, churches are shrinking or dying all around us. In fact, statistics tell us that over the past twenty years, over half of our evangelical churches have plateaued or are declining. And that doesn't mean that the other half is doing well! You and I know that isn't the truth. Let's pause and address the reality that all churches go through life cycles, just like people do. Every church goes through a pattern of developing, plateauing, and declining over its life cycle. Many writers and speakers have repackaged the concept, addressing the critical issue of change. An early writer to unpack the issue was Robert Dale. In his book, *To Dream Again*, Dale's nine stages of a church's life cycle were dream, beliefs, goals, structure, ministry, nostalgia, questioning, polarization and dropout. [26] Most churches quickly plateau as soon as they gain structure and begin a downhill descent. If they don't see the need for effective and continual change, they will blindly continue on a road to their inevitable end. This norm has been with us from the beginning. But what we're seeing today is far worse. We're seeing an ongoing decline of Christianity on our continent!

Prophets have arisen all around us, addressing the urgency and critical condition of today's church. Now, there have always been voices speaking into the blindness and gradual drift within the church. And hundreds of books written by passionate preachers and teachers have pointed to the deterioration of Biblical mission and values during the second half of the twentieth century. One that has always stood out to me is Robert Coleman's *Master Plan of Evangelism*. Back in 1963, Coleman wrote of the stark contrast between what the church had become and what Jesus had intended for it to be! "When His plan is reflected on, the basic philosophy is so different from that of the modern church that it's implications are nothing less than revolutionary." [27] Of course, the difference is that Jesus intended for us to actually make real disciples!

It feels like the voices of concern have turned into a growing shout in the last ten to fifteen years. It's getting louder and louder, as more and more seers have joined in a chorus of concern and urgency. Each year, books are addressing the issue by the dozens. Is this the latest fad or the easiest sell in the Christian marketplace? It could be! But personally, I believe God is speaking, louder and louder, warning the North American church to wake up before it's too late!!! Kyle Idleman, in his book, *Not a Fan*, shares these profound words as he looks at today's church.

> My concern is that many of our churches in America have gone from being sanctuaries to becoming stadiums. And every week all the fans come to the stadium where they cheer for Jesus but have no interest in truly following him. The biggest threat to the church today is fans who call themselves Christians but aren't actually interested in following Christ. They want to be close enough to Jesus to get all the benefits, but not so close that it requires anything from them. [28]

Now, our writers and circuit-riding speakers are coming from different places. We're hearing the contrasting voices of men like Alan Hirsch, Erwin McManus, Andy Stanley, Neil Cole, George Barna, Ed Stetzer, Leonard Sweet, Thom Rainer, Michael Frost, David Ferguson, Reggie McNeil and Nelson Searcy, to name a few.

But one message is clearly coming from every one of them- the church, as we know it, will die if we don't reclaim the life and mission that God called us to in the first place! By the way, there also is an increasing sense of hope and conviction that the crisis within the church can be turned around! It's not too late!

Again, there are huge differences of opinion about structures and form. Some call for a complete change to missional communities without the trappings of what they would consider the congregational era. The cell church movement has pressed this ideal for decades. Reggie McNeal, for example, says that the survival and momentum of the church of this century will only come through our adoption of a missional mindset by leaders and believers alike. "This missional church engages the community with the intention of being a blessing. It looks for ways to connect with the world beyond the walls of church real estate and program." [29] So there are leaders who feel that the only way to truly bring about this great a change is to start over without the trappings of the structures and systems of the past. Neil Cole, in his book, *Organic Church,* says, "We want to lower the bar of how church is done and raise the bar of what it means to be a disciple." [30] That doesn't sound too bad, does it? Others call for a rebooting of the traditional church with all of its structure and buildings, focusing on greater relevance and better programming to keep attenders and to attract new people. And there are those who are working aggressively to blend the two paradigms, bringing together the best of the attractional models and the missional community models. Hugh Halter and Matt Sway, in their book, *And,* have wrestled personally with bringing together the best of ideals. "When people push us for our 'model,' I generally say, 'We're sort of a hybrid. We have a missionary thrust that forces us out of the church walls into a network of incarnational communities, but we also deeply value our collective calling, our corporate essence, and our consistent larger gatherings.' Our website now articulates that Adullam (their church) is a 'congregational network of incarnational communities." [31] I've watched many authors and speakers actually shift and reshape their positions over the past ten years, from principled ideals to practical realities, as they've listened both to God and man.

Alan Hirsch, in his book, "The Forgotten Ways," presses his desire to see the North American church regaining a lifestyle beginning with a passionate love for God, a life of radical discipleship and relevant forms of organization and structure. In premise, Alan points out that the potential for movement-like characteristics in God's people seems to be hindered the more we as the church become over-organized and institutionalized. [32] And it's true! The more organized and systematic we become, the more we seem to lose the dynamic, the vision and the passion that we began with. I've been saddened as I've watched so many church planters and pastors who started out well appear to lose their way as the job of running the church has superseded their original vision to change their world for Christ! And that usually happens in a few short years!

While forms, structure and programming have to keep evolving in a changing world, I'm not convinced that forms and structures are the real enemy! We certainly need many different models to reach the great diversity of people across our continent, but the real issue isn't the model.

> We're to love God and love each so passionately, so demonstratively, that the watching world believes and wants to join the family!

I watch younger generational churches springing up everywhere successfully reaching peers for Christ and making them into disciples! They're reaching across cultural lines and filling up with people who would never walk into a traditional church. Their gatherings and styles look bold and new and relevant to today's culture, and yet, they're adopting so many of the very same forms and structures of churches around them! They may have announcements and worship teams and altar calls. Nothing's wrong with that! I'll say it again- I don't believe our models and structures are the big problem. Here's our biggest problem!

3) **We've Forgotten Who We Are! And we've forgotten what our purpose is both as believers and as a community.** Here's perhaps the greatest reason for change. We are the light of the world! We're commanded to shine in such a way that people everywhere are turning to Him. We're to love God and love each other so passionately, so demonstratively, that the watching world is amazed, believes and wants to join the family! In Matthew 5:16, Jesus tells us to let our light and lives shine in such a way that people watching us see our good works and they end glorifying God as a result of what they see. In other words, they get saved! Our ultimate purpose is to make disciples who go! We're called to raise up a community of goers, mobilized to continually multiply throughout their communities. That's the call. That's our purpose. There are no exceptions. There are no excuses.

If that's true, then you can see how many of the programs and structures that we've developed down through the years are defeating the very purposes of God! Now, I believe that most of our programs and systems were developed with the right intentions. Look at church plants as an example. Most church plants down through the years started with the intention of reaching communities and winning new converts to Christ. And the programs and systems developed were created with the goal of making disciples of all ages. Over time, though, as churches settled in and no one new from the outside was coming to Christ, the programs focused more and more on teaching and training Christians to know and to live as Christians.

Christian Women's Club was established as a citywide ministry aimed at evangelistic outreach. For years, Christian women would bring their

71

non-believing friends for a morning at a local hotel event center. Hundreds of women would gather for brunch, and a host would guide them through special music, a craft or hobby presentation and a guest speaker. There was always a gospel presentation and, through the years, many women were saved! It was an excellent ministry.

As a young couple, my wife and I were invited to sing at our local Christian Women's Club. We have heard of its great reputation. You can imagine our surprise when we arrived and discovered a room filled with well-dressed, elderly Christian women. I don't think a non-believer was in the room, apart from hotel staff. The ministry had run its course. And as the ladies had aged, they had completely forgotten the purpose of this event. It had become a wonderful social gathering, certainly meeting their needs, but missing the mark! They were still presenting the gospel and giving opportunity for the lost. But the lost didn't appear to be present. The event had lost its meaning, its reason for being. It wasn't long before the ministry passed away!

Somehow, somewhere along the way, perhaps we misinterpreted what Jesus originally said. He told us, "Make Disciples who Go!" But somehow, translated over time from the Aramaic to the Hebrew, into Greek and for a King named James, and finally, into today's English, we thought He said, "Make Believers who Know!" Of course, I'm making fun of us. But look at what we've done. We've created classes and groups and programs to fill our minds full of godly information, so often without any measurable expectation of life transformation. We've shot ourselves with good intentions! Obviously we need to Know, but we forgot about the Go. We forgot that to live as a Christian demands that we go. We forgot that loving God has to include loving our neighbor. **We Forgot!** We've ended up creating programs and systems that allow us to remain comfortable and satisfied as closed communities, protected from the cruel world we live in. We've learned to measure ourselves by our busyness and attendance and how much we know and give and how good we are. It almost sounds Pharisaical, doesn't it? Yet God has called us to step outside and be faithful, intentional transformers among the people who surround us. All of us! Everyone! Again, no exceptions!

> We've ended up creating programs and systems that allow us to remain comfortable and satisfied as closed communities, protected from the cruel world we live in.

This is what's killing us! The world is changing all around us and we often aren't. So many of our methods and much of our programming has lost its relevance, even to our own people, let alone the very people we want to reach! But, most of all, we've lost the very foundations upon which the church was build! **Make Disciples Who Go!** This conflict will drive so much of what we will look at throughout this book. There's one more concept that we will major in.

4) **Many of our churches are not attracting new people!** And the visitors that we are attracting are largely Christians, hopping from one church to another! Here are just a few initial reasons why visitors aren't flocking to many of our churches. We're often not attractive. We're not prepared. It's not our plan or strategy to deal with visitors. We wouldn't know what to do with them if they did come. Our people aren't really prepared to bring them. In fact, most of our people don't have a consistent or strategic lifestyle that would allow for a friend to be brought to church. Many don't really have any non-believing friends in the first place.

I've already said that there are those today who would say that the current evangelical model of doing church is a lost cause. It can't be turned around. Decades with believers living a defined lifestyle will be impossible to change. The only solution is to start new church communities, on mission, centered around cells and small groups, plus-or-minus a centralized gathering. A gathering creates watchers and a whole system of in-grown ministries. All the energy put into a building and the gathering defeats the very lifestyle of going out and making disciples! The gathering itself has become an enemy. This "attractional" model trains us to watch and clap and sit and vegetate! Believers feel satisfied through in-house service and weekly attendance instead of an everyday life of service to the Lord! Some would say that a simple non-entertaining gathering once a month or, in time, once a week could complement other smaller groups. The focus would certainly not be on great worship or a single speaker. All of the structure and programming should center on one thing- building relationships and commitment levels that will produce true disciples who go and make more disciples! I agree completely with their fears and their goals. But I'm convinced that this is NOT the time to give up on the North American church! I believe a transformation is possible if we, as leaders, truly understand what is at stake, what needs to change, what that will take and we commit ourselves to do it!

> Out of a lifestyle of going, we also come together to gather, to grow and refuel, to collectively help to grow new disciples, to serve and reach the world- Together! But the focus can't be on the Gathering- it's got to be on the Going!

There is a clear contrast between what Alan Hirsch has defined as the attractional model and the missional model. [33] The first method seems to focus on attracting people to a church while the other method mobilizes believers to attract people to Jesus through their love and lives. Let's be honest. To think that we can attract people to Christ by simply pulling them into our Sunday services and then preaching to them is weak at best! Relationships mean everything! They always have! And that has been the missing ingredient in much of the programming of the church over the past fifty plus years. The majority of believers have been systematically programmed to see themselves as attenders at a place called the church. We go to church and, periodically, some of us even bring our friends with us. We've created a culture of watchers attending an event rather than participants in the great mission of God. The more entertaining the event, the better the music, the more articulate the pastor, the more we like our church. And we tell our friends. And many of them leave their churches, which are not nearly as attractive! The vast majority of our growth in our growing churches today and for decades has come from other churches shrinking. And when non-believers do come and believe, they become watchers just like us!

The truth is- the greatest emphasis of the church has been on making believers who know. Certainly we need to know God's Word and we need to know how to live the Christian life. So we teach and preach and expect godly living, loving, giving, serving and attendance. So much of what we ask for is focused on the development and maintenance of what goes on in our structures and buildings called the church. But we **are** the Church! And we've been called to be far more than attenders and believers who know. We've been called to be Disciples who **GO!** That does include world missions, which we often have been good at, but it really must start with all of us living out the life of Christ in our own communities, at home, at work and at play! Out of a lifestyle of going, we also come together to gather, to grow and refuel, to collectively grow new disciples, to serve and to reach the world- Together! **But the focus can't be on the Gathering- it's got to be on the Going!**

I do think we need to take an honest look at this issue as we compare the two primary models that we're looking at. We can say that the institutional church focuses on its gatherings and programs, and the cell church focuses on a missional lifestyle, with fewer distractions. That's true. But my observation is that both models can be very effective in making and mobilizing disciples, and both models can completely miss the mark! For example, I've seen large churches aggressively working to creative systems of relational accountability and disciplemaking so that movement and multiplication does take place. And a missional lifestyle and its fruit is clearly evident throughout those churches. By the way, I've never seen that happen without small groups being part of the structure of those churches. And I've also seen many cell churches with that same sense of intentionality and mission. Those leaders are also focused, intentional, strategic and unafraid of creating systems of accountability and multiplication.

At the same time, I've seen cell churches attracting lazy believers who are tired of all the programs. They just want to sit and soak and love on God and each other. And they attract more believers just like them. The leaders enjoy far more free time. For what? And with an attitude about programming, there's little value placed on teaming up for outreach. An authentic, missional lifestyle may develop, but evangelism and multiplication is haphazard at best. These cell churches are going nowhere fast! Guess what? They are matched with thousands of traditional churches across the country that also are directionless and are moving toward extinction! I don't believe the issue is to cell or not to cell! The issue is to wake up or not to wake up!!!

There is still great hope for the evangelical church, as it exists today. Our buildings are filled with believers, many who would be excited to embark on the Mission- a whole new way of living. They just need to be led! They need to be deprogrammed and reprogrammed. They need to be discipled. You as the leaders of the church hold the keys to the great awakening that we need across this land. I don't believe we need to scrap everything we have. I also don't think we need to eliminate the desire to have attractive gatherings and events and programs and facilities and leaders and workers. In fact, one of the reasons why so many churches are plateaued or dying is because they aren't attractive! Most of our churches aren't suffering because we're too attractive. We're suffering because we aren't missional, and we aren't attractive! Many of our churches have become like religious country clubs, catering to an aging base of members, with the greatest focus being on membership benefits! Isn't that true?

Here's a developing concept- we need to be and can be both attractive and missional! Away with any attractional model that simply inspires our people to sit, clap and go home satisfied! We'll have to really work to change this inbred way of doing church. This simply has to go! But, at the same time, let's do everything we can do be as excellent and attractive as we can be. Away with sloppiness and mediocrity! What we really need to be is **Attracti-Missional!** Jesus was attractive and missional and we should be too! Nelson Searcy, in his book *Ignite*, points to Rick Warren's concept of a deepening circle of commitment by church attenders. He says, "I like to refer to evangelism as attracting a crowd to worship. In other words, it's a process of moving someone from the community to the crowd so they can ultimately be moved into the congregation and then the core!" Searcy describes "come see" evangelism and "go tell" evangelism and concludes that we should be doing both! [34] None of this thinking, of course, is new, and the problem is most believers don't do both! As we wrestle with these issues, we will need to rethink everything we do in our church, from the top to the bottom! This will require hard work and a commitment to stay the course, whatever the cost! But we can do it! We'll need to carefully reconstruct and realign our vision, values and programming to the mission that God has called us to! We'll need to live it, model it, preach, teach and train it, in everything we do. And we'll need to begin raising up a new breed of believers, disciples who go, a few at a time. As they multiply, over time, our goal must be to raise up a majority of believers who are living out this incredible Great Commandment/Great Commission life! We'll go into detail on these issues and more as we move through this book together.

> Most of our churches aren't suffering because
> we're too attractive. We're suffering because
> we aren't missional, and we aren't attractive!

I greatly appreciate the merging of two fine thinkers, younger and older, in the book, *On the Verge,* **by Alan Hirsch and Dave Ferguson.** Alan is a missional movement leader and Dave is a church planting, emerging mega-movement leader. Both come from opposite corners in the world of ideology, but they've realized that the blending of their two worlds truly crafts a solution for the sleeping giant called the church. They share- "Whatever terminology we might employ, we do believe we're on the threshold of something that has profound significance for the future of western and therefore global, Christianity. What were once conflicting approaches to church (such as incarnational or attractional) are beginning to seriously interact." [35]

It's worth a moment to journey with these two men. Alan allows us to see the difficulty that he went through to come to these conclusions.

> I (Alan) admit that in my own early days as a church
> planter, leadership developer, and missional strategist
> for my denomination, I was much more inclined to
> this oppositional kind of thinking. The breakthrough
> happened for me in researching for *The Forgotten
> Ways*, when I came to the astonishing realization
> that every church, incarnational and attractional and
> everything in between, already has the full potential
> of Apostolic Genius resident in it, and all that is
> needed is for us to reactivate it. This is a very powerful idea you should ponder for a while, because if
> it's true- and I am convinced it is- then it changes
> everything. [36]

He does go on to say: But let us be clear: we believe church can be attractional and missional at the same time only if the organizational genetics, our core ideas, the paradigmatic brain at the center, legitimizes both impulses as important and justifiable expressions of what it means to contextualize the gospel in the Western world. [37]

I'm not surprised to hear of the skepticism that both Alan and Dave have received as they've shared about merging established models with missional living. The task is beyond comprehension. The chance of failure is great. It's easier to predict the demise of the established church as we invest in new, smaller, more flexible models. But here are two questions. What is the will of God? And what will happen if the evangelical church actually begins to live missionally? Everything will change! The decline will re-climb! If our churches, in cells, in homes, in rented facilities and in traditional facilities, actually begin filling up with authentic disciples, truly living out the life of Christ, we'll see the awakening we've all been longing for!

There are those who would say that our purpose is not to be attractive to non-believers as a church community and that that is the ruin of the church today. But I say why shouldn't we be attractive to non-believers as a community? Why aren't we attractive? Is it because we are so righteous and heavenly or is it because we've lost our way? Could it be that we're simply excusing the reality that we've lost our purpose, our power and our potency in a world that desperately needs to see the Church alive, vibrant, Spirit-empowered, making a difference?

I will contend throughout this book that the purpose of the church is to make disciples who go! That was His great command! If the entire structure and programming of the church is focused on mobilizing disciples to go and bring their friends to Christ, then those friends will be coming to Christ, coming to church, growing into disciples and then going after their friends! This Biblical mindset needs to drive everything! Everything must change that's not moving us toward God's actual will for our churches. If the entire structure and programming of the church has deteriorated into something that simply maintains itself, like an old folk's home, we will die! New life won't come with great new ideas, new programs or new structures. New life will rise out of a fresh awakening to an old, but ageless truth- go and make disciples who go!

Foundational Keys to the Kingdom

Here are three foundational keys that we need to build on before we dive into our details about how to attract visitors to our churches. These keys lay out a critical framework upon which we can build our entire strategy for a healthy church.

> We as leaders can get so busy and visionary and excited and distracted that we end up forgetting the main thing!

1. **Change will only bring true value when it's built on the right foundation.** Let's not fool ourselves! "Unless the Lord builds the house, they labor in vain that build it." I'm sure you've heard that somewhere before! In other words, we can work hard, dial in all the details and some of us can build very successful churches from man's point of view. But they're here today and gone tomorrow from God's point of view! I've seen some of those churches. Many of them are sitting near-empty or remodeled into office buildings, serving as tragic reminders for all of us! No credit! No brownie points! Like dust in the wind! Who wants that? Why work so hard for a fleeting moment of self-glory? It's not worth it! On top of that, think of doing it without the power of God. Think of doing it without the guidance of the Holy Spirit! Think of doing it without His protection. Now, how crazy is that? It sounds like a disaster waiting to

happen! Why in the world wouldn't we want God right in the center of what we're doing?

Unfortunately, ministries and churches are built or rebuilt every day all around the world, outside of the will of God. How in the world do they miss the mark? I actually think it's quite easy! We as leaders can get so busy and visionary and excited and distracted that we end up forgetting the main thing! We quietly move back into the trap of dependence on our own strength and ideas. And we can forget who we are. We can forget what we're really here for. So, before we talk about changing it up, I want to talk about firming it up and laying down the unchangeable foundations that God has laid down for everyone of us! God always comes first. What is His will, His plan, His desire, His purpose in what we would like to do? Are we close to Him, listening to Him, walking in Him? Is this His timing, His priority? Are these the changes that He is guiding us to make right now? Now, how can we know that? Well, for one thing, we don't plan first and then ask for God's approval later. We start with God! Let me quote Solomon again: "Trust in the Lord with all your heart. Don't lean on your own understanding. In all your ways acknowledge Him and He will guide your steps" Solomon was pretty smart. We should listen to him, don't you think?

2. **Change will only bring true success if it moves us toward God's original intention for His church.** We've got to be doing this for one purpose- to live out the life that Jesus has called us to live! If we truly love God, we will first draw close to Him and then we'll obey Him. Look at these three commands: Love Me with all your heart, soul, mind and strength. Love your neighbor as yourself. Now, go and make disciples who go! These three commands lay out the essence of Christianity. It's a dynamic relationship with a life-transforming God who commissions every one of us on a life-long mission to change the world. Everything that we do in our church attending and programming must be about

growing and deepening us, equipping us and mobilizing us to go out and reach others for Christ. There is no higher cause! There is no higher purpose! Certainly we'll care about other things. And certainly we'll care about each other. But that brings us to the problem with the church today. We often care so much about ourselves and each other and our causes that we completely lose sight of the Mission! It's the Mission that we've been called to and everything else must be organized and strategized to most effectively achieve that goal. The purpose of our changes must be to actively reach more people for Christ and not simply to be more culturally relevant and to feel better about ourselves. That would be so foolish. Rick Warren, in his book, *The Purpose-Driven Church,* says that the key issue in our churches isn't a growth problem- it's a health problem! "The task of church leadership is to discover and remove growth-restricting diseases and barriers so that natural, normal growth can occur. . .I believe the key issue for churches in the twenty-first century will be church health, not church growth." [38] And isn't it true?

> Our spiritual journey has to drive us first to a passionate love for God, each other and the lost. That personal commitment to spiritual balance and excellence in everything we do will then overflow throughout our church.

3. **Change will only bring true satisfaction when our goals and end results are about changing lives and not simply about growing numbers.** I'm writing this book from the view of the visitor- from the outside in. That's where we begin. But you'll discover as you read it that the real keys to growing a strong, vibrant church begin from the inside out! In fact, you'll see that it all begins with the heart. Your heart drives the future of your church. It will come down to that! So for thirteen chapters, we'll look at hundreds of details that will trigger thoughts about hundreds of other details. They

all matter deeply and affect where you will be ten and twenty and thirty years from now. But **none** of them will make any difference if you don't deal with the heart issues! The details will simply create window dressings! Our spiritual journey has to drive us first to a passionate love for God, each other and the lost. That personal commitment to spiritual balance and excellence in everything we do will then overflow throughout our church. We tend to get this backwards! We tend to forget that everything concerning the church and the kingdom is about our relationship with God! And it's about His purposes and His will in the lives of people. The details that we will look at in this book simply aid us in getting to His primary objective- making disciples who make disciples so we can reach our world for Christ!

Why I Wrote this Book and Assessment

There is still time and a place for the church as we know it in North America! I'm absolutely convinced of that! We need to be committed to trying all kinds of new forms and methodologies to plant churches and to restructure and give fresh starts to dying and stagnant institutions. But, as I've said over and over again, I don't think our greatest enemy is form and structure. Institutions often adapt to the right new forms and structures when they are driven by the right values and vision. But when they lose vision and forget the right values, no structures will give them a future, new or old! The problem isn't about new or old wineskins- it's about the quiet evaporation of the wine! The church has lost its way. It's forgotten what it's here for. The church desperately needs a fresh inoculation of new life and power. Imagine what that would look like here in North America. If the people of God are again filled with the Spirit and power of God, the right structures for each situation will flow right from the heart of God.

> I don't believe wineskins become old because churches grow out of touch with culture. I believe they become old because churches grow out of touch with God.

Here's what I've seen. Walk with me inside this gymnasium. The music is loud, the images are blazing on screens, the energy is intense, the preaching passionate and forceful, the room is packed, all generations and cultures are represented. Now walk with me inside this living room. The music is quiet and contemplative, there are no projectors, but songs are printed out, the energy is passive, the preaching soft, heartfelt, tender, the room isn't full, and most of the attenders live nearby. In both rooms, everyone is meeting God, with all their hearts. They are growing, caring, and dreaming about how to reach people and advance God's kingdom. They both take offerings- one in the gathering and the other in a basket at the door. They both have leaders- one is paid and the other is not. Both gatherings are attractive, to regulars and visitors alike, not because of any flash factor, but because of the life of God in His people! These churches can be in every community across North America and they will grow and reach many people for Christ! Both are new wineskins, because both churches are filled with fresh wine! I don't believe wineskins become old because churches grow out of touch with culture. I believe they become old because churches grow out of touch with God. I'm not talking about staying religious and upright and doctrinally correct. I'm talking about staying so close to Jesus that His passion and love within us overwhelmingly forces us to stay close to lost people and His mission to draw them into multiplying discipleship!

I wrote this book and assessment because I believe that many of us as pastors and leaders simply do not know what to do to reach our communities! We don't know where to begin. We don't know how to attract visitors to our churches. We don't know why we're not attractive. We don't really know how to get ready for visitors. I travel across the continent regularly and have taught, coached and consulted with thousands of church leaders over many years. I visit different churches every Sunday and I see the tremendous need for ideas and answers about so many different issues in the church. Here's a tragic reality- most believers and therefore most churches rarely think about reaching new people with the good news about Jesus. There's no understanding of missional living. It's just not on the agenda! Life is too busy and the distant memories of that "issue" only resurface when we come to a holiday or something else that reminds us of the call.

A survey unpacked in several articles in *Church and Faith Trends*, written by the Evangelical Fellowship of Canada, concluded that perhaps only 15% of Canadians invited to church will accept that invitation. My question is: why would they? Are they in close relationship to their inviters? Do they hang out together? Do they go out for dinner and see movies and sunsets and hockey and soccer games? Do they feel like friends or like a project? Has the life of Jesus been demonstrated by their Christian friends over time? Is it the right time to invite them to church? Have they already invited them to other opportunities to get to know believers, like Starbucks or a picnic or back-yard barbecue? Is the facility, the program and the gathering or event that they are being invited to really attractive and matching the healthy expectations of the visitors? And is the church family actually prepared for an influx of real, live non-believing visitors? That Canadian study went on to summarize: "In other words, the reason institutional religion is failing in Canada is not primarily because people lack interest in church, but because churches are not interested enough in ministering to people outside their walls." [39] I would guess that, for years, a decreasing percentage of North Americans invited to normal churches by normal attenders have accepted that invitation to church. There are loads of reasons why! And, over time, we, the inviters, in most evangelical churches, have slowed down or stopped inviting our friends altogether. Isn't that true?

I want to say one more time that I believe that creating small groups or cell churches doesn't automatically solve this problem.

With strong, missional leadership, disciple-multiplying and healthy systems of accountability, so much can be done and needs to be done through new, more flexible ways of doing church. Let's be creative and go for it! But many small groups and cell churches have become comfortable and complacent, like their larger counterparts. They have no plan, no preparation, and no strategy for pre-believers and new believers when they do show up. There's no commitment to excellence and attractiveness. They've lost the way! They too have forgotten who they are! They're on cruise control, like so many other churches across this land. Throughout this book, I'm pressing for our need to change! It doesn't matter how large or small your church or cell system is. Take the concept of each chapter and apply it to your world! I'm walking down the halls and looking at every detail. I'm looking in your living room to see if you are ready. When new people do show up, whether it's a friend you've brought or a neighbor, do you know what to do? Are you ready? As individuals, we need to change the way we walk, the way we talk and the way we think. As leaders, we need to change our strategies and structures so our focus clearly is outward, movement-like, prepared for visitors and prepared to make and multiply real disciples. This needs to happen in missional communities of every size and design. The ultimate secret for a great tomorrow is not in our clinging to old methods or coming up with creative new ones. The secret is returning to God's plan that He laid down in the first place!

From the Outside In

This book has been written with the outsider in mind! Lost people matter to God and He wants them found! How do they see us both as individuals and as a church? How do we see them as non-believers all around us? What will it take to bridge that gap between un-belief and faith? How do we prepare ourselves as a people so we are fully invested in God's original plan for our lives and our church? We can turn this around right now!

There are literally hundreds of incredible books out there that can challenge us and help us see where we need to be! Read them! Let's look at several sources filled with great insight. Years ago, Lee Strobel wrote *Inside the Mind of Unchurched Harry and Mary*. He challenged us to be relevant and to get in the shoes of ordinary people who don't go to church.

> Without frequent heart-to-heart conversations with unchurched people, it's easy to forget how they think. That's why I wrote this book: to help advance your understanding of unchurched people so that your personal evangelistic efforts and the efforts of your church might become more effective. . .That's my goal because, frankly, I love irreligious people. Some of my best friends are, in reality, hellbound pagans, and I an impassioned about wanting to see them transformed by the same amazing grace that radically redirected the trajectory of my own life. [40]

More recently, Jim Henderson hired and took an atheist, Matt Casper, to a dozen churches and then told us all about it in *Jim and Casper Go to Church*. It's a provocative and eye-opening book. The most intriguing question that Matt had about the church was this: "Jim, is this what Jesus told you guys to do?" [41] Is this what Jesus told us to do? Buildings and budgets and boards and. . . I'll stop with the b's, but you get the point. Matt found it hard to believe that the most important thing that Jesus' followers should be doing is holding church services. What an amazing observation. Last, and perhaps the most current source, *Outreach Magazine* constantly shares interviews with pre- and new believers and their observations as they visit churches across our land. It's a must-have magazine! Subscribe!

These are all invaluable tools to read and learn from. My contribution is to provide you with a boatload of details about what church should look like so you can see yourselves and what your ministries look like right now. This book is like a roadmap that will help you prepare to walk with pre-believing friends, in community, from their homes and neighborhoods all the way to a missional life of discipleship and disciplemaking. We'll begin with pre-believers, new believers and other visitors as they make their journey toward you as a church family. But the big picture of the book walks us through a process of preparation to become a community and movement of devoted disciples, committed to impact our world for Christ! All the chapters in this book supply you with essential components of the whole picture. And I've saved the best for last. Every chapter builds toward the final product- turning self-serving people into glorious, multiplying disciples, filled with the Spirit and focused on the Mission! That's what He's called us to be and that's what He's called us to do. So let's do it! Let's dive in and get started. But first, let's gather together on the front porch.

The Front Porch

Go back with me in time to one of the great, rich stories that Jesus told his disciples. It's a story of a father and his two sons.

There was a man who had two sons. The younger one said to his father, 'Father, give me my share of the estate.' So he divided his property between them. Not long after that, the younger son got together all he had, set off for a distant country and there squandered his wealth in wild living. After he had spent everything, there was a severe famine in that whole country, and he began to be in need. So he went and hired himself out to a citizen of that country, who sent him to his fields to feed pigs. He longed to fill his stomach with the pods that the pigs were eating, but no one gave him anything.

When he came to his senses, he said, 'How many of my father's hired servants have food to spare, and here I am starving to death! I will set out and go back to my father and say to him: Father, I have sinned against heaven and against you. I am no longer worthy to be called your son; make me like one of your hired servants.' So he got up and went to his father.

But while he was still a long way off, his father saw him and was filled with compassion for him; he ran to his son, threw his arms around him and kissed him. The son said to him, 'Father, I have sinned against heaven and against you. I am no longer worthy to be called your son.'

But the father said to his servants, 'Quick! Bring the best robe and put it on him. Put a ring on his finger and sandals on his feet. Bring the fattened calf and kill it. Let's have a feast and celebrate. For this son of mine was dead and is alive again; he was lost and is found.' So they began to celebrate.

Meanwhile, the older son was in the field. When he came near the house, he heard music and dancing. So he called one of the servants and asked him what was going on. 'Your brother has come,' he replied, 'and your father has killed the fattened calf because he has him back safe and sound.'

The older brother became angry and refused to go in. So his father went out and pleaded with him. But he answered his father, 'Look! All these years I've been slaving for you and never disobeyed your orders. Yet you never gave me even a young goat so I could celebrate with my friends. But when this son of yours who has squandered your property with prostitutes comes home, you kill the fattened calf for him!' 'My son,' the father said, 'you are always with me, and everything I have is yours. But we had to celebrate and be glad, because this brother of yours was dead and is alive again; he was lost and is found.'

Luke 15:11-32

What's the point of the parable? Let's look at it, first of all, in context. Jesus tells three stories in a row about lost possessions—a lost sheep, a lost coin and a lost son. All three are precious, and all three are found. What's the point of the parables? God wants lost people found! Lost people matter to God, and He wants them found! There is the core value that we see all through His Word! The father could appear to be the least involved, passively waiting on the front porch. But that's simply not true. The shepherd, the woman and the father all were passionate pursuers! The shepherd and the woman actively looked for the lost sheep and coin. The father had to wait for the son to come home! But he was waiting, watching and longing for his son's return.

As we read through this third parable, we clearly see into the heart of all three of the characters in our story. First, we have the rebellious son who later becomes the repentance son. We have the judgmental and sulking older brother. And we have the ever loving, patient, responsive father who runs! We generally see the father as our heavenly Father, who waits for us and continues to be patient with us, even when we stumble and fall. But here's an intriguing interpretation of the passage. In a sermon series on this topic, Nathan Edwardson, lead pastor at the Stirring in Redding, California, painted a picture of the father, ever watching and waiting on the front porch. Nate, who also happens to be my son, contended that all of us, representing the Father and filled with His love, should be on the front porch, waiting for the next prodigal to come around the corner! In fact, we all should be competing over who gets to run to meet the next one!

I want you to capture everything that you've already believed about the father's posture on the front porch. Picture the father, patient, yet waiting with anticipation and hope, filled with love, ready to run at any moment. Now, representing the Father, picture your entire church packed on that front porch. That's right! The whole church! You may have to picture a very large front porch! Picture everyone earnestly waiting, praying, and ready to run and meet the next prodigal rounding the bend. The prodigals, of course, include our friends, neighbors, and relatives, the people we work with and people throughout our community. I believe this reflects the heart of God!

This is God's will for your church! Everyone on the front porch! Everyone! And here's our conflicting reality. Our churches are filled with prodigals, older brothers and nice attenders. Very few are intentionally poised on the front porch. The older brothers are protecting the church from the prodigals. The prodigals in the church are hiding, hoping not to be found–especially by an older brother. And all the nice attenders are clapping for the handful of believers on the front porch. How sad! How unexciting! How predictable! And how far from God's call on his church.

Sometimes we create structures and systems to try to get everyone on the front porch. Ready or not, we will train, shame and guilt everyone onto that porch. We want a front porch church. The prodigals and older brothers on the porch have to work harder at hiding their reality. And everyone on the porch cheers loudly as the same people always manage to run for the next prodigal coming around the corner. That's certainly not God's plan! God wants us gathering on the front porch, truly representing Him–filled with His love, His compassion, and His heart to run. He wants older brothers softened and filled with the father's heart. He wants prodigals restored and standing on the porch, now waiting for their friends to come. He wants the front porch to be so safe, that, when any of us slip and have a prodigal relapse, we are embraced, restored, renewed and ready to go! Let's not forget that all of us have that potential to easily slip back into being a prodigal or older brother. I hate it when I do that. But that's our default when we aren't filled with the Father's love. As that reality continually humbles us, and as we, ourselves, receive the Father's embrace, strength and love, we shine! Together! On the front porch! That's what this book is all about. Shining together on the front porch! Can you imagine what the world around you will think when they see your porch, crowded, alive, vibrant and shining so brightly?

> *Let your light so shine before others that they may see your good deeds and glorify your Father in heaven.*

Jesus

Notes

PART TWO

THE JOURNEY

Journey to Discipleship

A Movement of Devoted Disciples

Outreach Plans

Roadmap to Maturity

Programs / Facilities

Assimilation

The Gathering

The Family

Entry Plan

Inside the Door

Drive In-Walk Up

Getting There

THOUGHTS ON CHANGE

If there is no struggle, there is no progress.
Frederick Douglass

He who rejects change is the architect of decay.
The only human institution which rejects progress
is the cemetery.
Harold Wilson

If you want to change the culture, you will have
to start by changing the organization.
Mary Douglas

3. GETTING THERE
You Can Built It. . .But They may NOT Come!!

Are You Ready??? That's the Big question! Ready for What? That's the Big problem! Many of our churches are absolutely unprepared for any visitors showing up, for any reason, in any spiritual condition. I know. I show up at churches all the time that demonstrate that they have no idea what to do with visitors and they don't seem to care. Now, showing up at church may not be the best entry strategy for our visitors. We would like them in relationship with our people first. And we would probably plan that their first encounter with the church would be a special event made just for them. But, at some point, we want them to arrive and walk into a gathering, large or small. Are we ready? Are we prepared? We'll keep asking questions like these throughout the book.

Think about all of the places that we could begin our journey together. We could start by talking about your facility, or friendly people, or great music and preaching. This book is like a route map. The diagram across the page lets you see all of the stops along the way. There is an ultimate destination. We want to turn self-serving people into healthy, multiplying disciples who reflect the mind, character and priorities of Christ. But first, they have to find us! How do we get on their map? How do we as believers get into relationship with them? How do we help them get in the front door, whether it's a cell, a home group, an event or a gathering? And then, how do we walk them, step by step, through a process that will turn them into authentic disciples? Let's start at the beginning! Let's look at how we look as a church to our community.

If you want a healthy, growing church, people have to get there! As simplistic as that sounds, all churches that aren't growing aren't growing because people aren't coming. It's been said- "If you build it, they will come!" But that's not the truth! There are church buildings sitting empty all over the country. They built them and

99

something went wrong. You may be in one of those buildings. If you want people to come to your church, people have to know you are there. You have to get on the map in their minds. People pass by church buildings everyday that are simply invisible to them. They're off the map! Thousands of others drive within miles of our facilities without knowing we are there. There are always reasons why. **The first thing we need to look at is how we look to our community and how we look at our community.**

Community Image

How do we look to our community? The people who have had contact with us in the past all have an attitude about us. The neighbors who have watched us through the years carry a variety of opinions about us. What is our **church history**? How has it impacted our community? Does the community know us at all? Have we worked to develop a healthy relationship with the neighbors? If we haven't, why would we expect them to ever visit our church? To them, we may look like a building filled with very strange, religious people. If we haven't worked to improve it, that image may be the reputation that they are passing throughout our town. How's that for advertising! Is there negative history to overcome? We can't ignore the impact that the difficulties of the past have on the present. Bad reputations must be overcome! How did we approach the community when our church was planted? Has that been good or bad for us? Are there things that we need to do to get past the past and move to a great tomorrow?

What sort of image do we want to have in our community? What image do we have? What image would cause people to come to visit us? Sometimes we have all the right components in our church, but nobody knows us on the outside. How do we get our image out?

What are people looking for in a church? First of all, most people aren't looking for a church. It's not on their agenda. Their time is already filled to the max. But, if they ever were interested, somewhere down the road of life, there would be an invisible list that they would come with. Now, the music and the preacher would need to be **good**. But, even more important- that church would have to be **friendly**. The church folk would need to be **real**. Why would they ever come and why would they ever come back if the people weren't authentic and happy? The people would also have to **care**. Everyone is looking for some sort of connection. People find connections everywhere- at work, at home, at the club, at the bar, over a barbecue. They would expect to make connections at church as well. And, they expect those connections to build on genuine care. If that wouldn't happen, they wouldn't be back. Does our church care? How is it demonstrated? How would people know we care? How would people in the community know we care? Our church would need to look like it's **alive and active**, filled with energy and a reason for its existence. Our church would need a reputation of **honesty and integrity**. There are so many churches out there that have somehow gained a bad reputation in the community. Why would people ever visit one of them?

He was a bold, visionary church planter whom God used to start churches all around the world. But he tells the story of one church plant that was destined to fail. Months into its start, another struggling local church offered to merge with the new plant. Everyone knows that there always is baggage that comes with the joining of two churches. Church planting normally frees a planter from the encumbrances of a past. But, in this case, the greatest benefit was inheriting property and a nice, large facility in a fairly good location. After lots of prayer and talks, the merger took place and the new plant suddenly grew and had a permanent home! Everything looked great- on the inside. But there was more to the story than one could see! Church planters- listen

very carefully now. No one had talked about the church's past!

Here's the rest of the story. Moving into their new facility, the church plant advertised, promoted, invited, and did everything to reach out to the neighborhood. But no one would ever come to anything at the church. It was the strangest thing! One day, the pastor was walking in the community and he began to talk with one of the neighbors. At first, the old man acted hostile toward the pastor. And then, suddenly, he said, " I want to show you something! He led the pastor, who happened to be my dad, into his garage and pointed to a photo of a beautiful, old historic church. My dad had never seen that church before. He soon found out why.

The old man began to tell the story. That beautiful church had been built ages ago on the property that the new plant had just taken over. It was a landmark church, a piece of history. It had been a part of their community from generation to generation! Everyone in the neighborhood loved it and expected it to stay there forever. But a new pastor had arrived in recent years, and, you guessed it. He wanted to tear down the old church to build a new and better facility! Who would blame him? But when the people of the community heard of the church's plans, they rose up together in mass and told him he couldn't tear down their beautiful historic landmark. He refused to listen to them. They proceeded to go to court for an injunction to stop the destruction of "their" church building. But, that night, the day before the hearing, the bulldozers swept in and knocked the old building down. A beautiful new church building was erected in its place. The pastor had won the

battle. But he lost the entire community! They would never, ever set foot in that new building! Never! And they perhaps would also never hear the claims of Jesus, His love, His patience and His mercy! Of course, the church died!

Your church has to be visible for visitors to come! Some churches are invisible. Is yours? Some churches become invisible to even their own neighbors because they've had no contact for years. The church people don't talk about their church, so no one hears about their church! Other churches are rundown and have become very unattractive to their neighborhood. Some churches are located in neighborhoods where most people would never find them. Visitors would only come if they heard something great about that church!

Many churches gain an image by becoming actively involved in various parts of the community. Some churches have floats in community parades. Some set up booths and pass out free water at festivals and events. Other churches have aggressively worked at **contributing** to various needs that they see around them. Some have worked on special projects to help the community- cleaning up poor neighborhoods, helping to renovate or equip schools, doing yard work for the elderly, teaching English to immigrants. You can imagine the impact a church can have and how positive it can look through the eyes of the community if it is giving generously with no strings attached!

Cordova Neighborhood Church, in Rancho Cordova, California, is just one great example of a church constantly reaching out to its community. They feed the poor on a weekly basis; they teach marriage enrichment classes for couples in the community; the building is filled with activities reflecting a heart for the community; the pastor has been actively involved in city council. They are building a youth center intentionally designed for community use as well as for the church. Large churches with significant ministries impacting their communities all started out like this church and have grown because of it!

What happens inside our churches is often the neighborhood's best-kept secret. Wonderful things can be going on and no one knows outside the doors of the church. Word does generally leak out over time and reputations are gained. Some churches are known for doing very **strange** things- that's unattractive. Some churches are known to be **stiff and formal**. Others have earned the reputation of being **warm and inviting**! Some churches appear to be very **legal-istic**- they specialize in right and wrong. Some are very **social**- they love to have fun. Some are known for being very **spiritual**- they are passionate about God. People looking from the outside in aren't looking at how scripturally accurate we are; they don't know what that means, and they don't care! They do know it if they see life and love, warmth and care, integrity, spirituality, commitment, involvement and generosity! What do we look like to people looking in?

Marketing- Getting on the Map

The dictionary tells us that marketing is the activity of presenting a product or service to potential customers in such a way that it makes them eager to buy it. Just the thought of marketing the church can cause some believers to run for cover. The last thing we want to do is commercialize the church and market it like a cheap religious idol! On the other hand, there has to be a way for people to get to our church. Some people want to simply trust God to grow their churches. I'm afraid it doesn't work that way. God is clearly involved in the process, softening hearts and preparing lives. But He commands us to do our part- Go! Go and make disciples! Let your light Shine! Be fishers of men! Make your words count!

Compare advertising to fishing. If you don't fish, you won't catch fish. The more you fish, the more likely you will catch more fish. Remember, fish will only eat when they are hungry, not when you want them to eat. Three normal handicaps are fishing poorly, fishing with the wrong bait or fishing where there are no fish. Parallel that to fishing for men. So **the first thing we need to look at is how we look to our community. The second thing we need to do is get our church on the map.**

How do we "market" the church? How do we let people know that we have something great that they need to be a part of? Let's look at four different ways of marketing- advertising, direct mail, social networking and word of mouth. We'll save the best two for last!

A. **Advertising**- One of the easiest ways to market is to advertise. There are always people looking for a good church- even in the 21st century. They're new to the community and they don't know where to join their next church family. Or they're looking for a new church home. Or they've been thinking about it for years and they've finally decided to take the plunge. When that moment of need happens, the advertisers often win! He who has the most attractive website or ad through the eyes of that beholder gets the visitor. Visitors may go through two to ten churches before they decide where they want to attend. If you don't make yourself visible to your world, you lower your chances of visitors significantly. If you advertise a little, you'll get a little response. If you advertise consistently, you have the greatest chance of attracting visitors when they are looking. Some churches will only use word of mouth as their way to market themselves. Although we'll see that that's the best way to draw people, many churches will miss out on the percentage of people who are looking for a new place of worship and family.

Remember these principles-

> 1) **Advertise where people are reading.** Know your community and the reading habits in your community. Figure out who reads what newspapers or flyers or local magazines. Learn how to get your website out there and easily findable. Find out the costs on all your options so you can make your best decision on how to spend your money.

2) Advertise well! Focus on quality. Bigger is unfortunately better in advertising, but what you can afford is better than nothing. Make sure that your website and advertising are attractive or you will waste your money. Grab their attention. Have fun. Tell them enough to make them interested. Put yourself in their shoes. Don't be boring. Don't clutter your website or ad. Be sure to include critical details like location, date and times, phone numbers, and something that identifies distinctively who you are. **You've got to get on their map!** So put **Your** map on all of your advertising. You want them to memorize your location long before they decide to come for a visit.

3) Advertise consistently. Make your church a part of your community. Keep your name and information current and out there so people begin to know what you are about. It's always money well-spent. In almost every community, the people who come through your advertising will easily pay for it.

4) Target the right people with the right ads. Who do you want to attract through your ads? You can't target everyone. Be sure to target people you can reach. And make sure that the people you are after know that you are after them. Will your ad really attract them? Will your church match your ad when those visitors arrive, or will they be disappointed? Your ads need to represent you.

Let's talk about the homogeneous principle of life. Birds of a feather flock together! That's the bottom line. We constantly fight that principle in the church and we lose every time. Forcing people to come together only works under high levels of commitment or pressure. We live in an age of rapidly-changing levels of commitment. People won't simply do what we tell them to do or go where we tell them to go. Either we learn to go with the flow of human nature or we will never really reach our potential in changing lives, touching our community and growing our church. Here are some pictures of reality. We've forced our young to tolerate our forms of worship, music and preaching. Then most of them have left home and they also have left the church. Why? Because what we've providing for them hasn't been relevant, at least from their point of view. Then, we've tried to force our middle-aged adults to stay with our traditional worship styles. But in recent decades, they've left in droves. And finally, we've tried to throw in a hymn or two in our blended contemporary worship services to satisfy the church of the past. But we haven't made them happy either. The blending of cultures is like swimming upstream. You've got to want to do it, and most people don't.

I've watched this for years. And I see the same thing today. This reality doesn't change. Cultures are constantly changing. North America is constantly changing. The homogeneous units of our nation are changing. New groups are forming as populations, communities, nationalities and economies shift. New groups are happy together that didn't get along 20 years ago. Younger, multicultural generations are joining together while their parents, as believers, still harbor prejudices toward each other. And they are creating a dozen new homogeneous units, each developing their own distinctiveness. By the way, the homogeneous principle is about what we have in common and where we feel comfortable. A next-generation church may be filled with young adults of many races and may have attenders of all ages, but it won't take long to see that they have some specific distinctives that have brought them together! Another church may clearly cross barriers between the rich and the poor because of their passionate spirituality and the obvious love demonstrated by the people toward each other. I watch people today searching for the right church, often ignoring race, economics, age and education. But where they decide to attend, almost invariably, fits them on some cultural and predictable level. Birds of a feather do still find each other!

Think about this example. One young English-speaking Hispanic couple will look for a Hispanic church. Nothing will stop them. They will find cultural joy and safety there, driving past a dozen multicultural churches. They may not want to be a minority on Sunday. They may want one or two Hispanic cultural experiences a week. They may want to be around family and friends. They may not know how great it is to be in a culturally diverse church. And they may not care. This is their choice! Another identical couple doesn't want to attend a Hispanic church. They long for identity in a multicultural setting and will search until they find that church. Both churches are meeting valid needs! Both couples will not be swayed! This isn't necessarily an issue of maturity. It could be an issue of prejudice, but it doesn't have to be. It's probably an example of taste. Let's celebrate with both couples and with both churches as they attract specific people first to themselves and then to God.

Many of us today would like to reject a homogeneous principle as a symbol of segregation and sin in the church. We would like all of us worshiping cross-culturally, blending our styles and distinctives into one. Now, heaven will look like that, but we're still here on Earth. The prejudicial attitudes that have created racial and religious silos across the land are wrong and sinful! The idea that a Black man can't fellowship and worship with a White man is atrocious! It's godless! If that Black man wants to worship in an Anglo, Asian or Hispanic church, he should be welcomed without question. It happens every day. But if that Black man wants to attend a church with other Black brothers and sisters, unifying around age-old African-American cultural distinctives, isn't that also good? Is he wrong to enjoy a style of music and service that doesn't match other cultures? I don't think so. And will he bring his friends with him because he loves his church? I believe he will. Now, there's the homogeneous principal working for us. Distinctive cultural groups of people reaching others for Christ that perhaps no one else will reach. What about a younger African-American generation that rejects that older culture? That's where culturally-diverse church plants must be springing up everywhere. I'm talking about choice, and we are a people of choice!

As I travel across our land, I find absolute diversity–a multiplicity of age groups, cultures and nationalities in each state and

community. As newer churches plateau and older churches need to reinvent themselves, it's essential that they listen carefully and pay attention to the changing culture of their communities. Who are they as a church family? What are their homogeneous distinctives? Who can they reach for Christ with their own unique culture and attractiveness? What do they need to change to reach more people for Christ? How can they become more diverse and multicultural? What would it take to cross cultures and begin an entirely new ministry? Is that really possible? Where do they start?

What all of this means is we need to carefully appraise who we are and match who we are to our target group. We can't be what we aren't! Let's face it. An Anglo church won't be and can't be attractive to their neighboring Hispanic community without radical change. There are immense cultural and language barriers, both ways. But this church has a growing desire to impact their neighbors for Christ! Now, it would totally make sense that God is prodding the leadership to reach out to their neighbors. Why wouldn't He put that on our hearts? But if they want to successfully reach a whole new target group, they will need to create another leadership team and a completely different service or church and set of structures. The new leaders of this Hispanic ministry will need a framework within which they will be comfortable, excited about serving and attractive to their "homogeneous" group of people. The primary target of the mother church would still have to be community people who would naturally be attracted to them. A second target group, the Hispanic community, would require an entirely new strategy to reach these people for Christ.

So let's look at marketing what we are and what we want to be. For example, we may want our church to be far more multicultural than it is, looking more like our community. Time will tell if this change is possible. The people of the church have to really want it, and they also have to be attractive to the people of the community. The atmosphere of the church has to be very inviting to them. And the people of the church have to actually invite them. Churches almost always multiply who they are. It's next to impossible to change the entire culture of the church. A pastor friend of mine in a multicultural community deeply longs to be more diverse in his church. The church is multi-cultural, but the Anglos outnumber everyone else. Here's the problem: as the church has grown, even more Anglos are visiting and are staying. As frustrating as that is, my friend simply can't control that. The good news is you only see diversity in their Sunday gathering. The blending of many races and cultures has made the "whiteness" of the majority simply fade away!

Let's come back to marketing- a Chinese or Filipino or Vietnamese congregation needs to make sure their advertising is culturally relevant to reach their own people group. For example, some Chinese churches advertise in local Chinese newspapers. But that won't work for English-speaking Chinese congregations for obvious reasons. If an African-American pastor is planting an African-American church, he needs to make sure that his advertising clarifies the target group for the church. If he sends out a generic advertising flyer, he will completely miss his audience and he'll waste all of that money. If you're targeting a multi-cultural group of people, make sure that your advertising clearly demonstrates that.

Where should we be advertising?

> **1) The Internet - Here's the Number One place that people go to look for a church before they visit. Everyone!** Tell a friend about your church and she'll look it up on the web. I always use the church website to find current service times and clear directions to the church. It's essential that you develop and maintain a **quality, attractive** web site for your church. It's well worth the cost to have someone create an excellent site. There are options for every budget, great and small. It will be inexpensive to maintain and the reward of visitors will certainly pay for the effort. Don't expect people to pour into your church because of your website or any advertising, for that matter. No advertising will produce quick results, but it will be well worth it over time.

Your advertisements, flyers and business cards can refer to your website and people can immediately learn more about you. Again, the quality of that website will make people want to visit you or **not!** Don't waste your time on a website if you won't build quality into it. I come across simple, unattractive websites all the time. And I'm also pleasantly surprised when I find many smaller churches or plants with great websites. Finding the right designer or program goes a long way. And remember to keep your site current. Occasionally, I'll find a church web page that hasn't been updated in three to six months or longer. They're still advertising Easter and its July. That looks sloppy and very unattractive. Sometimes the church has moved or changed their service times, but they've forgotten to update their website. Maybe they don't want us to visit their church. But I doubt that. Again, we're talking about attractors and distractors. We want to eliminate everything that will distract people from what we're trying to accomplish.

2) Local/Regional Newspapers- The local newspaper has often been a valuable choice. An ad on the church page can still grab the attention of newcomers moving to town and looking for a great church home. In larger cities, there are often regional papers that are actively read and are also far less expensive to advertise in. You never know when someone is looking, so advertise every week if you can. One new tithing family will pay for a year of advertising.

3) Yellow Pages- The Yellow Pages has been more important than the newspaper. But times have changed! Cell phones and the web have almost eliminated the use of home phones. Disruptive technology! And the yellow pages seem to be disappearing as well. Some people use the white and yellow pages online. If it's useful in your community and by your people, advertise in it. Otherwise, pass.

4) Nickel/Target Newspapers/Magazines/Flyers- Other options like the local "penny saver" newspapers are usually far less expensive, and they do have a reading audience. There are many newspapers, magazine and flyers targeting a specific audience that can be very helpful. For example, there are publications and flyers sold or sent out, specifically targeting local Chinese or Filipino or Arab households. These can get your message right to the people who need to read it. This strategy is especially for first generation churches that struggle trying to target a minority scattered throughout a city. This puts you on the map- a valuable step.

5) Radio/T.V./Cable- A well-placed ad on radio or T.V. can be heard or seen by large numbers of people. Think about stories that touch the heart! Most of this advertising can be very expensive and it may not be possible or productive for you. There are still reasonable opportunities using ads on cable.

6) Your Answering Machine- Every time someone calls your church, you are attracting visitors or turning them off. How the phone is answered and how the "potential visitor" is treated and helped makes all the difference in the world. And the voice and presentation on your answering machine really counts. Believe me, thousands of people decide to visit a different church based on a poor presentation on an answering machine. It represents who you are! It's often your first place of contact. Take the time to create a quality message with an attractive voice. Again, find the right voice. Don't try to sound like a local radio station, but do try to sound like you care about the quality of your message. Make sure that you get them to the information that they have called for as quickly as possible.

Some churches have paid big bucks for complicated phone systems that make you wander through a maze of endless options. Some of them never do get you to your desired goal. These systems are often designed to protect the church receptionist from having to talk to you! Why even try? Wait a minute! Perhaps these are actually God-given early warning indicators of a corporate business structure that should be avoided. Watch out! Always get in the shoes of the visitor. Always! I personally hate calling churches and taking five minutes to discover that I can't find anyone home. But they are home. It's office hours. I'm lost in the system. Help! It drives me crazy. Answer that stupid phone. Pay someone to answer the phone! If you're large, pay five people to answer the phone. I do have some feelings about this. Ask me sometime and I'll tell you what I really think. Here's my question- are you a church or a corporation? Then act like a church! Do you deal with sheep or clients? Come on! Make me feel like a person and like you actually care. While I'm on a roll, here are two more problems I find. Some churches don't tell their service times on their message. What? I've also found churches that have forgotten to bring their message up to date. Picture your visitors coming at the wrong service time. Now picture them not coming back. This may be a bigger deal than you think.

7) Signage- Signs are extremely essential to get people to your property. Attractive, well-placed signs will guide them in for a smooth landing. No signs will leave them wandering. Poor signs will send them running! A frustrating attempt at a visit because of poor signage will often be the last visit. We'll talk more about this in our next chapter. Be appropriate and visible.

B. Direct Mail- Direct mail is one of the easiest ways to get into neighborhoods all around your church. Church plants use direct mailings as a primary tool to establish their presence in a community. It's an effective tool over time. If the mailing has quality and grabs their attention, it will leave a lasting memory in the minds of the readers. Most people will glance at it and toss it, but they'll begin to remember your name.

I've been surprised to discover how many church planters stop doing direct mail just a few years after they've begun their church plant. Many of them saw good results in the beginning. Start-up resources do dry up several years into a church plant. But that's when new churches have to become innovative. Many planters get frustrated when their churches plateau and aren't growing like they first did. I believe that they would see continued results if they would again do what they did at the beginning.

The real key to direct mail is doing it strategically over time. Don't try it once or twice and expect any visitors. As your community sees the consistency of quality events and opportunities arriving in their mail, they will know that you are there and there to stay. Focus on special events like an outreach picnic or concert, or an Easter or Christmas event. Direct mail reinforces the other forms of marketing that you are doing. Search to find the cheapest way to put out your best product. It's great when we can afford a top-quality product like those produced by Outreach Marketing. With limited budgets, many churches have learned to create their own postcards and flyers to save costs. When cost is a factor, focus on specific neighborhoods, rotate your target neighborhoods, and send it only once a year if that's all you can do. Stay on the map! It's better to send something once a year than to send nothing at all.

C. Word of Mouth- I have saved the two best for last. I believe that word of mouth is absolutely the best way to market your church! It's the cheapest means of marketing. It's the most personal. It guarantees a hearing with the right neighbors and it produces the best results. No other form of marketing even comes close to word of mouth. Our goal is to have our churches filled with people stirred up and passionate about making friends who need Jesus. As they build relationships with their neighbors and friends, they will look for the next step and opportunity to involve their friends with other believers. Show them those opportunities. Motivate your congregation to talk about your church and the Lord- all the time. Encourage them to invite their friends- to the right event. Keep the concept of visitors before your people- every weekend. Talk to your visitors- in every gathering. Create events and opportunities for visitors- on a regular basis.

As the pastor, I constantly encouraged my people to invite their friends. I was the Number One marketer! And we constantly had visitors! We gained the habit of bringing friends to church and to special events. And the church was continually growing. Most of the churches that I visit never address the subject of visitors. The people aren't regularly encouraged to invite their friends and neighbors. **And they don't!**

Continually give your people attractive handouts and flyers to take home to their neighbors and friends. This is critical. This is such a valuable use of your marketing energy and budget. Give your people a tool that they're proud of and want to give away. Make inviting visitors to church and events one of the main things. By the way, people talk about the things that excite them. If they're not talking about their church, it could be because they've lost the habit. But it could also be because they've lost the excitement! Sometimes we need to give them something to talk about. Think about it.

> It's critical that you assess the responsiveness of your marketing strategies. What worked yesterday may not work today.

D. Social Networking- This is the wave of the future and it's right here, right now! I've already said that social networking will continue to grow to be perhaps the greatest tool to connect people with people. I can't emphasize enough how valuable and essential it can be in the life of the church. A growing number of our people have been interacting with each other for years. I predict that this lifestyle will continue to grow until a vast majority of us are interacting, in some form, in this way. Dozens of companies are competing to network all of us categorically, by profession, by congregation or denomination, by interests and hobbies, and the list goes on. Churches and loyal subjects promote Jesus and events all over their pages. Major companies are hoping to friend us so they can show us their wares. Now, networks like Facebook will become overcrowded and annoying, forcing some to retreat to smaller, less distractive circles of friendship. But these and new evolving vehicles will provide you and others in your church family the opportunity to celebrate your faith and your church with all of your friends. As your pre-believing friends watch you and your friends demonstrate the love and life of Christ online, it provides one more opportunity to move them toward the Savior.

Marketing Responsiveness- It's critical that you assess the responsiveness of your marketing strategies. What worked yesterday may not work today. One type of marketing may work for someone else, but it may not work for you. Community demographics make a world of difference. For example, direct mail may not be useful in a small community where everyone knows each other. Our neighborhoods across this land are like night and day! What works in Southern California or in Minneapolis probably won't work in Boston or New Orleans. You as a church or as a church planter also define some of what works. I've seen church communities try everything and still fail to penetrate their cities. And suddenly, a new church in town succeeds where everyone else has failed. They may be able to do something that you simply cannot do. That's life! On the other hand, maybe you can learn from them and try again! Don't be afraid to try again. But take the time to listen and to sort out what seems to be working in your world. What has worked for you in the past? Are you doing it today? Why or why not?

Sometimes we discover that we have stopped doing something that was really helpful. Why would we do that? Some churches stop doing strategies that are working because they think they can't afford the expenditure. They don't realize that they can't afford not to do it! What hasn't seemed to work in the past? Why not? Ask the hard questions. Maybe you should try it again. What various forms of marketing are you doing today? Are they working? Why or why not? How responsive are people to each type of marketing? Dig in to the reasons why some things are working and other things are not. What can you do to improve the quality of your marketing that is working? What marketing is proving to be a waste of time or money? What marketing should you try that you aren't doing right now? Do it!

Marketing Openness- Here's a big question. How open is your church leadership to marketing? Some leaders will say they are open to marketing as long as it doesn't cost them any money! How open is that? Every church has to make up its own mind on how much money should be spent on marketing. Remember that doing the right marketing will always pay for itself. Word of mouth should be happening all the time. But you need to be sending your people home with good-looking flyers and invitations and that will cost you money. Good advertising and direct mail will complement your people talking about their church. An appropriate amount of money spent on marketing will bring in a continual flow of new people, who will pay for that marketing ten times over. Step out on faith. Put it in the budget!

> All the marketing in the world would be a waste of resources if we didn't have God doing the main part of the work!

Marketing and the Power of God- I don't want to overlook the work of the Holy Spirit in drawing people to Himself. God works in wonderful ways and gets people to the right places on time all the time! He's involved in our lives and in the lives of the people that He wants to save or add to our church. Certainly God has drawn people to church with no help from anyone. I've seen it happen over and over again. But most of the time, God chooses to use you and me as His partners in this great work of rescuing the lost and growing His church. We do the advertising, mailing and telling our friends and He stirs their hearts and helps them decide to visit. We tell them about the good news and He convinces, convicts and saves them! What a deal!

One of the interesting observations from pastoring the same church for many years was watching the pattern of visitor attendance. There were predictable patterns that aligned themselves with the seasons and the weather. There also were patterns that fit with the mood of the church. But there were unusual seasons when visitors just poured in week after week and others when there simply were no visitors. There was no explanation for it other than God drawing people to visit in His timing. But how did He get them there? He probably used advertising, direct mail, an invite or the memory of a friend's invitation.

All the marketing in the world would be a waste of resources if we didn't have God doing the main part of the work. This is His Mission and we are called to do our best on our part. You can see why all of our marketing must be combined with a whole lot of prayer and a humble spirit in total reliance on God. We will not really succeed without His Power! It may look like it, feel like it, and may even get the attention of the watching world. But watch out! Without His power, imitations of the real thing have a way of falling fast and hard.

Outreach Mindset

Most of what we are trying to accomplish will fail over time if the church body doesn't have a genuine concern for the lost around us. We shouldn't simply want to grow our church because we want it to be bigger and supposedly better. It's not motivating enough to grow larger if no one is finding Jesus. Most churches that have lost their heart for the unsaved are going nowhere and are slowly dying away. Look at the churches in your community. Are you one of them? The ultimate mission of the church is to reach lost people for Christ and to grow them into reproducing disciples. If that's not the mindset of the majority of people in your church, then that's where you have to start. Why would your church members invite someone to church or a church event if they don't have concern for the lost? They probably wouldn't. And if someone did get invited and they did come, why would they come back if they saw that no one really cared about them. One of **the** greatest ways to put your church on the map is to help your own people care about their friends and neighbors who don't know Christ.

Unfortunately, many churches today have lost their understanding of and their heart for the Mission. We've become ingrown. We've become content serving ourselves and trying to meet all of our own needs. And we've lost sight of one of the greatest purposes of the church. Audrey Malphurs, in his book, *Advanced Strategic Planning*, says:

> Far too many evangelical churches have assumed the ostrich position when it comes to knowing and understanding the world that Christ commands us to reach. They have buried their heads in the sand. They have no idea what is going on. . .If our churches want to relate to and reach our culture, they must spend time exegeting the culture as well as the Bible. In short, they must become culture watchers. [42]

The starting point has to be an assessment of what is actually happening in the church, starting with the lives of the people. Do we as a church have a genuine concern for the local lost? Some of us are concerned for the lost all around the world, but we've made little effort to reach out to the people who live all around us. The Great Commission starts right next door! **Are we excited about Jesus?** And are we excited about our church? **Are we intentionally developing friendships with pre-Christians with the hope that they will someday come to Christ?** If we aren't telling people about our church, why aren't we? **Do our church people want outreach events scheduled so they can have the opportunity to invite and bring their friends to them?** Or are events and activities all scheduled by the leadership and pressed upon the body? In many churches, events are planned and encouraged from the top down, but most of the people have no heart to participate.

119

Church leadership in this area of Great Commission/Great Commandment living makes all the difference in the world. Leaders have to lead or the sheep won't follow. It has to begin with the pastor and other leaders modeling this intentional lifestyle of making friends for Christ. What is the outreach lifestyle of most of the leadership in your church? If we aren't modeling a lifestyle of intentionally building friendships with nonbelievers, how and when will we change that? It needs to happen now!

What is the outreach focus of the leadership? Are we committed to doing whatever it takes to reach lost people in our community? Maybe that needs to become the special focus among our leadership. Grab some training material. You'll find great examples at sonlife-classic.com or pastors.net or willowcreekassociation.net or at your local bookstore. *Becoming a Contagious Christian* and *Becoming a Contagious Church* are great books. [43] *Growing a Healthy Church / Eternal CPR* disciple-making training can be life-changing. [44] So settle on a book or some training. And then use it with your leadership. Do some retreats or some weekend sessions. Bring in a consultant. **Do something!**

How much money is being spent on outreach in the church budget? Many churches haven't ever thought of making outreach a line item in their budget. It's just never crossed their mind. Jesus said that where our treasure is, that's where our heart will also be. If we really want to be fully invested in outreach, we need to put our money behind it as well. We need to be generous. We're talking about lives here. And we need to teach our people to do the same thing with their time and money.

Outreach Programming

One of the greatest ways to help our people reach their friends for Christ is through outreach programming. We'll be dedicating an entire chapter to the detail of programming for effective outreach. But now we want to look briefly at what you're already doing. If we want visitors to come to our church, we've got to have a plan. Most people won't just come to church- especially if they aren't Christians. There's got to be a reason for them to come. Marketing is valuable, but what are we marketing? It's critical that we put our church on the map, but usually it's an activity or an event that will get people there. Word of mouth is the best way to market our church, but what are we talking about? Some of our people will talk about how great our church is, but usually we're pointing to something special, like a church picnic or concert or Easter Sunday. We have to have year-round outreach plans for both the entire church and for each of our segment ministries. The events themselves need to be well-planned and calendared so they can be planned for and counted on by everyone in the church. We need to help our people to get into the rhythm of corporate outreach.

Here are two critical thoughts that we'll talk more about later-

1) **We don't want to do too many events and activities, or we'll burn our people out.**
2) **We don't want to do too few of them, or they'll lose the vision and value of doing evangelism together!**

How are you doing with outreach programming? Is it on your hearts, minds and calendars? Are you planning and doing consistent, well-planned outreach events and activities, both as an entire church and as segment ministries? Have you learned to produce attractive marketing tools to help your people invite their friends to these events? Again, we'll spend a great deal of time going into detail in this area later in this book. My goal now is to get you thinking and looking at your current situation before we examine future possibilities.

Outreach Participation

The greatest crisis in the church today lies in the heart of man rather than in the programming of the church! Without a heart for lost people, all the great programming in the world will eventually fade away! Good programming complements a lifestyle of evangelism and can actually inspire people as they become involved in a pattern of corporate outreach. But until people have a heart to reach out to their friends, most outreach programming will only be an aid to the few and faithful. What's the story in your church? What percentages of your people are participating in outreach activities? Are people bringing their friends to the events and activities that you have planned? Look at each of your segment ministry outreach events. What percentages of your people are inviting friends? What percentages are actually bringing friends? Are those friends coming back to other events? At each outreach event, what is the ratio of believers to visitors? What do you think are the reasons for these percentages and this ratio at your events? Take the time to look at each of your events during this last year, both as an entire church and in each of your segment ministries. It would be good to assess all of the ministries to see what the differences are and to evaluate why there are significant differences. What can you learn from each other and from your past as you do this evaluation? As painful as this assessment may be, the truth will set you free!

Notes

THOUGHTS ON CHANGE

All change is not growth, as all movement is not forward.
Ellen Glasgow

Change before you have to.
Jack Welch

*To improve is to change;
to be perfect is to change often.*
Winston Churchill

4. THE DRIVE-IN/WALK UP - 10 minutes and counting!
What You See IS What They Get!

What your church facility looks like makes all the difference in the world! As much as we may not want to believe that or think about that, it's the truth! First impressions are everything, and your first impression is usually what people see from the street. Remember, we're normally not attracting mature, spiritually hungry people who want exactly what you have to offer. Most of those people are already well established in another church! People visiting churches are looking for something that will please them and their family, like a new restaurant. If you don't care about how your church looks, they won't care to visit it! And the non-believers that we bring to church will be as "observant" as everyone else is.

Think about your own shopping experience. Do you like to go to newer stores and restaurants or old ones, businesses that are well kept or ones that are run down? I think that most of us usually drive to malls, stores and restaurants that are either newer or ones that are kept clean and attractive. Then there are always the places that we have become familiar with over time. We don't really care about the appearance because we like the service! But you rarely see new faces in businesses like that, and you rarely see new faces in churches like that either.

One of the problems that can take place in many churches is that things around the property begin to deteriorate and we don't really notice. Most of us would never allow our homes to deteriorate the way we let our churches begin to get run down. But we simply don't notice. Or we don't really worry about it. Or we realize the church is strapped financially and can't do anything about it. A lot of churches get trapped in the "we're always broke" syndrome and they limit their ability to bring about the necessary changes that they really need to make.

Most of us would never let our business buildings or personal property get run down the way some of our church properties or buildings get run down. We'd never stay in business! As stewards of God's house, we should make sure that our churches look at least as well kept and attractive as our homes and businesses. If we really care, we'll raise the money. If we really care, we'll organize, show up at workdays and work nights and get the job done! We don't need to have new property and a new church to be attractive. But we do need to care!

What is Ten Minutes and Counting? Visitors are registering every sight, sound and smell as they approach the church building. The data will add up quickly, with pluses and minuses. Within the next ten minutes, they will have decided whether they will come back, or not! Most of them make up their minds long before they even hear the preacher preach! Again, first impressions are everything! You can see why it's so important that we do our best to remove the things that will turn people off and send them running.

Property

Where do we begin? Let's do the drive in and the walk up. Let's be the visitors. For some reason, we've picked this church- out of their website, off the Saturday church pages, or perhaps a friend has invited us to come. First of all, it better not be too hard to find. We're not completely sure about attending this church anyway. Give us a few obstacles and we'll turn around and go home! As we drive or walk down the street and begin to approach the church property, we begin ten minutes and counting.

What do we see from the street? What do we catch at first glance? Are there attractive, well-designed signs letting us know that we have arrived? Is the sign inviting and visitor-friendly, or is it a relic of the past? Is it attractive to visitors or is it attractive to the church regulars? Is the property beautiful? Is it well-groomed? Is it obvious that someone is mowing, pulling weeds, and trimming the landscaping on a weekly basis? Are the plants fresh and beautiful? Is the property weed-free, poop-free and junk-free?

Be honest. Look around. Look down at the end of the building. Look at the part of the property that's seen from the street. Is there attractive landscaping? Is it obvious that someone cares and that the property landscaping was well-planned and attractively designed? Are there borders framing the property and are the borders attractive and kept-up? Is the parking lot attractive, or is it run down? Are its lines fresh and clean, or are they fading? If there is gravel, is it well-manicured and looking good? Or is it thinning out and spreading everywhere? Is there lots of parking so I know that I will easily find a space? Is there visitor parking for me right up front? That would make it really easy for us. Does the property seem safe and carefree so we can drive in and get out of our cars without concern? Does it feel clean and inviting? If it's nighttime, is the parking lot and property well-lit so we will feel safe when we get out of our car? Does the property feel well-mapped? Is it easy to see where we need to go first? Is it clear that this church holds to a high standard of excellence when it comes to the beauty and upkeep of its property?

Imagine arriving to a church property that clearly is deteriorating and not appropriately looked after. Why would you want to even drive in? Why would you want to go to a church where the people don't care? That's the message that we're giving to the outside world. Picture a sign that looks like it's been there for twenty years and nothing's changed. All of us would guess that what we find on the inside would be the same! And it often is! These are the distractors that we've been talking about.

Watch any church on a Sunday morning where there is no visible parking and you will see visitors slowing down, looking and driving away. It happens everywhere, every week. It's critical to leave lots of clearly visible parking for visitors and everyone else if you want to grow a church. Lack of parking is a killer for church growth. Our entire church staff parked far away from our church building to model a philosophy of ministry and care for visitors. We were then able to ask our people to park as far away from the building as possible to leave lots of parking space near the building for visitors, newer people and latecomers. We modeled it, they agreed with it and it worked!

Buildings

Church buildings certainly count too. As you make that drive up to the church property, the buildings will tell you as much or even more about the care of the church. Some churches seem like they are as old as the nation, but they are beautiful! They are well-kept, clean and are very attractive. Other churches are only ten or twenty years old, but they've deteriorated and are desperately in need of a face-lift.

Let's drive up to your church building again. Is it attractive and clean in appearance? Does it demonstrate quality and care? Is it well-trimmed? Does it have attractive lines as a building? Some churches were built in the hardest of times with very little money. Some were built without a legitimate architect. Costs were saved at every turn. And it's obvious when you look at those buildings. Maybe it's time to do some appropriate remodeling. Could some trim on the windows bring them up to date? Do the windows and doors look clean and new and attractive? Maybe they need to be replaced. How about the general appearance of the outside of your building? Do the lights look like they have been maintained? Do the fixtures look good, or should they be replaced? Are all of the lights checked and replaced on a regular basis? Does the building have attractive lighting at night? Does the building look like it's been freshly painted? Or does it have that aging and stained look? Here's another thought: what looked attractive in the 80's and 90's often looks pretty foreign now in this new millennium. What could we do to help our look? We're all attracted to buildings that look new and clean and cobweb free. Most of our church buildings start to fade and lose that fresh look in a couple of years. That's when we need to repaint them. We need to be proud of our church buildings and we need to make them look great. Make sure that the cobwebs are taken care of on a regular basis, depending on how good your spiders are. Spray the place! Treat it better than your homes.

Take a quick look around for junk. Is there a pile of anything around or up against the building? Why is it there? Get rid of it! Is there a storage shed in sight? Hide that thing- where no one can see it. You may be used to it, but it's a great, big eyesore to visitors. By the way, hide the garbage cans! Don't leave them out where your company can see them- especially on Sunday. One more question in summary- Do your church buildings demonstrate a standard of excellence? Do they show the watching world that you really care about your church? How you care for your buildings and property could send a message about how you care for your religion and God and how you care for people.

A Word about Rental Facilities- Many of you don't own the buildings that you are using for your church services. Some of you are involved in a church plant and this is a first step. Others of you have been renting for years and there may be no immediate way out. Here are the facts about renting space and growing a church. It is true that it is often easier to grow a church on your own property in your own building than in a rented facility. In almost every case, you will accelerate your growth when you move into your permanent facility. Your people will tell all their friends and they will come to see it! The community will also be more responsive to your permanent home.

That being said, some churches will use that obstacle as their reason for not growing in a rental situation. They're dead wrong! They're usually not growing for one hundred other reasons. On any given Sunday, you will find thousands of churches across North America in rental facilities growing rapidly with no problem. They do have to work a little harder. They have to really make sure that they get on the map! The key comes right back to you as the renter. Don't let your circumstances be an obstacle to where God wants to take you. Are you in an attractive rental facility? If not, find another one. Figure it out! If it costs you more and you start growing, the change will quickly pay for itself. The facility may not be your only problem, so changing locations may be the least of your worries.

Many rented facilities can be improved. Work with the owners and see if you can make that happen. Many church plants are pouring a lot of money into rented buildings and it's paying off in the end. It's a lot cheaper than buying the whole thing and it works financially. Offer to paint the building if it helps. It's critical that you make sure that your rented facility is attractive and clean. Treat the grass and landscaping as your own. Step in and keep it beautiful and well cared for.

New Hope Community Church in Hawaii made the decision years ago to remain in a rented school facility and to plant dozens of daughter churches. With that decision, New Hope began investing in the auditorium infrastructure- sounds, lights, etc. The school loves the church and the church loves the school. By the way, the mother church alone is running over 8000 in attendance each week. How's that for overcoming obstacles!

Signs are extremely important in a rental situation. Make sure there's great-looking signage helping people to get to the right parking lot and to the right door. I've visited many churches where there are literally dozens of signs plus friendly people all pointing me to my next stop. I've also driven around entire buildings looking for the church. I've found no or minimal signs. What were they thinking? In fact, recently, I visited a church renting a school facility. There were just enough signs to let me know a church was meeting somewhere in the massive building. I wandered and wondered why I had to work so hard to find any people! I finally arrived at the service and discovered that I was half an hour late. They had forgotten to change their service times on their website. Now, what if I had been a normal visitor? Do you think I would have come back? Are you kidding? Spend the money and get the signs! Put them everywhere. Let people know what's happening inside. How sad if visitors drive by and can't find you. It's the first step.

Atmosphere

There is an atmosphere that envelops visitors as they come to church. They often bring with them a sense of apprehension and fear of the unknown. That can turn to a sense of excitement and anticipation if their early experiences go really well. We can help to create that mood from the moment they drive on to our property. I can still remember visiting Chuck Smith's Calvary Chapel as a young man back in the 70's. As I drove into their new church parking lot, there were cars and people everywhere. I got out of my car and, can you believe it, there was energized music playing from speakers on the light fixtures. That atmosphere immediate grabbed me and made me want to get inside as quickly as possible. It also made me decide that that was what I wanted to do when I built a church. And I did!

We want to do everything we can to make church a positive, friendly, exciting experience, both with man and God. All of that can start outside the church buildings. Let's again be that visiting family or single. Imagine driving in to the church parking lot and seeing a whole group of friendly, smiling, happy people, guiding cars in the right direction and greeting people as they get out of their cars. Imagine the other people getting out of their cars being warm and friendly too. As you gather your family and begin to walk toward the buildings, you're met by friendly people all along the way. You hear music playing, you see banners and balloons, tents and tables with information and coffee and donuts. People are standing all around the entry area talking with each other and some come on up and actually begin to talk with you. You can't help but have a positive feeling about this place. And you haven't even gone inside. Now, I'm not talking about a circus atmosphere. I'm describing what I've personally experienced at so many churches across the country. I love it! It makes me feel like I've arrived at something worth coming to. It also makes me feel like this church really cares about people and has taken the time and effort to demonstrate that care.

Mark Waltz, pastor of Connections at Granger Community Church, writes about what he calls the WOW factor in his books *First Impressions and Lasting Impressions.* The WOW factor is creating experiences in your church that will make people remember that you care and that made them feel valued! Like getting a fresh-baked cookie at a Doubletree Hotel, or greeting customers at the front door. "If our guests can't say, 'Wow! I'm impressed!' within their first ten minutes on campus, then we've failed." Mark goes on to describe the opposite of the WOW factor- having experiences that will negatively affect the visitors. "When your guests are distracted from the real purpose of their visit to your church, you'll have a difficult time re-engaging them. In order for people to see Jesus, potential distractions must be identified and eliminated." [45] You can tell that Mark represents leaders in churches across our land who truly are committed to the very best experience for their visitors each week. Of course, every experience and every church will be different! Some will be more resourced than others. But all of us can demonstrate care. That's the real WOW factor that everyone's looking for! And we all can work to eliminate the distractions that will be there if we don't have a plan.

This can and will happen at your church if you plan it and get organized. Train your people to be friendly- especially to people they don't know. In fact, help them to stop focusing on their own friends so they can reach out to people they don't know that well. Recruit your friendliest people as greeters. Don't put them in a uniform or put a button on them. Let them be normal-looking- like everyone else at church. Place some of your greeters as helpers in the parking lot. Have others greeting on the way in to the entrance of your building. Wire some speakers so they can play outside your building. Set up some area for food, fellowship and information. Put up some banners and balloons. If that can be outdoors, you may want to build an information kiosk. Many churches will set up booths or tents and tables to display ministry opportunities. Some will set up an area with tables and umbrellas and an espresso and coffee bar with donuts and other refreshments. Why not make every Sunday a special day of excitement and celebration. All of this takes extra work, but you will love what you have created. And so will your visitors!

Of course, none of this will happen if you don't establish these ingredients as critical and permanent components of your strategy. Most warm and caring churches become unfriendly simply because that's what happens as churches grow larger. The **only** way to turn that around is to be intentional and to train and model and then train and model.

Notes

THOUGHTS ON CHANGE

Without change, something sleeps inside us, and seldom awakens. The sleeper must awaken.
Frank Herbert

Just when I think I have learned the way to live, life changes.
Hugh Prather

Change is the only constant. Hanging on is the only sin.
Denise McCluggage

The first step toward change is awareness. The second step is acceptance.
Nathaniel Branden

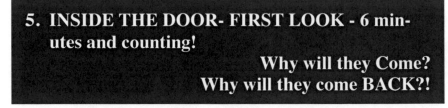

Now we begin that critical countdown with only six minutes on the clock. Impressions are being formed. Our visitors are already beginning to decide whether they want to come back or not. They like our church. Or they don't! As they walk in the door, the sensors continue to go off. Scores are unconsciously being added up on both sides of the spectrum. And if it's a family visiting, everyone's participating. They may not be talking to each other-yet. But decisions are being made and the consensus will tell all.

Let's make it clear that, above everything else, people make all the difference. Wonderful, friendly, happy people can make up for a lot of other negatives when it comes to looking for a church. In fact, many people will shop and pass right over the perfect church to settle for a loving, friendly church where they feel at home. That needs to encourage us to **be** that warm and caring church family. But it doesn't give us an excuse to be slackers when it comes to caring about the quality and excellence of our facility!

Facility

Walk in the front door as the visiting family and take a look around at your church, through their eyes. The first question on our minds is, "Where do we go from here?" We've never been in this building before. We have no idea what comes next. We may never have attended church before. Our visitors probably are nervous and at least a little apprehensive. It's so important that the next few moments are easy and help to relieve their fears. We'll look over and over again at the importance of friendly, caring people in this process. But let's start with what our visitors see and feel.

> Wonderful, friendly, happy people can make up for a lot of other negatives when it comes to looking for a church.

What are the first impressions that our visitors have as they step inside the door? One of their greatest needs is to be able to easily navigate our facility and find their way around. I visit churches all the time and often discover the difficulty that newcomers face if they are arriving for the first time. We become so familiar with our facility that we don't even think about a visitor's ease of discovery. Where do we go from here? Where are the bathrooms? Do our children stay with us or do we take them somewhere?

Walk into any mall in the country and you will find a well-placed map at every entrance. There is a "You are Here!" X on every map. As you look for the stores that you want to shop at, you can quickly determine which direction you need to go to get there. The stores, restaurants, restrooms and other services are clearly labeled so everyone, child or adult, can know where they are and where they are going. Mall developers have learned over time how essential it is that customers don't feel lost and can easily find what they are looking for. We need to do the same thing in our churches!

So there needs to be some purposeful mapping of your facility. You need to create two types of maps- one in print and the other in plain view. Many churches hand the visitor a map of their buildings to help them clearly move from point A to point B. Other churches actually have that map at various locations on walls throughout the building. Having clearly defined and understandable maps is an essential first step to making your visitor comfortable. Having your building well-labeled is the second step. Have clear, visible and attractive signs everywhere! Be creative. Go and look at some churches that are known for having quality and creativity. You will find that they have taken the time and money to design and mount beautiful, well-placed signs throughout their buildings. Don't throw up a cheap sign! Don't let a well-intentioned volunteer build or buy something that you will regret for years. Many of us have done that once. Let's not do it again. **Don't sacrifice your visitors with mediocrity!**

═══════════════════════════════════════

Money, Money, Money, Money, Money, Money, Money, Money!

As we walk through this process, the issue of money and costs will come up over and over again. Some of us have more money than others of us to do the improvements that we would like to do. But we can all start somewhere! Decide what you need to do first and get going! Money follows vision! People begin giving when they are presented with a clear vision and understand what the real need is. The purpose of this manual is not to help us create the perfect little church so we can be happy and satisfied with ourselves! God help us if we get caught in that trap! Our goal is to eliminate the obstacles that will keep people from coming to church with the ultimate intention that they become fully devoted followers of Jesus Christ! Now, giving with that goal in mind should be absolutely thrilling!

═══════════════════════════════════════

Decide to demonstrate excellence even if you don't have much money to spend. Have signs to and at the restrooms. Have signs to and at the auditorium. Have signs to all of the main ministry rooms, both for Sunday and throughout the week. Make it easy to get to the nursery, the children's, youth and adult classrooms, the kitchen, the offices, the welcome center, the coffee corner, the CD sales, and this list goes on and on. Assume that people don't know anything. Label everything so few questions need to be asked. Try walking in on a gathering like you are the visitor and think about all the questions that would be settled if there were appropriate signs. Your goal is to help your visitors to get anywhere from everywhere! We'll talk more about maps in hand in our next chapter.

Think about your own home and how nice you want it to be on the inside! Most of us work at keeping our walls painted and our carpets fresh and clean. We try to have current furnishings that are attractive and enjoyable to our family. Some of us like everything in its place all the time so we feel a sense of quality in our homes. Others of us work hard to clean up and prepare when we are having company over to our homes for dinner. Often the whole family will work together to clean rooms and to get ready for friends. In our home, my wife wanted everything to be as perfect as possible. My three sons and I worked to make that happen. Now, if we care that much about company in our homes, shouldn't we care even more about visitors in our church?

Let's step back into the shoes of our visitor and have a look around! How does everything look? Is everything clean and neat and well cared for? Are the walls nicely painted and trimmed? Are the wall-coverings, trim and decorations attractive and warm? Does everything look nice and un-distracting? Nice is normal. Nice is comfortable. Most of us won't be able to "WOW" them with our facilities. But if we're sloppy or messy, we may lose them! I walk into churches and often see poorly-trimmed corners and fading foyer walls. I'll see bulletin boards that look like they haven't changed in twenty years! I'll notice a lost and found area that no one's thought about for months, or years. Or a pile of clothes left in a corner for someone hopefully to remember and collect someday. All of this can so easily happen in any church. But these distractions make visitors think twice about coming back again. "WOW- what a mess! They sure are friendly, but they don't take care of their stuff!" Now, that's the wrong WOW factor! Let's admit it. It's normal to relax and get used to a little bit of sloppiness here or there. Unfortunately, we can end up caring less for our church than we even care for our own homes. How sad, but how true. That's why it's critical that we 1) hold to a philosophy of excellence in all we say or do in our churches and that we 2) assess and reassess ourselves on a regular basis to make sure these things don't happen- for long.

> Our goal is to eliminate the obstacles that will keep people from coming to church with the ultimate intention that they become fully devoted followers of Jesus Christ!

Your foyer is the first section of your living room. It's also the first thing that visitors see. It needs to be warm and friendly and inviting. Paint it and furnish it like a family room. Trim it out and get some nice pictures. Use soft colors on the walls. Add some couches and tables and lamps. Floor coverings are important. And the right lighting makes all the difference in the world. Make it so people will want to live there! It's so helpful to go look at other innovative churches to see what they have done. Learn everything you can from everyone.

Let's walk down a hallway. In fact, how do all the hallways look? Again, are they attractive, with nice lighting, warm and well-maintained? Hallways can be boring or beautiful. Hallways can also be distracting if they are poorly painted or dark or too sterile. Many churches have worked to make their hallways as well-trimmed and as beautiful as their foyer. Some churches have done very unique designs and paintings down their hallways to carry a theme and to excite the children and young people as they come to church. What a great idea! It's important to realize that all churches start small and their creativity and ability to do unique things grows as they grow! Most of us can't do everything, and it usually will take time to do the things that we want to get done. We need to envision those changes that we want to make, create our priority list and then start at the beginning of the list.

Most of our newer restaurants and businesses work hard to stay clean, smell-free and attractive to the visiting public. Most of them have designed their restrooms for good airflow, with electronic air-fresheners. Many of them have someone scheduled to check of cleanliness, supplies and smells every 30 minutes on the clock. It's a neutral experience to use a clean and refreshed restroom. But it's a nasty experience to walk into smells, spillage and overflowing wastebaskets, or toilets! It makes me think that they don't care. If they don't care about their restrooms, they probably don't care about the quality of their food or other services. When I look at the staff and management of that restaurant or business, I often see people who appear to be undisciplined and carefree. They haven't yet learned the importance of detail and the parallel between that and visitor-retention. I'm gone, and I won't be back! Transfer that thought to your own church.

There are three primary location targets that most visitors care about- they are the restrooms, childcare and the main auditorium. They all need to be easily identifiable. They need to be attractive and inviting. They also need to be **clean and smell-free!** Clean and smell-free may be Nos. 68-74 out of 400 distractions in our assessment. But they are Number One when churches truly don't care. And, to a lot of our visitors, we prove that we don't care when we don't deal with this issue. Most of us usually take it for granted when a building or room is clean and not smelly. Our senses are neutralized and we are able to take in all the other details that surround us. But add dirtiness or smelliness and everything changes. Some of us grow desensitized to cleanliness and smells when nothing changes over time. But our visitors are not used to our dirty or smelly restrooms or classrooms and will choose to head straight out the door. I'm personally amazed at what is tolerated in some of the churches that I visit. Why do some children's classrooms smell fresh and neutral at the end of the day and others smell like a stockyard? If we care about our visitors and if we care about the quality of our ministry, we need to care enough to keep our facility clean and smell-free! Do we want that restroom clean and attractive, with plenty of towels and with no piles, when the last visitor uses it just as he or she is exiting the building? That means that there needs to be a sanitation plan for every room and section of our buildings.

That means that someone has to be in charge and others have to be assigned to do this systematic job, from beginning to end. That means that excellence and quality are the standard of our church and we will settle for nothing less! So what do you think?

Each of these rooms, again, needs to be attractive and not distracting. Think about the restrooms, the children's rooms and the auditorium, at first glance. Do they alarm visitors or disarm them? The restrooms can be rundown or they can be beautiful! Many churches are redesigning their restrooms to make them more attractive. Look at what you have and do what you need to do. We'll look in detail at the children's classrooms later in our process. But, at first glance, do they warm the hearts of parents and children, or do they make them want to run? As visitors walk into the auditorium, at first glance, does it feel warm and comfortable and inviting, or is it cold, sterile, and uninviting? Do the seats look comfortable? Does this feel like a place that I would like to visit again? All of these questions are very subjective, but every visitor processes these same questions in their journey through our building. Is there a clearly identifiable place to go if my baby starts crying? Will I feel at home if I'm handicapped, and especially if I am in a wheelchair?

Let's talk about food and the kitchen before we exit an overview of the facility. Food and a great kitchen provide an important springboard to newcomer ministry. The kitchen and food service areas of the church are often invisible to the visitor, but what they provide can make a significant difference. Some churches opt to do without food and beverages because of cost and hassle. I believe they are missing out on a foundational truth. **Eating makes the meeting!** People will stay much longer and just hang out when there is food involved. The better the food, the more people will stay. If it's good and if it's free, it brings the best results. But quality food and beverages at reasonable prices will also draw a crowd. Build a great kitchen and use it often. Enough said. More later.

Atmosphere

Exiting two identical stores can leave completely different impressions, and much of that has to do with atmosphere. No, I'm not talking about the air that you breath. I'm talking about the environment that they've created. One store has worked hard to capture your heart and attention. The other store has assumed that they will draw you in through other ways. I believe that the store with a more energized atmosphere often wins our ongoing business. They may not have the best pricing or product, but many of us will go back to shop for more simply because we like the atmosphere. Unfortunately, people often will pick their churches the same way. They're not looking for great theology or many of the other ways that should count when you're looking for a church. Their hearts are often won by far more carnal things, like a good cup of coffee.

Let's not get hung up on their level of maturity. Our desire isn't necessarily to attract mature people to our church. Our ultimate goal should be to turn self-centered seekers into fully devoted followers of Jesus Christ! So let's give them that cup of coffee! As I've said before, we want to do everything we can to make church a positive and friendly experience.

We've talked about creating an exciting atmosphere outside the building. Whether or not your weather will allow for aggressive creativity on the outside, let's bring all of that creativity inside as well! We want visitors to walk through those front doors and into a foyer filled with energy and anticipation. How you've set up that foyer makes such a difference. It needs to be warm and attractive, with lots of thought put into colors and décor, couches and wall-coverings. Well-placed banners and balloons and information and visitor booths can all add to that atmosphere.

> It's better to be less creative and to do something well than to try to do too much and to do it poorly!

Let's look at the three top contributors to atmosphere- music, food and people! First of all, music is so important. Selecting the right music, not too loud and not too soft, is so important. Have speakers everywhere- in the foyer and hallways and restrooms and in all of your rooms. When you build new buildings, always wire everything for sound. If you are playing an auditorium feed as your music source, everyone everywhere will know when the service has started. That will draw people from the foyer and other rooms to the auditorium when the church service is starting.

Many churches are hanging television monitors in their foyers and entry areas. This creates a great tool both for atmosphere and for communication. Sometimes churches will play music videos before and after church. Often they will use the monitors as a place to show announcements through videos or slides. Many churches will switch to a live feed from a camera in the auditorium so people can see that the service has started. You don't have to be a big church to do all of this. But you do need workers who will make sure that it works and that it works smoothly. Visitors may give you an A for effort, but they're most impressed when everything is working and nothing is distracting. Take one step at a time and build on quality.

Food is the second critical contributor to atmosphere. Visitors and regulars alike will stay around talking for half an hour with the right food and beverages provided. And most will leave fairly quickly with no food. Because churches are built on relationship, we want to do everything we can to create an atmosphere that entices relationship. Visitors will more likely come back if they have established a number of friendships on that first Sunday. So set up that cappuccino bar, put out that Starbucks coffee and those Krispy Kreme donuts. Buy some great veggies and pastries! Do it Right! It takes a good amount of effort and organization, but the returns are worth all of it.

The third great contributor to atmosphere is people. Your people make all the difference in the world! If your congregation is truly friendly, they will be like a magnet to visitors. According to John

Maxwell, the average church would grow if the people would just smile. All visitors come with an invisible shopping list when they visit your church. They often are not even conscious of their list. But it gets checked off as they spend their time with you. People and relationships are at the very top of their list. "Do these people really care? Are they like me? Will they like me? Will they judge me? Will they care what I wear? Will I like them? Will I find any of my friends? Do we hold the same values? Are there people here who are my age and like to do the things we like to do? Are there children or young people here for my kids to enjoy and hang out with? Will my family like being here?" These are just a few of the questions that run through the visitor's mind in his or her opening seconds upon walking through that door. Again, within moments, they will be deciding whether they will come back or not.

> We need to clearly define our goals and plans
> so we can do exactly what we intend to do.

You can see why it is so important that everyone is warm and encouraging from the moment the visitor walks in. We need to be inviting, happy and positive- from the heart. We need to be helpful and aware that they may know nothing about life inside this building. We may need to help them find their way to the nursery or rest rooms or auditorium. We want our visitors to feel safe. We want them to feel normal and unafraid. We want to do all we can do to encourage them and make them feel at home. Think about this- **happy people multiply**! All of this will only happen if we are intentional. We need to staff our volunteers with intentionally. We need to clearly define our goals and plans so we can do exactly what we intend to do. We need to have a plan for before the service and a plan for after the service. We'll go into more detail on these important subjects in our next two sections.

Let's take one more moment to think about the condition of our visitors as they arrive. They arrive believing and skeptical, friendly and fearful, healthy and damaged. Many don't know the language, the culture, or the reasons for doing anything we do. Some are happy and some are really scared. Some are ready for friends and will jump in right away. Some are circling our churches and looking for the right home. Some are wounded and angry. They're coming for answers, but they don't show it. They may show sadness or quietness or antagonism. Not every visitor wants a hug. They may need it, but they don't know it! Some will run from any hint of friendship. They've come to hide. In fact, many people will pick a large church so they can hide out in the bleachers.

How confusing! One shoe doesn't fit all! It would be so easy if we could expect the same results from all of our visitors. That won't happen. I still remember one visiting family standing up against a foyer wall, week after week. They looked so angry, ready to kill. Months later, the husband told me how angry he was that no one ever talked to him. Are you kidding? Of course, no one talked to him. If looks could kill, we would have all died. We thought he was telling us to stay away. In reality, he wanted to be loved and cared for. But he and his wife were so wounded that they only had pain and anger pouring out of their faces. By the way, they were long–time believers, coming wounded from another church. You never know! So here's the truth–some visitors want to be loved and others don't- yet. You just won't know. So do your best. Love them anyway. Listen to the Lord. Depend on Him. Be sensitive to people. You will err. But if you're going to err, always, always, always do it on the side of love. Love wins!

Notes

THOUGHTS ON CHANGE

In times of rapid change, experience could be your worst enemy.
J. Paul Getty

People don't resist change. They resist being changed!
Peter Senge

A small group of thoughtful people could change the world. Indeed, it's the only thing that ever has.
Margaret Mead

6. ENTRY PLAN- 5 minutes and counting!
All Dressed Up- On Your Mark,. . .

We've set the ground rules for our visitors arriving at our property and building. But are we organized and ready for them? We can work hard on the preparation of our facility, our atmosphere and the attitudes of our personnel. But we've got to have an entry plan! As they drive onto our property, as they walk up to our doors, as they enter and walk through our buildings, are we ready? In the next five minutes, our organizational preparedness will either help us accomplish our goal, or we will have to learn the hard way! We learn the hard way when we have a plan but we haven't worked through all the details. We learn the hard way when no one is really in charge or the wrong person is in charge. To accomplish a great plan, you need the visionaries to create the plan, organizers to put the plan together, analysts to tweak the plan and worker bees to do the plan! This takes time and effort and can't simply come together. Let's look at the overview and a few details of that entry plan.

Welcome

We need an entire team of greeters who are especially prepared and personality-gifted to meet everyone as they come to church. They need to be naturally happy, friendly people. They need to be outgoing communicators. They need to like people! Sometimes individuals will volunteer to greet because of the need, but, in reality, they are either shy or they really don't like people. You don't want those people greeting your visitors, and they don't really want to be there either. Help them find that right place of ministry that better suits their personality and gifts! But make sure they don't greet. Here are some details that can't be overlooked. You need a greeter plan. You need a pre-service and post-service greeter plan. Many churches will work hard with greeters before the service and completely drop the ball when the service is over.

Imagine walking into a store, hotel or restaurant where everyone is friendly and polite. They smile, they greet you, and they ask if they can help you in any way. They really seem to care. I'm not talking about salesmen on commission. I'm talking about salaried workers who know that the first priority of their job is to truly care about the well being of the clients in the store. If the customers are happy and get what they want, they'll come to buy again! Occasionally, I'll discover a business like that! I can picture a few restaurants, hotels and stores that I've gone to for the first time. As I've entered or sat down, everyone has been happy, cordial and attentive to me. They've functioned like a team. They've appeared to truly like each other, working together. I've really enjoyed shopping, staying or eating there. Now, that's a business that I want to go back to again and again! Translate that into a church gathering and you'll win Big-Time!

I watched a video several years ago at Kauai Christian Fellowship in Hawaii created for the morning service to demonstrate this very point. The greeters and ushers were enthusiastic and caring before the service, but the same people were rude, bored or inattentive after the service. The visitors were amazed and left quickly. Can you see how distracting and disappointing this would be? The video was so funny and so sad! If we think that first impressions are important, imagine how important last impressions are. Create teams that see their assignment as before and after ministries, or create two separate teams if that works better. Do whatever works! Going that extra mile will make a major impact, both on visitors and on the rest of your church.

You need at least one greeter organizer. You need someone to recruit and train and schedule and remind the greeters when they are greeting. As your church grows in size, someone will need to organize the greeters into segment teams. You will need greeters in the parking lot, greeters at the main doors, and you'll need greeters at other doors if visitors are using them. You will need greeters at the entry door of each children's and youth department throughout the church. Picture the right greeters welcoming parents at the nursery entry door. Think of the encouragement that that will give to them as they think about leaving their baby. Now picture warm, loving greeters outside of every children's department. Can you see what a difference that will make to visitors? The purpose of those greeters is to take away the fears of both parents and children alike. What about department guides to take people to their classrooms?

> If we think that first impressions are important, imagine how important last impressions are!

When your visitors walk through that door, they have no idea where they are suppose to go next. Some of your greeters will be busy welcoming people as they pour into the building. So other greeters also need to be at the door assigned to point the way so visitors don't get lost. But why not have guides waiting to actually take visitors to the nursery or children's departments or auditorium? Why not have some friendly young people ready to take junior-high or high-school students back to their rooms. Can you imagine how welcomed they will feel?

You can see the importance of having an excellent plan in place for greeting people as they come to church. This is such a valuable ministry. People need to be recruited with a clear picture of just how vital their service will be to the mission of the kingdom. It's truly a spiritual ministry- they not only represent a first point of contact with the church but with the Lord as well. The greeters need to see themselves as a team working together. They need to enjoy each other and have fun together. They also need to be brought together for encouragement and continued training. The greeters need to understand that they are on the job and need to be early, prayed up, happy, alert and undistracted. Amazing and unique opportunities for care and encouragement will happen on a regular basis for greeters who are alert and listening to the Lord.

The number of greeters necessary to really do the job well at your church may be overwhelming! But it also provides a great opportunity. Think of all the unemployed Christians who come on Sunday and just stand or sit around! In churches small or large, there are so many people who could be helping in this area. By recruiting them, it meets an important need. It makes them part of the team. It gives them purpose. What they are doing is significant. And the church gets healthier for it. Can you see how this ministry builds character, values and vision for both adults and young people? Think about how you can use this as a tool to activate and mobilize a whole new set of workers to get involved in the vision and life of the church.

I would personally recommend that the greeters come dressed like everyone else in the church. I don't believe it impresses people anymore to have greeters wearing special clothes or nametags. Sometimes it does make the greeters feel important. But this ministry is not about them. It's about the visitor and regular attendees. I think it's most attractive to visit a church and to have ordinary people greeting me and talking to me all along the way. By the way, I want to reaffirm that the greeting team should never be seem as an alternative to the rest of the church being friendly and caring and happy. We must be training and encouraging and helping our entire church to demonstrate this kind of love and interest in others. The greeters are simply the advance team for the rest of the church, complementing everything else we do.

Information

If the first thing that visitors need is to be warmly welcomed, the second thing they need is information. Assume that many of them have never gone to church. Most of them haven't visited your church before. They clearly need to know some basic who, what, when, where and maybe why. There needs to be a detailed information plan. Someone must be in charge of looking at the big picture of what information needs to be offered to the visitors and attendees and when, where, and how it needs to be delivered. Many different ministries will put together their own flyers and pieces of information. But what a mess if no one coordinates the gathering and delivery of that info! A leader or team needs to look at and decide all the pieces of information delivered throughout the church. Left to their own design, some ministries will crank out too much data and others won't create anything. Someone needs to decide what really matters so people can receive what they need to know when they need to know it!

Your information needs to be attractive, clear and concise. It needs to inform, including a precise time and place, so outsiders know exactly what you are talking about. Never assume that people know anything about your ministry or opportunity. People on the inside may not even read your flyer, so your target always has to be the outsider. I'm continually amazed at the missing information on many church flyers simply because the creators are writing to the inside crowd instead of to me, the visitor. Be sure to let your readers know whom you are targeting so there is no confusion.

Once you've gathered your information, you have to decide the best way to get it to your visitors. Traditionally, the greeters and ushers are the ones who hand out bulletins at the door to visitors. And that works. What's most important is that the information giver is truly helping the visitor get the direction they need at the moment.

Probably the first thing that a visitor needs to be offered as they walk in the door is a map of the building. Picture the greeter welcoming our visitors, taking a few moments to get to know them, handing them a map and a bulletin and walking them over to a large map on the wall to tell them even more. That sounds like a really caring plan! Or picture that same greeter walking the visitors over to several workers helping at an information table or booth. Many churches have lots of information placed on tables in the foyer, but lots of them don't have anyone at those tables explaining anything about the information. I'll bet that most visitors never make it to those tables. And if they do, they don't know what to pick up.

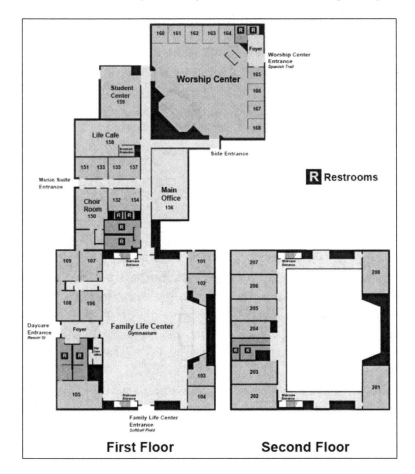

More and more churches are setting up information booths, tables, gazebos or tents manned by happy, trained greeters who

can guide the visitors through their introductory process. If you do set up a visitor's information area, use signs to make it clearly identifiable. Some great churches have so many booths and ministry and information areas that the visitor has no idea where to begin. Make it clear! Meet your objective.

Packaging your information will also make a difference in how easily your visitor will understand what they are to do next. We all hand the visitor a church bulletin. Many of us prepare a visitor packet of information about our church. That usually includes info on our ministries, major events and opportunities for all ages. It also may include our history, denominational info and our doctrine. Think about adding a brochure or sheet to hand out along with your visitor pack that focuses on the very simple questions of a first-time attendee. "We're glad you're here. We know you are new and probably have some questions. Here's what we do on Sunday mornings. . . If you have children, here are your options. . . Here's what we will be doing during our church service. . . Please don't feel any pressure to give when we take our offering. . . We hope you come back next week to visit us again. . . We also would like to invite you to meet us by the information booth after the service and / or at our newcomer's dessert. . ." Walk them through their initial questions and they will find it a lot more comfortable coming back the next week. By the way, many churches are putting all of this info on their website so people can find it at their own leisure.

Segment Plan

If you intend to meet the needs of a variety of people, then you need to specifically focus on the individual needs of each segment group as they arrive at your church door. You may have great programs and ministries, but if they aren't clearly presented, you won't get people to them! Let's name some of the segment groups that have very individual needs- adults of many age groups, women, men, singles, young married couples, seniors, babies, children, families, youth, college-aged adults, special needs visitors, people in recovery and more. You may want to add the component of racial and language diversity to this discussion. Each individual represented by one of these segment groups arrives with very specific needs.

What is your entry plan for each of these groupings of people? They all have very unique needs. They are often arriving at your door with objectives based on those unique needs. "I'm lonely. I'm discouraged. I'm empty. I'm looking for friends. I'm looking for a family. I'm looking for God. I'm a mess. I need someone to talk to. " Everything may change when you add, "I'm recovering and I need someone to talk to" or "I have special needs. Do you guys care about me? I need someone to talk to."

For example, seniors often arrive looking for other seniors. They want to know if seniors have a place in your church. They want to know if the seniors will really allow them to become a part of their group or if they'll be left on the outside. And if the seniors have a group, they want to know when they meet, where they meet, and what they do when they get together. Those are all good questions and need to be answered. What you must decide is how and when you answer those specific questions. How important is it that they know those answers the first time they walk into your church? How will you communicate with them? Is printed information enough, or do they need personal contact? Should someone, perhaps another senior, be strategically watching to make that first contact with a senior couple on their first Sunday? If you don't make that contact, will they come back to visit you again? If the seniors are a minority group in your church, they may not be very visible to other visiting seniors. Perhaps the only way that they will return will be because you've created a plan to draw them in.

> Most visitors who aren't a part of your church's majority don't want to be spotlighted or treated differently than any other visitor.

A first or second generation Hispanic or Asian or Jamaican or Caucasian couple visits your church. Do they feel welcome? Is there anyone else like them in the church? Will they feel at home? Will their children be accepted? Is there anything for their parents if they invite them? Is there another service in Spanish or Mandarin or French or Canadian? Aye? How will these questions be answered? Racial diversity is growing rapidly across this land and it is the future. The church needs to be modeling it Now! Most visitors who aren't a part of your church's majority don't want to be spotlighted or treated differently than any other visitor. At the same time, they don't want to feel isolated or insulated from the majority who call your church home. I will share over and over again how much visitors and attenders need to feel loved, welcomed and embraced by the people of the church, or they won't think twice about coming back! If it's important for visitors in general, it's even more important for visitors who are not of the majority culture. They will walk in consciously or subconsciously wondering if they will be welcomed or rejected. They have had years of prejudice conditioning them to think that they won't be accepted. The immediate warmth and embrace of your church family will be critical if you want that individual or family to return and become part of you. I'll talk over and over again about training your people to demonstrate love, kindness and hospitality. We need to teach them to become color-blind, racially and generationally-sensitive and very intentional and purposeful in their interaction on Sundays and throughout the week. All of this begins with the power of the Holy Spirit working in our lives. He's the One who touches our hearts. That makes training the easy part. Tools can easily be molded and shaped when they've been surrendered and softened in the hands of a loving God! We've got to talk about these issues and plan ahead if we want our visitors to truly feel welcomed and if we want them to become a part of our church family.

Let's be realistic. We can't meet every need! Most churches end up specializing in meeting certain needs better than other churches. A lot of that has to do with the gifting, personalities and vision of the church leaders and their people as they've grown and developed through the years. As churches grow larger, they can become more diverse, as more people arrive with different visions for ministry. Unfortunately, the less we plan and prepare for the unique needs of visitors, the less we will attract them to visit again. It was always disappointing to me as a pastor when it was obvious that we were not able to offer specific ministries at our church. For example, a deaf person would attend and we didn't have someone who could offer sign language. No matter how hard we tried, we simply could not meet every need. That's just the way it is! It's actually healthy to accept that reality and then focus in on the areas that you can do well in. It's always better to do fewer things well.

Every church has to work through these questions considering their own demographics, size, organizational strength and visitor retention. Your church is unique and how you attack these issues of care will be different than the church down the street. But it must be addressed! People want to be cared about, and they all arrive with a special set of needs. Some of those unique needs can be immediately identified and we can address them. I believe that the more quickly we throw the net, the more likely we'll catch the fish. Again, this concept of the first contact must be organized, with someone giving oversight to the plan, recruitment, training, accountability, actual oversight, and encouragement. Each segment ministry will have its own strategy for recruitment and distribution of information. But there also needs to be church-wide coordination that looks at the big picture and helps the consistency of that effort. Some segment ministries could completely miss the opportunity of a first contact. Thinking this process through with all of your ministries will help everyone get the big picture and get on the same page

Notes

THOUGHTS ON CHANGE

All great change in America begins
at the dinner table.
Ronald Reagan

I cannot say whether things will get better if we
change; what I can say is they must change if they
are to get better.
George C. Lichtenberg

Things alter for the worse spontaneously, if they
be not altered for the better designedly.
Francis Bacon

7. THE FAMILY - ARE THEY READY? - 4 minutes and counting!
Friendly- But to Whom?

We've got everything in place for the arrival of our visitors. We're organized, we've prepared our workers, and we have our entry plan ready to go. But now we come to one of the most important components of attraction. It's time to meet the Family. That can be a scary thought. Think about all the movies where the daughter brings her boyfriend home to meet the family. What comedy. What diversity. What warmth and tenderness. Or not! And the family makes all the difference. Picture yourself walking our visitors toward the family room. This is it! It's like the dating game. We've done everything we can to create an attractive entrance to our church, but here is where the truth will be known. When they walk through Door Number Two, will they like our family? Will they be attracted to us? Will they want to stay and become a part of our church? For all the drama of that moment, there is an even greater set of questions. Are We Ready? Have we dressed up? As a family, are we prepared for those visitors to walk through that door? Will our kids behave themselves? **The first thing we need to look at is our attitude and how we look to those visitors who are walking in.**

Attitude

How do we look to our visitors? When they walk through that door, are we like a family, standing there, waiting for them, arms outstretched, anticipating their arrival? Are we excited to meet them, to get to know them, to hear their story and to tell them ours? Let's assume that the Father has set this date up. He's arranged the whole thing. He's even pulled some strings to get these visitors through the front door. He's invested a lot in this moment. It's an answer to

161

many prayers! It's part of His great plan. He wants them in, saved, sanctified, serving and reaching out to others. Are we ready?

> The last people many of us usually are thinking about are visitors- especially if they're not like us.

You can see why it's so important that everyone is warm and encouraging from the moment the visitor walks in. We need to be inviting, happy and positive. Unfortunately, a lot of this doesn't come naturally to us, and that's because we, by nature, are self-centered and self-serving. Let's admit it. We often come to church for ourselves and we look for our friends and our favorite spot to sit. The last people many of us usually are thinking about are visitors-especially if they're not like us. They don't normally attract us if they are older or younger, shorter or taller, larger or thinner, darker or lighter, better looking or funny-looking, and our list goes on. If we don't repent of and break this normal mindset, and if we don't get intentional about becoming warm and encouraging to strangers, we won't have to worry about them for long. They are looking at us through that same lens, and we can't expect them to change.

I visit different churches most Sundays as a consultant. I can almost guarantee that only one or two people at most will talk to me. I'm including unfriendly and friendly churches. My experience in friendly churches is that most people are friendly to each other, but not to me. They stand in circles of conversation throughout the building, but most of them don't even see me. And they're clearly not interested in talking to me! I'm not counting the official greeters positioned at the door. I'm not discounting the importance of friendly greeters, but that's their job. And I'm not

counting the "level one" acknowledgement that I may get at the greeting time. Most of that contact is extremely impersonal and doesn't count on my relational and attractive list. In fact, the way I am usually turned to and then immediately brushed off like a completed assignment would make me never want to come back if I were a visitor! On the other hand, I am always pleasantly surprised when someone purposefully comes up to me, greets me and enters into a genuine conversation about me and why I am visiting. That makes me feel welcome. That makes me feel like someone actually cares. Let's assume that all visitors are like me. What that means is that it's critical that our visitors and new attendees experience a number of meaningful conversations before they leave our building. What would we have to do differently to make that happen?

Now, some of us are quiet and some of us are loud. Wouldn't it be terrible if all of us were loud? This isn't about loud. It's about love! And it's about being intentional. People who are more introverted will demonstrate love and care in a different way than people who are extroverts. They may, in fact, be better at sensing real needs and approaching quieter visitors who arrive at church. God's wired us all in unique ways so we can work together to love people toward Him! But we have to be intentional.

By the way, I believe this is both a spiritual issue and a training issue. God wants us to demonstrate His love all the time wherever we are. So God clearly wants us to be loving and caring to visitors and newer attendees as they begin to come to our church. If we aren't naturally demonstrating this kind of love, we need to repent, draw closer to the Lord and allow Him to fill us with His Holy Spirit. What takes a lot of effort and remains prejudicial becomes so much easier and natural when God's love is flowing through us. This **is** a fruit of the Spirit- the evidence of His presence in you. We need to pray that God will soften our hearts and give us that consistent, free-flowing love that He wants all of us to have and to demonstrate!

At the same time, it's essential that we train our people to know how to approach visitors and what to say in those early conversations. Many people don't really know what to say to strangers and so they don't say anything at all! No wonder greeting times can come off so sterile and artificial. By the way, the size of the church can make a difference. Smaller congregations in smaller rooms can demonstrate care more easily than larger congregations in larger rooms. It's more obvious when a stranger walks into a small setting. And smaller congregations often are looking for visitors to add to their numbers. Of course, small congregations can also be very cliquish and unfriendly to any one who is new. On the other hand, visitors can easily disappear in a large congregation. And congregations can give up and grow complacent as they grow in numbers simply because they feel overwhelmed by their size. That's why it's essential that the leadership in growing churches remain committed to figuring out how to demonstrate the life and love of Christ despite the obstacles. In either case, training is a critical key to setting congregations free in this important area of need.

All of this reminds us that the greatest changes that must take place in most of our churches are in people. Sometimes we have the illusion that if we get a bigger or nicer or better facility, in the right location, at the right time, everything will be good. While those options may help, the real attractional issue is so much more about our people and relationships! Brian Orme, the editor of *Outreach Magazine*, shares this: "Change isn't really about brick and mortar, systems and structures. At its root, change is about people. . .It's not enough to have steely resolve to make change happen; change requires wisdom, prayer and ultimately, the power of God!"[46] Amen! By the way, subscribe to Outreach Magazine. It's a refreshing wave of current thought on this entire issue of transforming our churches into missional launching pads for the Kingdom.

I pastored a church that was small and personable, warm and very friendly. Visitors were embraced and easily integrated into our growing family. Love was in the air and everyone could feel it! The church was happy! And we grew larger and larger! The excitement was contagious. People told their friends, and they came too! And we continued to grow. We were forced to go to two services and then to three.

Everything seemed to change. The body was divided, and people didn't see their friends. The growth was overwhelming. It was impossible to remember everyone's name. It became harder to try. People began to give up on caring. They became more focused on their own friends and small groups.

Visitors and growth bring both blessings and complexities to every church! If we had surrendered to the difficulties of our circumstances, all would have been lost. For what does it profit a man to grow a big, fat church and lose the very essence of what the church is called to be? We had to do everything possible to stay focused on maintaining an atmosphere of love and a people committed to caring for each other, including visitors. That demands intentionality! But is there really any choice?

Where in the world do we begin in this area of training people to be warm and caring? We begin with a core value- every believer needs to demonstrate intentional, unconditional love all the time to people everywhere. This core value needs to be part of the foundational training throughout the church. It needs to be proven Biblically and then articulated practically so people understand what it looks like. The congregation needs to be taught that they should be sensitive to and caring for people they don't know all through their week. Sunday then is not the exception to the rule, but a continuation of a lifestyle. We need to train **all** of our people to be greeters so that assignment is not simply handed out to the few. They need to be trained to be friendly and sensitive, to listen, to know what questions they need to ask and to remember the answers for years to come. They need to be taught how to give their full attention to the people to whom they are talking so the beginning of a friendship develops. And they need to try to find those same visitors in the following weeks so they truly do feel loved and like they are a growing part of a family.

This can't simply be a plan for first-time visitors. Imagine how bad it would feel to be cared about on your first Sunday and ignored after that. That actually happens in many churches that get intentional but miss the bigger picture. Visitors become the mission and our friends get the rest of our time. Unfortunately, many regular attenders can get lost in the crowd!

I've had to learn the hard way just how much sheep love to be petted by their shepherds. As the pastor of a small church, I determined to pet as many sheep as possible every Sunday and everywhere I went through the week. My wife and I especially focused on new sheep as they arrived at our door. We knew it was the right thing to do and the sheep loved us for caring for them! I believe that a significant contributor to the great growth of our church was because the sheep felt loved and the sheep in turn loved each other. As the church became large, we couldn't pet all the

sheep! And it was natural to become more task-oriented at times and less sheep-conscious. In fact, there were moments that I was so focused on the task that I completely ignored the sheep that I was walking by.

It didn't take long until some courageous older sheep shared with me the pain of not being petted by their shepherd. I soon discovered that other pastors and elders and leaders in our church were doing the same thing! In our growth, we had lost some of our heart! We had to step back, reaffirm our values and get back to our priorities. We did have to multiply our shepherds and we did need to change the expectations of our sheep. Lead shepherds can't be all things to all people! But, at the same time, I learned the critical balance in both loving and leading! I decided that I couldn't pet all the sheep, but I still could pet all the sheep that were around me! I had to reaffirm my personal priority of putting people before programs and tasks. I realized that most sheep would not stay long for feeding in a fold if they didn't think the shepherd really loved them. Somebody ends up leaving!

How do we train an entire church to care? What an amazing question. We know it should be happening naturally. But we know it doesn't and it won't. We have two choices. Ignore it, but it won't go away. Or set a plan in motion that will bring about necessary change.

Where do we start? Train your pastors and pastors' wives. Train your board and their spouses. Train your leaders and their spouses. Train your ministry leaders. Train your workers. Train your small group members. Train your church members. Train your discipleship trainees and ministry class attendees. Bring the body through a series of classes and train everyone. Talk about it in sermons, in classes, in disciplemaking, at leadership events and in meetings of every kind- over and over again. If this is important, and it is, this theme should play center stage until the cows come in.

By the way, there is often a sizable group of people, in many of our churches, who would love to serve the Lord in some simple way. They're just waiting to be asked, but they don't know it. They faithfully arrive at each gathering. They're filled with the love of God, but they don't know what to do. So they find a friend, or go to a class, or they go and sit down. If they were simply asked and shown what to do, they would. I believe there are dozens or hundreds or thousands of people who would love to be mobilized to spread love and joy and compassion. Find them. Ask them. Organize them. Release them and watch what happens!

I've shared some nice stories about churches. But I recently visited another type of church. It was a wonderful and friendly church and everyone really enjoyed talking to each other. But they wouldn't talk to me. I walked all around them, waiting for someone to notice me, but no one would look me in the eye. I even felt avoided! It was weird. Now, I was a racial minority, so that may have made a difference. But I clearly stood out as a visitor. I didn't need a nametag or identifying mark. My racial uniqueness may have created an obstacle to the friendliness of these otherwise warm individuals. Or perhaps they simply did not care! Either way, if I had been a "normal" visitor, I surely would not have come back. And, by the way, no one would have missed me!

Think about that! How do "minorities" feel when they walk in your church? They already feel uncomfortable. They are already prepared not to be accepted. They perhaps need even more loving and care than the average visitor! Here's one more thought for free. The average visitor feels like a minority when they walk in your building-especially if he or she is not a Christian! How will you compensate for that?

Modeling, of course, is so essential to this core value if the majority of a congregation is going to live it. And modeling always begins with the staff and their wives or husbands. All the shepherds need to be involved in petting as many of the sheep as possible. Hugs for everyone! If the shepherds aggressively demonstrate care for their sheep and for visitors to their fold, the sheep will learn to do the same thing.

As a young pastor, I attended every conference under the sun. I wanted to learn everything I could from the pros who had traveled before me. And one of the principles that I grabbed on to was that people had to come before programs. **People first!** I heard it, I understood it, I strategized with that in mind and I said it over and over again. Clarity on that one issue alone helped us to stay focused on our priorities, and I also believe it helped us to grow larger and larger. People love friendly churches. They do! They love churches where they aren't simply a number, especially when the church size would normally create that result. But it takes focused intentionality to keep people first.

Ed Stetzer and Thom Rainer address the key components of a life-changing community in their book, *Transformational Church*. They describe church after church that has chosen to focus on the key factors that will truly create Christ-like, missional communities. In one chapter, they discuss the clash of being naturally

169

intentional and at the same time relational. They prescribe that, as we allow God to mold us to do both well, in His strength, we become all we are meant to be. But, from a leadership perspective, it takes focus and priority! Ed and Thom say, "No one system delivers relationships in transformational churches. Relationships can be intentional but are not a program. Could you imagine a staff position like minister of relationships? A relational approach to reaching and developing people is woven throughout every ministry and practice. Relationships are the substance of the church culture." [47] We often miss this critical way of thinking because we are so task-driven as leaders. But if we want a fresh start at rebuilding our church community God's way, loving relationships is one big factor.

So the shepherds need to look for and love the visitors. The elders, board members and their wives and husbands need to look for and love the visitors. The ministry leaders and their wives or husbands need to look for and love the visitors. The ministry workers need to look for and love the visitors. The worship team needs to look for and love the visitors. These are your leaders and workers. They can be expected to live out the Great Commandment! My conviction is that if your leadership team will be committed to model love and care, with continual training and reminders, this lifestyle can continue to permeate your entire congregation. It won't matter how large your church gets!

And what are we training our people to be? What are we teaching our children and young people and old people and new people and in-between people to be? **We're training them to be like Jesus!** What would Jesus do when a visitor walks into your family room? What will 50 or 500 or 5000 people do if they are Spirit-filled and intentionally focused? They will radiate love to everyone from wherever they are standing or sitting. They will be positive and encouraging, immediately accepting of all ages, races, appearances, clothing and hairstyles, accessories, size and condition. They will be blind to age and culture. Like the seventeen-year-old in the church I visited last Sunday. He had no reason to care about me or to pay any attention to me. There were far more important things to do and people to hang out with. We were surrounded by hundreds of people all leaving church. I was invisible- a nobody. But, for no good reason and without the slightest bit of coaching, he walked up to me and said, "Heh! What's your name?" We began a nice conversation. If I lived in town and continued to attend that church, he would be my friend. Why? Because he was friendly! What if everyone was like that young man? We need to be friendly and genuinely interested. We need to intentionally choose to step out of our comfort zones and stop hiding behind our excuses. We may be too busy or tired or shy or whatever, but none of those excuses cut it with God. We need to decide to be what God has created us to be, and then we need to ask Him for the power to live it out to the fullest!

Our first home was so small that, any time we had a group of people over, we had to sit on the floor and set up chairs inside and outside our living room. But we knew the only way we would really get to know visitors and regulars was to have them over. My wife's parents and my parents had modeled hospitality for years. We knew it was important. So we would have coffee, tea and pie one several evenings a month with 15 to 25 people. I was so bad with names that I would have to exit the living room with a little cheat sheet of paper and memorize as hard as I could. Fortunately, I would work to remember most names the next Sunday and from then on. I'm convinced that those experiences and others like that in homes throughout the church forged memories, deep-rooted bonds and harmony that have lasted for decades!

We need to be intentionally caring and acting on discovered information. If God helps us uncover a need, let's see if we can meet it. Isn't that what it's all about? That sounds a lot like Acts 2: 42-47. We need to be caring and friendly to everyone- all the time. And some of those people will be visitors. We need to keep our eyes open for visitors and lonely people and hurting people and shy people. Having the Holy Spirit inside us provides us with incredible built-in radar. If we are sensitive to God, He makes us sensitive to people. Ask Him for wisdom and guidance and compassion and appropriate sensitivity. Walk up to strangers or newer acquaintances. Pay attention to what they are saying. Focus! People who are paid to pay attention work harder at it. So act like a paid person. This is important! Remember what you are hearing. You'll be tested next week or next month when you talk with them again. Now, the mind can only handle so much. But you would be surprised at how much more it can do when you really commit yourself to try. I've had to write down names over and over again to remember for the next meeting. If I can do it, anyone can!

Let's talk for a moment about hospitality. Roman 12:13 commands us all to "practice hospitality." It's defined in the dictionary as the entertainment of guests, visitors, or strangers, with liberality and goodwill. That seems a lot like what we've been talking about as we think about our church family. But the command also is relevant to our own home and family. The more generous we are with our own homes and families, the more we personally will feel like a true participant in this celebration of life. It's becoming easier and easier to see our home as our castle. We drive into the garage and the drawbridge pulls up for the night. All the cares and conflicts of the world are kept outside by our walls and locked doors, but so are all the people who Jesus died for!

Let the drawbridge down- permanently. Open your home to the world. Become a generous giver of unending hospitality. It will feel so good. And it will make people on the outside feel so good as well. I've traveled for many years. It's been a surprising delight to have people open up their home to me for lunch or dinner or a swim or a night's sleep. It's been a blessing, it's met more than one need, and it's always endeared me to those who have opened their homes. And I've watched children learn to be hospitable because it was modeled right before their eyes. Hospitality is contagious. Don't let others have all the fun and blessing!

Attitude is Big. As we model and groom an atmosphere of love in our people, we'll create a contagious environment. People will want to bring their friends and their friends will not simply come back. They'll bring their friends too. That's what I'm talking about!

Heart and Responsiveness

If our attitude is important, our heart and responsiveness is an even bigger issue! Our heart is a reflection of God in our midst. Amway can create great attitude. What a family. But what I'm talking about here is a room filled with people with hearts turned to God! Imagine that gathering packed with people who are passionately spiritual. Some are quieter and shy and others are louder and more demonstrative. But the majority of people are hungry for God! They love Him, they are filled with His Spirit, and they have come with anticipation and expectation. They **love** the gathering. They **love** God's people. They **love** reaching out to newbies and oldies and everybody else. They can't wait until the music begins. They long to meet with God in the midst of His people. Arrogance and individualism disappear, and humility and unity reign. They don't watch the worship. They **do** the worship! They worship with all their heart, soul, mind and strength. They involve themselves in the components of the gathering, not as mere spectators, but as full participants. They haven't simply come to take. They've come to give- first to God and then to the Kingdom. They give with such generosity. And they give their hearts to the Truth. They are attentive hearers of the Word. They hunger to be doers!

And do they respond. While others may watch and nod and acknowledge the truth and goodness of the moment, these men, women and young people enter in. They change. They commit. They surrender. They celebrate. Having fully participated, they are full. Having connected with God, they are even more prepared to connect with others. What a fellowship. What sharing and listening and caring and praying and giving and laughing and crying. What responsive, open hearts and open homes with leaders leading and followers following- everyone a greeter, a listener, a servant, a doer of the Word. The Happiest Place on Earth. God's Disneyland.

Wake up! It was only a dream!

But it doesn't have to be!

This is God's plan for your church! This is what God wants to build into all of our churches. And is it attractive. Does it make visitors want to come back or what! These are the ingredients that make visitors become members and tell everybody they know about their church. This is what made the early church grow! And this is what will make your church grow too. People will drive for miles to see a fire. By the way, I do visit churches like this. And it doesn't just happen. There are leaders behind every door, clapping and thanking God for His wisdom and grace.

I often say that the top three things that people are looking for are good preaching, good music and good hugging. This is what real hugging is all about. It's a God thing! And let me tell you the truth. People will overlook some O.K. preaching, some O.K. music and a few hundred others details named in this manual when they experience the people of God coming together in life and power. It all begins with you. Be Contagious and Multiply!

Notes

THOUGHTS ON CHANGE

If you want to make enemies, try to change something.
Woodrow Wilson

We all have big changes in our lives that are more or less a second chance.
Harrison Ford

Change is such hard work.
Billy Crystal

8. THE GATHERING - ARE WE READY? 3 minutes and counting!

We've worked so hard to prepare for our visitors. And the Family is ready and waiting, for better or worse. Not every Family is attractive to every visitor, no matter what we do. We can be at our very best and our visitors will go to the church next door. Do we hang our heads and give up? Never! That's life and it's filled with opportunities and choices. You chose this church and they chose the one down the street. Isn't it great that there are such a variety of churches that allow us to pick the right one? But now, it's time for the gathering. The service is about to begin. **The most important thing that we need to focus on is being ready. Every Sunday! And every time the door is open. Are we Ready?**

Preparedness

I visit different churches every Sunday to be an encouragement and also an objective outsider who can speak to these issues. What I've discovered is that every church has a different standard for being ready. Some churches have clearly dialed every detail down to the minute, and they start right on time. Others hang out and go with the flow of the culture of the church. Sometimes they're waiting for the worship team to show up. Some churches have massive teams of people involved in a variety of ministries during the gathering. Others are hoping that someone will volunteer to lead the singing. Some of this has to do with the church size and a lot of it has to do with the church culture. We laugh and call it "Hawaiian time", "California time", "Filipino time", "Post-modern" or whatever time our culture represents. Nothing's wrong with a church reflecting its culture unless there are areas where the culture truly needs to be changed. Time precision and starting on time probably isn't one of those areas that God really cares about within a cultural context. But how we use our time when we are together does matter and we need to look at that.

Having a standard of excellence in everything we do is important and God does care! God cares about detail and He cares about planning ahead. Check out Leviticus, Numbers and Deuteronomy if you want to see God's attitude about precision and detail. For example, in Leviticus, God told Moses every precise detail in the exact order of what He wanted to have happen in each worship event. When it was done to perfection, God was very pleased. The leaders were told to get it right at the fear of their lives. Thank God we're not under the Law. But does grace give us the grounds to be sloppy, poorly prepared and unplanned in our gatherings? I don't think so. I believe that God wants our offering of praise and worship to be done with as much excellence as we possess.

Culture cannot become an excuse for us when it comes to having a standard of excellence. In fact, in every culture, there is excellence. People have worked hard to plan and produce with quality. So, in every culture, there are excellent hotels and run-down hotels, excellent restaurants and dirty restaurants, excellent worship services and sloppy worship services. And it all depends on how much effort, time and planning has been put into it.

Imagine a church where no one plans ahead. I've actually visited a number of them! The music is thrown together at the last minute and the worship leaders struggle to learn it and practice right before the gathering. Someone is recruited to do the announcements or the same person gets up and reads the bulletin. The order of service is predictable because the same thing is done week after week. The sermon content is the only surprise of the morning. Yesterday, the pastor didn't even know what he was going to preach on. Fortunately, he got inspired Saturday night. So here's the question. Who would ever want to visit this church and why would they ever come back? It lacks all creativity. It looks like no one really cares. How in the world could you expect quality and excellence to come out of that? Let's go to church down the street.

Some of us are far better at organizing and recruiting and planning than others of us- in any culture. That's why we often have to work as a team and recruit others who are gifted to help in these areas. Smaller churches and church plants often struggle with a limited number of people doing all the work. Their greatest challenge is to grow large enough to more easily attract others to their church. But most churches are filled with people who possess a great variety of gifts and talents, many which remain wrapped and unused! For example, men and women who plan, organize and implement all week long in their jobs could also be helping to bring greater quality and excellence to the gathering. But they're often not! It's critical that we find them and help them discover their valuable place of ministry, without feeling threatened.

> It's been said that if we fail to plan, then we plan to fail. And its true!

Big Picture Planning

If we want our visitors to have a great experience as they gather with us, we have to plan ahead. It's been said that if we fail to plan, then we plan to fail. And its true! Our gatherings will be the least distractive and the most attractive if we've taken the time to work through all of the details. Planning starts with a long view. If we can see the big picture first, then we can fill in all of the necessary details later.

Let's look at the big picture. We all know the main events that will repeat themselves each and every year. Most of them have seasonal or denominational roots, so they are predictable and easy to place on a calendar. The beginning of a great Sunday gathering is the planning of an entire year. Skip this section if you already plan everything in your church in detail one year out. But if you don't, walk through the process with me. Put all of your special events of on a calendar. If you've never done this before, let the past be your guide to the future. What events always happen in the winter? Write them down. What do you always do around Easter? What happens every summer? What do you do every fall, including around Thanksgiving time? What do you do every December and at Christmastime? What events would you have done in the past if you had had more time to plan ahead? Write those down. Are there special women's and men's and youth events? What about denominational meetings? Are there outside events that you will want your people to be a part of? You'll already find most of their dates for next year on the Internet. If you're working with other churches, help them to get organized and also plan ahead.

Recording the events of the past will help you create a blueprint for tomorrow. Now use this information as a guide to plan your next year's calendar. Don't do it in January. Do it in the summer or fall for the coming year. Fill in all the dates. Pull the leaders together in one meeting if you have to. **Now it's done!** You won't believe how many churches don't plan more than a week to a month ahead for almost everything. Or maybe you do believe it, because I'm talking about your church. Now you know you're not alone. But it's time to change! I can't emphasize enough how relieved you will feel when you plan ahead and don't have to always worry about scheduling events several weeks or months out.

Pastors- this one's for you. The year calendar is only the beginning. Now you can hang everything else around those events and seasons. Let's start with sermon passages and topics. As I work with hundreds of pastors, I discover that we are as different as night and day. Think about differences in background, education, training, personality, race, culture, gifting, vision and passion, to mention just a few. Add to that all of the same components reflected in the people of each of our churches.

Because of all of these factors, we approach ministry so differently from each other. Some of us prepare our sermons days ahead, others weeks ahead and still others months beforehand. And some of us don't prepare at all. We ask God to prepare our hearts and we let it flow. Now, I'm not addressing how or when we actually prepare our sermons. I am addressing the opportunity to plan the overview of what we believe God wants us to preach one year out. I believe that the same Holy Spirit who guides us in final preparation on Saturday and the actual delivery on Sunday knows what He wants to deliver one year early! Isn't that true? Doesn't He know? Can't He guide you?

For those of us who aren't used to planning our topics and passages that far ahead, it will be a difficult habit to break into. But let me tell you, the rewards will be wonderful. For you to know where you are going one year ahead will free you and God to deepen your vision, your passion, your understanding, and your content when you actually arrive at each sermon. Here's some practical help. Go away somewhere where you and God can get alone and think and dream together! Take some hours or days to pray and plan. Walk with God and talk with Him about where you've been, where you are and where you think you need to go as a church. Think and pray and think and pray and listen.

Think about what passages you believe you should preach through next. What are the key topics that God wants you to bring out to His people? Begin thinking in the context of the calendar year. What do you think you should preach in the fall when everyone comes back from the summer? Will you do anything different for Thanksgiving, December or the weeks around Christmas? What will you preach through in the winter? Will you preach some special sermons around the Easter season? What will you preach through as you move into the summer? What about other special speakers and conferences or events that are already on the calendar?

Take your thoughts and create a calendar sheet with those ideas on it. Create a sheet or two with 52 weeks on it. You may use a software program or you may just want to write it down first. Now make it specific to the next year's calendar. Write or type in all the seasonal topics, speakers, and events that you know are non-negotiable. What specifically do you want to preach on this next

Christmas and Easter? Think through those topics and write them down. Start writing in titles or topic concepts by the dates that they will be presented on. Begin to break down your topical series into component parts and write down a title or concept phrase for each presentation. Look at the passages that you plan to preach through. Divide them into sermon segments, and put a title or concept phrase for each sermon. Plug all of these titles into your 52-week calendar. Make it work. Now, what you have just accomplished in a few days is what you may have previously done over the course of an entire year. The good news is- it's done! You don't have to think about it for a year. You don't have to worry about what you're going to preach on next. How wonderful. How freeing!

One question that naturally pops up is this- what if I change may mind? What if I need to add something, or subtract someone? What if a topic needs to go twice as long? What if the passages need twice as long to preach as I estimated? Am I stuck? The answer is- absolutely not! Create the calendar knowing that it will flex. And it will. Do your best to estimate how you believe the year will go, but always plan to add appropriate change as the year goes by. Don't let the schedule trap you. Let it set you free. Now, you can see how all of this can flow very naturally once you step back and begin looking at it as a big picture. Until you've done it, it looks so difficult. Once you've created this habit, it will become like second nature to you. All you have to do is decide when you will plan every year and this part of the process will be conquered.

Here's what all that preparation will do for you. Now you can really get creative. Now you have a year to think about ideas and meanings and illustrations and testimonies and video clips that can go along with the sermon topic. Each gathering can now focus on a theme. Music and drama and other resources can be added to the plan for each gathering because everyone has plenty of notice. Teams can create. Individuals can be assigned. Music can be planned months ahead and everyone can be ready. Media and drama teams can plan and prepare for concept skits that fit right into the topic of the day. New ideas on ways of communicating God's truth can immerge. All of this sets the stage for a standard of excellence. Everyone works smarter and harder when they know where they are going and have adequate time to prepare. And all the other pieces that make up an excellent gathering can now have meaning, purpose and direction.

> Everyone works smarter and harder when they know where they are going and have adequate time to prepare.

Getting a plan in writing is invaluable. But, unfortunately, you can still be sloppy, wait until the last minute to prepare and ruin any chance of real excellence. For some of us, learning to plan ahead and to prepare all of the details ahead of time will take far more discipline and effort than for others of us. Working with church cultures that have learned to not plan ahead will be an even greater challenge. But it will be worth it in the end. Go for it. Start! Jump in and let the changes begin!

Now that we've worked through the planning process, we need to look at the detail of our actual gathering. Let's begin by evaluating our sensitivity to our visitors.

Seeker / New Believer / Visitor Sensitive

How sensitive are we to our visitors? They come packaged in all shapes and sizes! But they all have one thing in common. They want to be happy when they walk through that door into the auditorium. They want all their fears and concerns to be relieved. They only came to have a good experience. And they clearly won't come back if that doesn't happen. If they're believers, they're shopping for just the right family and preacher. If they are a seeker or a new believer, they probably don't have a clue what they're looking for. They just know that they're supposed to do this church thing. If it feels good and right, they'll stay. Let's do our best to help them.

Let's look at their journey into the auditorium. Is it easy? Is it understandable? Are the happiest, friendliest ushers waiting to invite them in? Does the atmosphere feel inviting and friendly? Is there a visitor information pack? Have they already received it or do they get it now? Do they know where to go to be seated? Does someone need to help them get there? Are people friendly inside the auditorium or was what they've already experienced simply staged? Is the atmosphere aiding or hindering friendliness? Are people talking to each other? Are they aware of new people coming in? Are they talking to them? Is there "good hugging?" Some visitors like to be invisible. Don't put a spotlight on them. Let them go to their seats and hide- for a while. Others really need to be visible and cared about. Is someone finding them and talking to them?

> What we are concerned about here is not being over-sensitive to visitors. We want to make sure we're not **insensitive** to visitors!

Some well-meaning brothers and sisters will raise concerns about being over-sensitive to seekers and visitors. Why are we ignoring the entire church and putting so much focus on the new people? Isn't the gathering supposed to be about us and about strengthening us? Yes, and it is! Almost everything that happens in most churches **is** about us. And as visitors come to check us out, our hope and prayer is that they too would join us. And if they're not yet believers, we want them to also become a part of the family of God. What we are concerned about here is not being over-sensitive to visitors. We want to make sure we're not **insensitive** to visitors! Most churches are not sensitive **enough** to visitors. If you have company over to your home, you want to make sure that they are comfortable, that they know where the bathroom is and what they're doing at your home. You're not so worried about the comfort of your own family, because they already are comfortable. In fact, the only concern might be that the children are well behaved and pay enough attention to the company. That's exactly what we're talking about here!

Form and Function

How do the things that we do come across to our visitors? Every church has a different set of unspoken rules of conduct. This is the way we do things around here. Unfortunately we often learn them the hard way. Some things come naturally as we go through a service. What we don't want to do is make it too difficult on our visitors. We clearly don't want to leave them standing with their eyes closed while everyone else is sitting. That might be funny in a movie, but you don't want it to happen to your friends at your church.

I believe that most church services are designed largely for the regulars. It's not that we mean to be Insider Clubs. It's just that we don't think like visitors. We think like a family. And we know that everyone knows That. So we don't say it. We assume it. And, unfortunately, not everybody does know That!

For example, as I visit churches, I'm often not told when to stand or sit. Some people stand when others sit. I'm a pastor. I know what to do. But what about visitors and especially non-believers? Verbal and written announcements about events are often missing the very details that a visitor would need. And why are they singing so much and where does all the money go and what do I do with his talk. Am I supposed to do something? Now do I just leave? I think I will.

So we want to walk through the details of our service looking at how visitor-friendly we are. We want to think like visitors watching us, listening to us, and trying to figure out what to do next. We want to make it a clear, understandable and enjoyable experience. Get rid of any distractions! Make this encounter as attractive as possible. We want make sure that there is clearly communicated information in front of them. That may be in a bulletin, it may be on a video screen, or hosts may be assigned the job of welcoming and explaining.

If you go to a movie, the messages are clearly in front of you. "We hope you'll have a wonderful experience. Turn off that cell phone! Don't talk once the movie has started. These other movies will be coming here soon. Go back outside and buy some of our overpriced food. Now sit back and relax." These are the main announcements for visitors when they arrive for the first time. But the theater has no problem saying these six concepts over and over again. And it's O.K. We need the reminder. Well, guess what? The same thing needs to happen at church. Repetition is good for us and critical for the visitor.

Here are a few examples of some questions that might come up. "Where do we sit? What do we do with our children during the service? Do you mind if I just stay here if my baby starts to cry? What happens next? How long will this last? By the way, I always leave my cell phone on in case of an emergency, except at the movies! What is this standing and sitting and standing and sitting? And the hands raised- I do that at all the concerts I go to. But I don't get it when people kneel!" We can't explain everything, but we can do our best to clarify the main things. Many churches are using videos or a repeating media presentation before and after the service to answer basic questions that anyone new might ask. A bulletin, handout or packet also can be extremely helpful.

Sometimes I'll visit churches where it seems like the entire service has been thrown together with no sense of planning or appropriate structure. The songs don't go with the drama. The drama doesn't go with the sermon. The sermon doesn't go with the solo ending the sermon. I've even visited gatherings in large, celebrated churches where it's felt like some of the segments had no logical reason for their order or existence. Picture segments that seem rushed and purposeless. "Get that greeting time over with so we can get on to more important things!" Well, then stop doing the greeting time! It feels fraudulent! What a great video clip, but no one tied it to anything else in the

service. Nice solo, but how does that fit in? What in the world did those dancing girls have to do with anything? Maybe it was the pastor's wife and they were ready to perform. Sometimes it feels like people are ready to do something that they've practiced, so we throw them into the gathering. Now, what if we had a one-year plan instead and there was a sense of continuity and harmony in our gatherings? What a thought.

Always assume that there are visitors coming to your gathering. Always be ready. That may be difficult if you are a smaller gathering and you know everyone. But if you don't plan, prepare and present like visitors are coming, you won't be ready when they do come. That sounds a little like the five virgins waiting for the groom! By the way, if you keep presenting like visitors are coming, your people may actually start bringing visitors! Think about that one. Let's look at some more details. How do we explain singing and dedications and communion and offerings and invitations? We don't want visitors to get in the way of what we are doing as a body. We want them to see the glory of God in our midst as we celebrate His greatness and goodness. At the same time, we want our visitors to join in with us, fully understanding and experiencing what's happening in the moment. We want them drawn in to our experience with God and each other. And we want pre-believers drawn toward Jesus, undistracted by misunderstandings and confusion.

Is what we are doing in our gatherings both spiritual and understandable? It may be mysterious, but most of us get it, and they should be able to too! Is everything visitor friendly? Is it sloppy, poorly delivered and distracting, or is it attractive, even to outsiders? We may put up with some fumbling and carelessness, but visitors probably won't. They're not used to that at other performances or presentations, and they won't expect it at your church either. Let's look at this for a moment. The gathering, for most of our churches, is not a show. It's not a great performance that waits for the applause of men. We are the family of God gathered in His name to celebrate, to meet with Him and His people and to hear from His Word! We don't what to surrender any of that for professionalism. But, at the same time, we shouldn't be shoddy and ill-prepared either. There's no good reason for that! We need to give our very best to God and His people. We need to be excellent in everything we do! There's no excuse for poorly-practiced music, dramas, readings or sermons!

I think we sometimes use our church culture as an excuse for our lack of adequate preparation. We need to stop excusing our sloppiness and start building a mindset that focuses on excellence before God and man! This isn't about visitors. This is about doing what's good and right for everybody. And the visitors will benefit along with everyone else! So is what we are doing attractive? Is the length of our gathering reasonable for our culture, or does it go on and on and on? Do we ask if our people really like the length? Will it work for new people? Will it work for younger generations? Is the structure and mechanics of our gathering logical and comfortable? Do the parts feel like they fit and like they are in the right place? Is there a natural flow and a smoothness that feels right? Does each part seem appropriate? And do the lengths of each segment seem good and unrushed, not too long and not too short? Are there boundaries and controls on the time of each segment? How do people get helped with the time management of their part? Is there a limit? Is there a clock?

Is there a way to end a run-away segment? Is that important to you? Is quality a value in each section of the service? Does everyone in charge, including those who are taking part in each segment, share that value? How much attention is given to the details of each gathering? Is the standard of excellence celebrated when you gather as a body?

One area of form and function that can easily be overlooked is taking care of special needs. Are you ready to help someone to their seat if they have a walking disability? Do you have special areas prepared for wheelchairs? Are you ready for people who are hearing impaired? Have you bought the right equipment? Is there someone who can do sign language and is there a special section for the deaf? What will you do if a family attends that speaks a different language? Not every church can be ready for every need that arrives at its front door. All of our communities are different. Which of these areas of special need will most likely become important to your church setting in coming years? Get ready!

Auditorium

How does our auditorium look to our visitors? When they walk through that door, what's their first impression? "Wow, this is sure small. How do they fit everyone in here?" Or "Wow, this is sure big! Where are we supposed to sit?" "Wow, this is old. This is filthy." Or, "This is nice. This is . . ." Not every church will draw a Wow as visitors walk in. In fact, it's probably better if they are less distracted by our family room and simply comfortable. Will they feel comfortable? What type of atmosphere have you tried to create in your family room? Have you made it bright or dark? And have you done it on purpose? Or did you inherit it from the last generation or last pastor? What are you trying to create in the family room? Do you want it to feel big and majestic? Or warm and intimate? Are you appealing to the older generations or younger generations? Or are you hoping that everyone will like it just the way it is? Because they won't! I hate to tell you, but people are very fussy and actually selfish about their personal tastes. Someone in charge wanted your family room to look and feel just the way it is. It might have been a committee, and they may have even taken a vote. They probably did their very best to decide how to paint and design the room. The question that you need to ask is this- Does that design and appearance, color and lighting, decor and staging represent your purposes right now?

Let's get back to the original question. Is our family room attractive or distracting? Is it warm and inviting, or does it need some help? Does it have purposeful lighting that can complement what you do at your gatherings? Is the sound system serving your purposes? Have you been intentional with your acoustics, so nothing gets in the way of what you're trying to accomplish. In other words, are your sound and lighting invisibly aiding all the segments of your service, or are they getting in the way? Effective sound and lighting should never be noticed and should simply enhance everything that you are doing. Everyone should hear clearly! No dead spots, no dark spots, no loud or soft spots.

Here are some of the things that distract me when I visit a church gathering. Walls that have been poorly painted and look like no one really cares distract me. I'm distracted by stages that look messy and uncared for. Mikes that aren't turned on until everyone in the entire room is aware that they aren't turned on distracts me. I'm distracted when the sound is killing my eardrums or when it's so soft that I can't hear what I see. So I'm distracted when people on stage are singing or playing, but their mikes aren't turned up. Media slides that never seem to come on in time so I can actually sing along with the worship team always distract me! I'm distracted when the stage is dark and I have to work at seeing. Now, do I sound fussy? Yes, I do! But I am the visitor. And I am distracted! Please, take away those distractions. It would be so easy. And I'll enjoy the hundreds of other wonderful components of your gathering so much more! That felt good. Now that I've gotten that off my chest, we can move on!

Are your lighting, sound and video equipment and personnel invisible to the gathering? They need to be. Listen, your media personnel need to see and hear everything that you are doing so they don't miss a beat. You want them in the room, in the back of the bus. But you don't want to hear or see them. You don't want to hear them talking. You don't what to hear their equipment clicking. Their operation needs to be so smooth that everyone forgets that they are even there. On occasion, everyone needs to turn around and clap. Don't, and, I repeat, don't place any of these people in the front row. How distracting! How distracting to watch someone try to find the right slide. How distracting to watch a little screen below the big one. How distracting to watch people move around when its time to do sound or video or media slides. Buy that cheap little cord at Radio Shack. Buy it today. Run it to the back of the room. Now that's over with.

> Let's have fun, be creative and take pride in making the family room a place that everyone really loves and enjoys.

Everything in your family room needs to be clean and uncluttered. And someone who truly loves clean and uncluttered needs to be in charge of that regular assignment. Is the auditorium clean before each gathering? We would always clean up our auditorium between services so it would be attractive for the next gathering. We just planned it and assigned it, so it always happened. Are the entry areas and corners of the room clean and uncluttered? Is the stage area clean and set up in an attractive way? Do the decorations, equipment and people on the platform look barren, overcrowded or just right? What would you change to make it better? Are window coverings being used, and, if so, are they attractive and convenient? What sort of decorations and banners are you using around the room and on the walls? Is it working? Does it look great to outsiders? Sometimes we feel stuck with something that dear Sister So-n-So made. Nobody likes it, but we're afraid to take it down. Figure it out! Be kind, be gentle and do the right thing. Don't be held hostage.

It will hurt, but she'll get over it, and so will you. There are so many great looking banners and resources that can be hung or placed around our family rooms. Let's have fun, be creative and take pride in making the family room a place that everyone really loves and enjoys. Maybe they'll start bringing their friends.

Here are a few more questions about the auditorium. Are the seats comfortable? And, if they're moveable, are they spaced appropriately? I understand that there are times that we have to pack 'em in. I've done it. But I hate it when my knees are jammed into someone else's back. And they don't like it either. Is the screen clearly visible to the entire room? Is it bright enough for everyone to see? Does the projector dissolve away into the room? Is the lighting adequate for people to see what they need to see? Sometimes we dim the lights for atmosphere, but we still expect everyone to read the bulletin. Let me tell you, if they don't read it in the family room, they probably won't read it at all. By the way, candles work great! Is the lighting on the stage bright enough and evenly distributed? Are the leaders bright and clearly visible to everyone? This is so important to a good presentation. Add some floodlights if you need to. I would walk all over the place when I preached, so we worked hard to have enough floodlights to cover all of the stage and down in the front of the stage. I've seen worship teams playing in the dark behind a bright leader. I've often seen speakers walking in and out of the light. I visited a church where everyone was visible except the worship leader, sitting at his piano, in the one dark spot at the corner of the stage. He didn't even know. Let's help each other get brighter! One more question- Are you committed to a standard of excellence in your auditorium?

Sound/Lighting/Video/. . .

Let's spend some more time talking about the media depart-ment. Your sound, lighting and projected media can be three of your greatest blessings in helping you deliver a wonderful celebration of worship and inspiration. They can also be your greatest enemy.

Again, so much of this comes down to a commitment to excellence. Are they attractive or distractive? If you as leaders decide that all of this must be operated at a high level of quality, then your recruitment, training, instructions and implementation will follow that foundation! If you leave it to chance, you know what you'll get.

Start with a plan. Here's what we want to happen every week with sound, lights and media. Who will be in charge of that plan? Is one person in charge of sound, lighting and media, or are there three people in charge? Is there a team under each person? Who recruits the team? How are they trained? How do they know exactly what you want them to do? Is it written down? Does it need to be in writing to get the quality that you want? Do the leaders and team members take their responsibility seriously? If they don't, you lose. Find someone else! I realize that smaller churches have limited pools of technicians to help in areas like this. But you can't afford to have someone in charge who doesn't really care about quality and excellence! Here's an observation. I've seen media staff fall asleep at the wheel and miss their cues because they are bored or distracted. Then I've seen teams of young people under good adult supervision do excellent media work, thrilled that they could demonstrate their usefulness. So here's the lesson- find the right people who are hungry to help, capable and teachable. Train them, use them and watch the great things that will happen. By the way, don't expect your people to simply figure out how to do a good job at sound, light and media. Help them meet up with some media personnel from other churches if they need to. We need to be available to help each other.

Let's talk about some details. Every Sunday is different and the media needs are different too. We can't walk in and turn everything on 15 minutes before the service and expect everything to work right. It won't! I've seen it over and over again. No one's tested the video before the service begins, and the sound doesn't come on when "play" is hit. The problem is, the youth group borrowed the audio cord Wednesday night and forgot to return it. Or the cord simply went bad during the week. The point is, the speakers, mikes, equipment, instruments, lights, projectors, players, computers and the actual software presentations down to the video all need to be tested long before the people arrive and the service begins.

I had worked for hours on the presentation. I had crafted the PowerPoint slides and videos to work together in perfect harmony. I had one shot to communicate the passion on my heart and wanted the message to ring clear. I had saved the best for last, building the videos to a moving ending. As the actual audience was watching and experiencing my presentation, suddenly, two minutes from the ending, the movie froze! It froze! I couldn't believe it. All was lost. The moment was gone forever. The impact died away. The computer had glitched the night before as I saved the presentation. But I didn't realize that it had ruined my video. I skimmed through the presentation in the morning without watching the video through to the end. If I had done that, I would have rescued my presentation and had my desired impact on my audience. By missing that one detail, I lost the moment and was totally embarrassed. Now, everyone makes mistakes. But, "I'll never do that again," he said.

Many worship teams and sound personnel set up and practice during the week, and that's good. But things change by church time. Besides, the demon of sound systems will show up- at least once a month. Count on it! So there needs to be a final and thorough check and arranging of everything long before the service begins. Equipment testing and preparation need to be done before people begin arriving for the service. Think about it. We shouldn't be testing sound and videos as people come in. The worship team shouldn't be still practicing as early visitors arrive. How sloppy! Poor planning and last-minute preparation will never produce excellence. Raise the standard! Create the discipline. At school and at work, all of us have to live by disciplines or we lose our jobs! Why should we give God a lower standard of commitment?

By the way, innovation in the world of media is fantastic. It used to cost a small fortune to buy good sound and media equipment. But digital technology has soared and costs have dropped significantly. With small budgets, many of us used to be limited to simple soundboards and PowerPoint slides. All that's changed! Now there are loads of alternatives when it comes to excellent sound systems. And great, new innovative programs and platforms keep arriving in the area of media production. Programs like ProPresenter, Easy Worship, Media Shout, Live Worship and Planning Center are just a few of many wonderful packages that help us plan, get organized and then offer smooth and undistracting presentations. And that leads me to my next point.

It's impossible to have a smooth, distraction-free service if the media people don't know where the service is going- in detail. It's impossible to guess at as many details as there are in most services and come out right every time. As few as the mistakes may be, they will appear sloppy and will reflect on the media personnel. That's not fair! They can't possibly get it right without detail. And that detail needs to be in writing- or they'll forget, and mistakes will be made. Many pastors will write out a complete page of details, dialing in everything from video clips and lighting to special music and the number and location of the mikes to be used. By the way, many will also designate the portion of time each segment gets in the service. That way, everyone knows what needs to be accomplished to get done on time. That becomes even more critical when there are multiple services.

By the way, the volume of your sound makes a difference. If it's too loud or too soft, people will be unhappy. If it's too late or if it feeds back, you'll be unhappy. Most of this can be solved by planning ahead. How loud do you want your mikes to be for talking, for singing, for videos? This doesn't have to be left to chance every week. Buy a sound level meter at Radio Shack for $50. Listen to various volumes over a month to decide what is perfect for your gathering. Write it down and train your sound personnel to honor the plan. Now, we all know there is no right volume level. That's why you decide what is best for your body and for each gathering. Most churches will set louder volumes for younger listeners because that's what they like! Mixed gatherings will usually dictate a compromise on volume so that no one is happy- it's too loud for some and too soft for others! Oh well. That's life.

So here are some questions that need to be asked. Do we know all the details for this service? Have we worked to make sure the sound is good and undistracting? Have we decided on our volume levels? Will the sound staff support our decision? Are we willing to lose people because of our decision to have the music too soft or too loud? Have we done a test on volume levels so there are no surprises? Do we have enough mikes and monitors? Have we tested all of our instruments and sound clips? Do we know what to do if there's feedback? Is the lighting ready? Is it bright enough and consistent across and in front of the stage? Is everyone going to be clearly seen? Are there lighting changes? Will they be smooth and undistracting? Is someone assigned? Are there any DVD clips or video clips? Have we pre-tested them for full-screen visibility and clean sound? Have we learned how to fade video presentations in from black-to-video and back to black? Do we know how to move smoothly between PowerPoint or other presentation software and movie clips? (No one needs to visibly see equipment switched and the word "play" appear on the screen. Isn't that annoying?) Are we clear about when each slide is supposed to go on the screen? Have we created blank slides for the times when we don't want anything up there? By the way, is the projector bright enough for everyone to see? Bulbs dim by 50% over time and their replacement every few years significantly improves their delivery. The last question to ask as the media personnel is- Are we truly committed to a standard of excellence and is that obvious to everyone? The final product of the media department each week makes a significant difference in the minds of most visitors as well as your regulars. A great, undistracted service has to be the goal!

Pre-Service and Beginnings

What are the first things that our visitors will experience as they walk into our family room? What you have planned is what they will see. If you have no plan, they will see that too! Let's look specifically at preparation times. Set-up and clean-up should be done long before people begin arriving. However long it takes, start early enough to be done at least 30 minutes before service time. Plan it, assign it, and do it! Don't lower your standard and get sloppy. Businesses expect this quality and people lose their jobs for less. Why should we accept anything less in the service of God? If you have multiple services, be sure to assign someone to be in charge of cleaning up and re-setting up the auditorium so it is excellent for the next set of worshippers and visitors.

Worship preparation also needs to be done at least 30 minutes before the service. We shouldn't be practicing as people come in. Come on! We've had all week! That's not the atmosphere that we want to meet people with as they come to church. We don't want them to tolerate our mistakes. We want them to hear our final product- one time. We need to have a thirty minutes-and-counting plan that happens every time we have a service. What lighting do we want visitors to arrive to? How bright should the auditorium be? Are we using candles? What lighting do we want on the stage? What music do we want to have playing thirty minutes before the service starts? Do we have videos or media slides that need to be running on the screens? What sort of atmosphere are we trying to create? Does that change from week to week? Does everyone know the plan long before the event? Does the plan change fifteen minutes before the service? What changes five minutes before the service? Is there a lighting or sound or video change to prepare people for the start of the service? Get creative. Set the mood. Do the lights come up on the stage? Does the worship team come up and start playing live music? What's the platform plan? Has anyone thought about it beforehand or does everyone just come up? Does it look planned? Does the service start with class and precision?

None of this will happen without a plan. And none of this will happen well unless everyone agrees with the plan. So have a plan. And then talk with all of your leaders and team members responsible for these areas about the plan. Talk about the purpose of each action. Help them understand the thought behind each detail of your plan. Here's an example. The worship team does a final sound check and ends thirty minutes before the service, whether they have practiced earlier or not. Everything is dialed in. The team goes to a back room for a time of worship and prayer. They focus on their Source and commit the service to the Lord and His purposes. When they're done praying, everyone goes into the auditorium and begins intentionally greeting, encouraging and loving on the sheep. They look specifically for visitors and people sitting or standing alone. Can you think of a better way to prepare people to worship than to be encouraged by the worship team and church leaders? When a visitor meets a worship team member, he or she will feel even more of a connection when they see them on the platform helping to lead worship. At five minutes to service time, the team breaks for the stage and they're off. Now, that's an excellent, purpose-driven beginning!

Music

Music makes the world go round! Music is the universal language. Almost everyone loves music. Unfortunately, music also is the great divider. People quit churches every week over music! People join churches every week because of the music they do like. It doesn't matter if we agree with it or not. It's the way it is! All we can do is assess what people like or don't like.

1) **First of all, let's talk about taste.** Some people like loud music and others like it soft. Some like rock and others like Bach. Some

like hymns and others like. . .- you get the point! Some leaders have grown great churches blending all the styles and volumes and tastes into each service. Some change it up every Sunday. Some have created multiple services to reach different types of people with different styles of music- like fishing. Others narrow their focus and target a specific segment of the population to build their church. Whatever you do, do it on purpose.

> A lot of the battle over personal preferences comes down to whether we are willing to surrender for the cause of Christ!

Think about what you want to accomplish through your music. Who are you doing your music for? We all know that we are doing our music for God. But He's not near as fussy as all of us are. God's taste in music is certainly broader than and different than your taste and mine. So here's the question: are you trying to please the older people, the younger people, the middle people or all of the above? Or are you simply picking music that you like? Oh, oh- now I'm getting personal. Here's a question- if visitors walked in the door, would they like the songs you're singing and the style that you've picked? If we want to reach the world, our music has to be relevant to them. Don't expect them to change their tastes to please you! It doesn't work that way. A lot of the battle over personal preferences comes down to whether we are willing to surrender for the cause of Christ. If my non-Christian or new believing friend gets bored attending 1st service with me and my music, am I willing to go with him to 2nd service and his kind of music? That answer should be a no-brainer! But I'm afraid many of us struggle with the idea of being missional with our music instead of simply feeding our own appetites. I know this paragraph will stir up feelings and controversy. Don't get mad! Work this through. I'm not talking about compromising and sacrificing spiritually and theologically for something weak and worldly. I'm asking you to look at the idea of laying down what you really like if it serves the purpose of reaching more and more people for Jesus. By the way, this is a critical teaching point. If we want our people to truly be missional in their own hearts and lifestyle, they'll have to surrender a whole lot of self. We'll have to preach and teach and walk them through that process. And music will always be a centerpiece issue- I guarantee it.

We invited ourselves to the board meeting because of the financial crisis that was developing in the church. If things continued the way they were going, the church had months before it would have to close its doors. We asked the leaders to tell us a little bit about their church history. One of the elders quickly became the spokesperson for the board. He talked about the glory days when the church was filled with 300 to 400 people. He talked about a church split and about the gradual deterioration of numbers down to the low 100's. And then he talked about music. He talked about a group of younger adults who wanted to start a contemporary worship service. This elder had personally worked through that process with the group. He was deeply concerned about the style, the drums and the volume of their music.

With great apprehension, the board decided to allow this group of adults to start an early service. This elder assigned himself to be the watchdog of the group, to monitor them and to make sure that their worship and music was appropriate. After four months, the elder told the young adults that their music was too loud, and he shut down their service! Can you believe it? Of course, the entire group of young adults left, never to be seen again. It was astonishing to listen to this elder as he told his story. Here's what was amazing- he was proud of what he had done! He had no regrets. He had

been the savior of the church! He had no idea that he had personally helped to kill the very thing the he loved so much.

Here's the rest of the story! The church leadership made slight, incidental, non-threatening, non-productive changes as a result of our meeting. That elder died within a short period of time, and the church died soon after!

2) Secondly, let's look at the issue of quality. No one likes music that's done poorly. Some will smile, praise it publicly and tolerate it privately. That's what family and friends are for. There's a time and a place for karaoke. But it's not during the worship service! Our music should be done with excellence, to the glory of God. This isn't a push for perfect people singing or playing perfect music. Sometimes that drive for perfection and performance strangles any sign of genuine humility and spirituality right out of the room. I'd rather have a good worship team with tender hearts than a great worship team with fat heads and inflated egos! Character is more important than competence! So I'm talking about godly people who have enough talent singing and playing that when they've practiced, they make beautiful music together. They aren't a distraction. But they also aren't the real attraction. They actually do so well that they disappear and Jesus takes center stage. That's what it's all about, isn't it?

I'll occasionally visit a church where it appears that very little thought has been put into the service. There's no special order or continuity to the songs that are being sung. Nothing is being said between the songs to give direction or meaning to what we are doing. That's bad enough for the regular attenders. But it's absolutely unfair for visitors! Let's picture this from God's point of view. Picture a pre-believing visitor attending a service. God's purpose is to use the content of the service and an atmosphere of love to draw this individual toward the Kingdom. Now, we know that God can speak through anything. He's even used donkeys! But He'd rather not. What a difference if someone has carefully and prayerfully picked and ordered the songs to weave together with the message and the rest of the morning's content. **That** is the excellence and quality that honors God. I also believe that it allows God to accomplish what He wants to do in a service.

By the way, many smaller churches have a smaller pool of musical talent. Now, isn't that a brilliant observation? It makes it far more difficult to put together a great worship team. The truth is, this is one of the primary reasons why smaller churches don't grow. It's of critical importance to solve this problem if you want to grow! Here are several thoughts. It's better to have no music than poor music. It's better to have one leader than several who don't sound very good. It's better to not use willing souls than to lose your potential to grow. You may even lose several people along the way, but you'll gain far more in the long run. Don't be held hostage by your mercy. Be kind, be sensitive, be loving and do the right thing. If you want visitors, and if you want them to come back, they will not tolerate what your regular attendees will put up with. They have no reason to! There are lots of other churches that they can visit. There are many churches and even church plants that use CD's and music videos as a healthy alternative to live worship done poorly. Grow the crowd and you will gain the larger pool from which you can develop a quality worship team.

3) Thirdly, let's look at the content of our music at each service. We've got to begin with a series of questions- what is our purpose? Where are we going? What are we trying to accomplish? How does everything tie together? What do we want as our End-Product? What do we want the body and visitors to experience by the time they leave the gathering? How should we begin our singing? How should we end our singing? Which songs best capture the expression and message that we want for this gathering? Are they understandable? Will the visitors and non-believers get it? Will I need to explain what the concept is so everyone can fully comprehend and participate? I love this song. But do other people like it? Is it singable? This song is so cool, but will it draw people closer to God? Or will it just rock the house? This song is so good theologically, but it's one hundred years old. Will anyone like the style? This song is beautiful, but its theology is terrible. We can't compromise what we believe just because we like the tune. Here's a great song that I've had on my mind for weeks. But it doesn't fit in with the direction of our service. I need to wait for a better time.

> You carefully construct your service so that everyone can arrive with a feeling of expectation and leave with a sense of resolution.

Church services should always be sensitive to visitors, whether they are seekers or believers. How do we look to our visitors? There's never a time when you should act like no one is watching and you can just be the family. This doesn't mean that you're always putting on a show. What it really means is that you are always being thoughtful of others. You are always aware that some in the room don't understand everything that you are doing. You carefully construct your service so that everyone can arrive with a feeling of expectation and leave with a sense of resolution. Something's been accomplished in us and in my life and heart. I've met with God!

By the way, there are seasons where we can create an entire service around the visitors in the room. Outreach events and seasonal Sundays like Easter and Christmas will often be planned with everything targeting the non-believing members of the audience. That's not seeker-sensitive. That's seeker-centered! That's focusing on a specific group with the intention of moving them on a journey toward salvation. So the songs, drama, videos and message all align on purpose. But a weekly seeker-sensitive service focuses on the body growing more and more into the likeness of Jesus. The family gathers, demonstrates God's love, worships, feeds on the Word and responds to God. As visitors and pre-believers attend and observe a gathering like that, they experience God among His people and often are deeply moved and impacted! A seeker-sensitive leadership team doesn't adjust the service to focus on the visitor or seeker. But they have clearly prepared with visitors on their minds. Visitors are welcomed and words are spoken so everyone can understand. Songs are occasionally defined. There is a sensitivity that people are in the house who may not know Jesus. Our goal is to make sure that nothing gets in the way of the Spirit of God drawing them to Himself.

4) Let's talk about the purpose of our music at the gathering. We sing to worship! It's as simple as that. With an audience of One, we sing as teams, choirs, leaders and soloists, to Him. Should our music be done with excellence? Of course. We've already said that. Can it be entertaining and fun? Absolutely! God loves creativity and fun, just like we do. Don't try to tell me something different. But let's never forget that our goal can't be to entertain or perform simply to achieve the praises of our audience. If that becomes our goal, we've missed the whole point. We've got the whole thing backwards.

We sing to worship!

We sing to honor Him!

We sing to respond to Him!

We sing to declare His goodness and 1000 other attributes!

We sing to draw close to Him!

We sing to love Him!

We sing for Him and Him alone!

More and more people are looking for worship that touches their hearts and connects them to a living God. A group of Christian leaders in the music industry gathered recently and were commenting on how their concerts events and CD sales are shifting away from entertainment toward music that draws people into an authentic encounter with God. Amazing! Steven Macchia, taking the temperature of the church, talks about this in his excellent book, *Becoming a Healthy Church*.

> . . .the people of God are hungering today for mean-ingful worship experiences. Not the kind of worship where they sit passively back in the pews- but the kind that engages and requires their full involve-ment. The key to effective worship in the healthiest of settings is engaging people's hearts, minds, souls and strength.

And he adds:

> A worship leader should be able to hear and interpret the heart of God. It's not just an issue of providing music. It is about seeing into the heart of God, hearing, and then bringing that to the people and helping them respond to that. Our mandate is to please God, not the masses. [48]

Does this ring true to you? Isn't this the purpose of our music as we gather? As much as this may contrast and contradict what we often see or participate in, this is the Way. This is the original intent! Matt Redman sang, "I'm coming back to the heart of worship, and it's all about You, all about You, Jesus, I'm sorry, Lord, for the thing I've made it!" What have we made it? What have we changed it into? And how can we come back to the heart of worship? Others may listen and respond, but it's all about Him.

God help us to not steal Your Glory.

God help us to not make it such a show that people leave enter-tained but no closer to You.

> *And God help us to not make it so boring*
> *and unexciting that people*
> *wonder why we sing.*

You, as worship leaders, play such an important role in creating an atmosphere for worship. The training of your instrumentalists and singers is so critical. Get them into the Word and prayer. Teach them to worship. Worship together! Coach them, help them understand, be patient with them, and hold them accountable. Everything in us and around us tells us to look good for the people we are performing for. Our egos fight our spirituality all the time. We can only win this battle with a clear understanding and constant reminder of our purpose and place in each gathering! Our goal is to make Jesus shine. And to stay out of the way! From the audience's point of view, what they see speaks far louder than words. The entire team on the stage helps to set the mood for the service. As a team, your personal commitment to model and reflect worship to the rest of the body makes all the difference in the world. First of all, God sees your heart and will bless and anoint you as a team for your posture before Him. Secondly, the people sense your sincerity and genuine offering of worship to God. Or not.

I've attended 1000's of gatherings. I've experienced countless moments where the worship leader and the team have disappeared and I've seen Jesus! They've clearly had fun when the music has been celebrative, and they've been passionate or contemplative when the music and mood has changed. They've truly been part of the worship, singing or playing from their hearts with all their hearts. They've connected with me, and I've connected with God. But I've also experienced a contrasting type of "worship" environment. Some of the musicians have looked like they're trying out for American Idol. The clothes, the moves- they're doing a Sunday gig! In absolute contrast, others have looked so bored that you wonder why they're singing or playing in the first place. Maybe they've been drafted at the last minute. Or maybe they've volunteered because no one else will. Some have seemed totally disconnected for the rest of the gathering. They're in their own world doing their own thing. I've watch some musicians leave as soon as the gig is over, go and talk and have coffee and donuts during the rest of the service and then return just in time for the encore. Give me a break. Stop it! I'm not saying that leadership needs to sit through multiple services every week. I am saying that I've seen leaders who aren't even there. Maybe they're simply the paid help. But they're not part of what's really going on. They have no idea what God is doing because they're not really present. Be present!

Listen- I realize we all have different personalities. People don't know us and can easily misinterpret our own heart for worship. We may look like we're having too much fun, but we're really worshipping with all our hearts. Like David. Some of us have amazing voices or are incredible instrumentalists. We can't help it that we draw some attention to ourselves. Should we sing or play badly so no one is distracted? Of course not! And people don't understand our circumstances. Someone may be coaching us on some changes, and it just takes time and patience. Maybe we've had a terrible week and we're working through some things. Or we may have already attended and participated in one service and we don't want to sit through all of them. People in the gathering can judge us day and night, and they do. We all know that we can't please everyone. But shouldn't our goal be to please Him? And He is pleased when our worship draws people to Him and not simply to us! Doesn't that make sense? So let's think about what we look or sound like. Let's ask others to help us from an outside point of view. If we look bored, let's fix it. If we look like a rock star, is this the time and place? Talk it out, figure it out and then worship with all your heart!

It's so important that you as leaders of worship lead us. Lead us in worship. Lead us into His presence! Some of us are far away. Some of us don't even know God. Dr. Richard Brown, Vice-President at Simpson University, teaching on worship, tells his students that so many people arrive to church services spiritually in their bathrobes, unshaven, un-showered and half-awake. It's your goal and responsibility as the worship leader to walk them through the process of waking up, cleaning up and moving forward into the Throne Room of God. What a great calling and opportunity. Take us on that journey of celebration, contemplation, cleansing and responding to Him. Tell us what to do. Don't assume anything! Don't leave me in my bathrobe. Should I stand? Should I sit? Talk to me. Give me permission. I don't know the rules here. This is so different from anything I've experienced. Why are you raising your hands? Why aren't you raising your hands? Or clapping? Too many believers never enter into more than a sing-along experience because no one leads them. Many worship leaders are great singers and instrumentalists, but they don't say enough. Talk to me. Identify with me. Draw me in!

So let's add it up. If we want our people to bring their friends, and if we want visitors to come back, we need good music. It needs to be purposeful. We need to be seeker-sensitive. We need to work at quality, with good vocals and good instrumentation. Songs and sounds need to be clear and understandable. Our service needs to be well-planned. Our volume levels need to be on purpose. The media presentation of the songs needs to be attractive. The words to the songs need to be clearly visible and easily readable. The slides need to be changed **before** the words are sung or no visitor will ever be able to sing along with the leader. Read that sentence again, just in case you missed it and you run the slides. All of the music presented or led should be done with excellence. And, most importantly, all of this must be done in the power of God! How tragic if we dial in the details and miss that whole point of worship! But it happens all the time.

Arts- Drama / Art / Dance / . . .

The creativity of your people can significantly enhance your corporate experience as you gather for worship. Releasing believers to participate in the service is both good for them and good for the body. I've always been amazed at the energy and excitement that's added to a service when flags are being waved during our singing or paintings are forming before us as the message is being delivered. Why not incorporate appropriate creativity into our services to add to our proclamation of the glory of God? Now, every church differs in style and talent. Some churches would never dream of doing what other churches take for granted. And that's O.K! Different strokes for different folks! That helps with the great variety of churches that visitors get to select from. One of the stark realities about doing creative things in your church is this- you have to have the right people to do creative things well. Don't try to be creative with willing people who are more talented in other areas. Help all of your people to serve the Lord in the ways that they are most talented and will be most effective. No one wins when someone does poorly in front of the entire church. I'm not talking about children trying to act and sing. We all like to laugh and enjoy our kids as they grow up. But we don't want to embarrass anyone as we move into an adult world. The question is- is this attractive or distractive? And does it receive glory or give God glory?

One of the hardest things is waiting for talented people to either reveal themselves or begin attending your church. There are small churches with lots of talent and large churches with limited creativity. That's life! Years ago, I was called to pastor a church with 75 people and an outstanding 25 voice choir. That was amazing! Yet, at a considerably larger size, we still had no one who really loved drama. Suddenly, the day arrived and Cathy and her husband walked through the front door as visitors. It didn't take long before we discovered her incredible talent at organizing and directing drama teams. The church was filled with talented people, but someone had to show up with the gifts and passion to pull it all together. We now had the opportunity for quality drama anytime anywhere. We had great skits for announcements, mini-dramas before, during and after sermons. We even had entire plays several times a year. Of course, this enhanced what we were already doing around our special seasons. None of this would have happened if God hadn't brought Cathy to our church. What if Cathy had never come? Then we would have continued to do our best with what we had. There are things we would never have done, and there are many churches that will never get to do the things we did with drama. But they will also do things that we never have done. No one ever showed up with the talent to do sign language for our congregation. I always wanted it. But God didn't give it to us. You can't have everything, and you're probably not meant to have everything. Maybe we're all supposed to take the talent that we **do** have, unwrap it and use **it** to the best of our ability. That sounds pretty Biblical to me.

> As we involve more and more people in ministry, they get blessed, the church gets blessed and God is happy too!

Sometimes there's talent right in front of us and we don't even see it. For example, I love watching artists paint a picture that speaks to a theme at the same time that someone is preaching the message. It's wonderful. It's beautiful. It enhances the sermon, just like a song or movie clip or mini-drama. But I personally never did it in the churches that I pastored. And that's because I never thought of it. It's as simple as that. If I had thought of it, we would have done it. I even had artists in the church paint for special events as a guest artist/speaker. But I would never have imagined the idea of someone painting a picture centered on my theme as I preached a sermon. That's one more reason why the sharing of great ideas in the Christian community at large can be so helpful. Why miss out on a good thing? Let's learn from each other.

It's essential to involve as many people as possible in ministry. Everyone is made to minister. That's what spiritual gifts and natural talents are for. As we involve more and more people in ministry, they get blessed, the church gets blessed and God is happy too. That being said, not every gift and talent is meant for group set-tings. Some people have a gift that is perfect for relational use, but it doesn't work in front of a group. They may think so, but you have to use your good judgment. As leaders, we are called to make hard decisions, and those decisions can't always be based on polls and politics!

Our services need to be purpose-driven. I'll repeat what I've already said. There have been many times when I have visited churches, and it's seemed more like a talent show than a service. What in the world were they thinking? There seemed to be no rhyme or reason for doing that. It didn't fit in with the songs or sermon or anything! The twins have a song they would like to sing. Brother Billy's ready with his saw. The youth group's practiced up and prepared. The women have a new dance number. Sister Sally would like to read a poem.

I don't want to stifle creativity! But what is your purpose? What are you trying to accomplish? How do we look to our visitors? What if God doesn't want **that** to be a part of His gathering? How would you know that? Don't just do something because someone volunteers or has a great idea. Don't just do something because another church has done it! I still remember reading in Time magazine about a liberal church allowing a stripper to demonstrate her talents during a Sunday morning service. You've got to be kidding! They were out of their minds! We'd never do that. It's too obvious. But are there components of our gathering that God would rather not have us do? What picture are you trying to paint both for the body and for visitors? Does this particular talent fit into the plan for this service? Will it be well-done? Will it be well-placed? Will it serve your purpose? Will it be tasteful and relevant for the whole audience? Will it please God and give Him glory? Will it demonstrate a standard of excellence? Then, do it!

Body Life

One of the greatest attractors to visitors is when they experience the body fully engaged with God and each other in a worship gathering. It's miraculous! The power of that setting is indescribable. How do we look to our visitors? We look glorious when we are united and filled with God's love and power. When they walk through that door, so many visitors will feel the presence of God in our midst. Something supernatural will happen- in Baptist churches,

Pentecostal churches and all the churches in-between. I've watched visitors sobbing uncontrollably and without understanding as we worship with all our hearts. I can't say enough about the impact that the body itself has on visitors as they worship with us. As they see our genuine love for them, as they see our passion in worship, and as they see us hunger during the delivery of the Word, they are drawn to Jesus. The power of God working though a loving, Spirit-filled body is as significant as the worship in song and the preaching of the sermon. They all work together like a fine-tuned orchestra.

You can see why it's so important that the family is ready for its visitors. We've already talked about the priority of continually modeling, training and helping our people to demonstrate love all the time, all week long. So I'm not talking about slapping on a happy face on Sunday to hide the sad reality of our daily lives. I'm talking about helping our people to learn to walk in genuine spirituality that then multiplies and overflows when we gather together.

Let's look at the parts of our gathering that reflect the life of the body. Some of those components are times for greeting, prayer, sharing, readings, communion, offerings, special music, other pre-sentations, and announcements, to name a few. When we look at all the things that we try to squeeze into a gathering, it's a wonder that there's any time to preach! Some churches solve the problem by dumping everything but the big three M's- music, the money and the message. Got to take that offering! Most of the body life then takes place in other venues, like small groups. This happens in many churches especially as they grow larger and larger. Expectations for personal interaction lessen in a sea of people. Unfortunately, the love of the body often fades along with that interaction. Churches can begin to feel sterile as the unity and bonding of the body decreases. Sometimes we throw out the very components that helped us grow in the first place.

When I was a young pastor, I visited Peninsula Bible Church in the San Francisco Bay area. I was so impressed with the life and energy of this large church. A theme presented everywhere was the concept of body life- the demonstration and participation of the church family being critical to the function and form of every aspect of church life. What intrigued me the most was a sharing time in every service. As large as they were, ten to fifteen minutes was dedicated to passing several mikes though the congregation so people could share what God was doing in their lives. Although only a handful of people shared, it was powerful for everyone listening and it gave glory to God! God was in the sharing! These moments were so dynamic and impressive to me that I incorporated them into my ministry. Having a regular sharing time became second nature to our church. People loved it. Visitors loved it! It was focused and very purposeful. We guided the subject matter each week and the length that each person shared. Some weeks we asked for lessons learned during the week from the Word, and other weeks we asked for praises, or prayer needs, or things that God was teaching them. This demonstration of authentic faith contributed significantly to our continued growth as a church.

I am convinced that that sharing time was a vital and perhaps even a critical part of what helped us grow! And the sharing time was as rich when we were large as it was when we were small! But as the church got larger and larger, the demands for other segments in the service also grew. We had more drama and more music and more

presentations and more announcements. With limited time, the sharing took place less and less and less! Pretty soon, we were hardly doing sharing times at all! Can you believe it? We practically stopped doing one of the very things that defined us as a church and helped us both grow and stay warm and healthy as we grew! How sad!

In stark contrast, some churches try to do it all, and the services go on and on and on. This may work in some church cultures, but those churches may not grow. Visitors who haven't adapted to that culture and time commitment have things to do and places to go. They will visit, but they may not ever come back. If you have looong services and you're not growing, that may be the problem.

We need to move back to the issue of purpose. The question is- what purpose does this serve? Is this necessary? Is it important to everyone? What would happen if we stopped doing that? What would happen if we improved it? What do we need to do to improve it? Are we clear, concise and appealing? Will we get the results that we are after? What will those results be? There are things that we will do in a small church that we need to eliminate, as the church gets larger. In fact, it won't get larger if we don't eliminate them. For example, when we meet together in a home with a group of fifteen to twenty people, there will and should be an informality that allows an open dialogue between everyone in the room. That is part of the purpose. Everyone gets to share and ask in that atmosphere. But that doesn't work well with one hundred people. It can feel sloppy, disordered, chaotic and even rude! It's impossible for a hundred people to all get an opportunity to talk. There's not enough time unless you plan to stay all day. If a church doesn't learn how to transition from fifteen to fifty to five hundred in areas like this, it will not grow! Visitors simply will not come back.

How do we keep the warmth and unity of family and still allow for growth as visitors come and want to join us? Lots of people simply do not want their churches to grow because they don't want to lose that warmth. How can we grow and still have a warm, loving gathering of believers? How can we keep an appropriate amount of body life in the service to maintain that element of warmth? Many churches work hard to find a balance between limited time and the demands of body life in a gathering. It takes planning and intentionality. It means that not everything will happen every time the body gathers. And not everything will happen in front of the entire gathering. It also means that everyone who plays a role in presenting or leading in the service has to be time-conscious. Many churches will plan out all of the components of their services months in advance, down to the detail and time allowed for each segment. Start- 3 minutes early; praise and worship- 20 minutes; welcome and hugs- 5 minutes; video clip- 3 minutes; announcements with 2 1-minute video clips- 5 minutes; offering- 6 minutes; message- 30 minutes; close- 10 minutes. Planners can then look at the big picture. What components need to happen which week to be most valuable and effective for our purpose? Let's look at some of those components.

Welcome and Greeting time- The welcome, of course, is meant for everyone. While some churches are very generic, many churches will use the welcome to recognize that there are visitors in the service. I personally believe it's healthy to welcome the visitors because they need it. They are new and it feels good to be welcomed. It's also good for the regulars to be reminded that there are visitors around them. It reminds them to be friendly and caring to strangers. Some churches use this opportunity to give out some type of visitor pack with a card to be filled out. Visitors are asked to put a hand up so ushers can give them the pack. It usually works out fine. Now, we don't want to embarrass visitors. They won't come back! But if a visitor doesn't want to be identified, they don't have to put their hand up! Some visitors truly want to hide when they first come to church. If that's what they want, let them. I am amazed at the churches that still make the visitors stand up and introduce themselves. I have learned that

that is expected and very honorable in certain cultures and it should be done. But, in most churches, that would almost guarantee that your visitor would never return! On the other hand, some churches are so afraid that they will offend the visitors that they miss one more opportunity to make contact.

Lots of churches will structure a segment of time in their service specifically designed for people to interact and get to know each other. I've seen them short, I've seen them long, and most of them are in-between. Sometimes the greeting time can be very caring and meaningful. I've visited several churches where everybody hugs everybody, time is not an issue, and visitors are enveloped into the family of God. But sometimes the greeting time can feel extremely artificial. I've attended churches where it was so short that it felt like something in the bulletin that had to be done. But they had forgotten why they did it. Listen- if you invite people to greet each other, give them time to do it. And give them instructions. Or don't do it at all! Many people have limited communication skills with strangers. They feel helpless at a greeting time. If we would simply coach our people on what to say and do, it would help them a great deal. I've watched churches actually do small skits to train their people to talk to strangers and visitors, right in front of those visitors!

Recently I watched a pastor model one of the best welcome and greeting times I've ever seen. He began with a typical welcome to everyone, including visitors. He encouraged all of the visitors to take a gift CD with a visitor pack and an information card. He told everyone the important info to fill out on the card. As helpers were passing out the packs, the pastor said he also had several free Starbucks certificates for any first-time visitors. As people put up their hands to get one, the pastor walked out with a mike and did a brief dialogue with the visitors as he gave them a certificate. It

felt friendly, warm and interactive. He then proceeded to set up the greeting time. He told us that a lot of people come to church and don't know anyone. One of the important components in the family of God is making friends. He instructed us on how to enter in to a conversation with someone we don't know. "Hi. My name is Bill. What's your name? What brought you here today? Well, I'm glad you came!" The pastor said, "Now, that's the beginning of a relationship." Then he told us all to stand up and try it. The actual greeting time went on for probably five minutes. Everybody was actively participating! I'm sure that this was modeled every week, so the body had been trained to care and to be friendly. It worked!

We really need to take the time to teach our people the purpose of a good greeting time. If they don't understand it, it's better not to do it! Sometimes the greeting time can feel so unfriendly. It can actually have a negative effect on visitors. Think about ten people all turning and saying "Hi" or "Good morning" to you and then immediately turning their backs to say it to someone else. That's not cool! Were those people truly unfriendly? I doubt it. They were simply doing what they had learned to do for years. The only way to change that would be to teach them a better way.

If you were visiting our church today, how would you want to be greeted during our greeting time? Would you want someone to say "Hi" and turn away, or would you want someone to actually take a personal interest in you? Heh, I know some of you would rather be left alone! But I think that most of us actually wouldn't mind if someone asked us why we came today. And wouldn't you want them to tell us why they picked this as their church home? Now, if that's how you would want to be treated, then that's how all of us need to respond to our visitors and to each other every week as people come and visit! Don't you agree? So let's take some time right now. Greet several people around you. Take some time to really get to know them. Don't be afraid to walk around to get to know some new people today.

Some churches will actually take a ten-minute break in the service with coffee and other refreshments so people can take time to fellowship and get to know each other and newer people. They've made greeting each other such a high value that it plays a pivotal role in their service. Other churches will use refreshments between or after services to intentionally help people move into relationships with each other.

My wife and I visited a church where a social hall right off the auditorium was filled with music and loads of snacks and desserts and coffee and people laughing and talking everywhere. It was amazing! They also had a great cappuccino and latte bar. It was well-decorated and warm. It looked so inviting. If I attended that church, I would definitely hang out and see my friends in that environment. I'd come early and stay late every Sunday. But, again, here's the problem. My wife and I walked in, grabbed some food and coffee, we stood around admiring the room and life and energy, and we left. Everyone was having a great time, but no one talked to us! So the room clearly met its purpose of creating a wonderful atmosphere for people to get to know each other and to stay connected. But there was no strategy in place to draw the visitors in. A team could easily have been trained to float around the room looking for

people like us. Why miss a great opportunity to draw people in? Seize the moment!

You need to do what works best for your church family. But you need to know that most visitors are looking for some sort of friendship and most of them won't know how to break into new relationships at your church. If you don't help them, they will come as strangers and they will leave as strangers. That's not what you want, and that's not what they want. An opportunity to greet and meet other people can provide one more way to help your visitors to make that decision to come back and visit again.

Sharing time- Many churches will designate a specific time for the body to share what is happening in their lives. Specific people may be asked beforehand to share a story or thought with the rest of the church. Many churches will video a sharing segment for the gathering. Doing a video allows for editing the very best of the story or testimony, and it also guarantees the length of the segment. That can be well worth the effort. Other churches will invite individuals up to the platform to share their story. Or spontaneous sharing may take place as people are given opportunity. Someone will float around the auditorium with a mike. The pastor will often focus the sharing so it varies in content. Some weeks, the sharing may be directed to set up the sermon and theme of the morning. Other times, the focus can be on a verse that was very meaningful that week, a lesson learned from the Lord during the week, a praise, a prayer request, or a mix of several of these components. If people are trained to share only one to two minutes each, four or five people can share in a ten-minute period. Or thirty people can express one sentence each of praise to the Lord.

> As much as we want quality and excellence, we also want authenticity. We want to look like real people with real lives, and we are!

Allowing for live, unrehearsed sharing is one of the greatest ways to authenticate Christianity to your visitors. So much of what we do can seem so staged and perfect in our services. As much as we want quality and excellence, we also want authenticity. We want to look like real people with real lives, and we are! We have problems and struggles and we have to work our way to real solutions. Allowing your people to share that reality with the rest of the church can be so dynamic. I believe it can be one of the most rewarding and purposeful parts of your service. If you think about it, it's also quite Biblical. Look at Paul's instructions to the church in 1st Corinthians 14. There clearly was more sharing in the early church than we have today. I don't believe the size of the congregation has to eliminate the opportunity for sharing. Ten minutes of meaningful sharing can significantly impact a group of five thousand as easily as a gathering of fifty. The structure may be different, but the value and benefit will be the same!

Introducing something like a sharing time as a new tool of expression in a congregation may not work at first. A gathering of people who aren't used to sharing in front of each other will probably need time to break in a new habit. As you listen for great testimonies from your people during the week, ask several of them to share those stories in the coming gathering. As you prime the pump and demonstrate to the family what good sharing is, it will catch on and more and more people will begin to share.

Here are some of the controls that have to come into play with a sharing time in a service. First of all, it probably can't be done every week because of the amount of time it takes in a service. Secondly, you can't have the same people sharing every week or you will kill your service! The person guiding the sharing time has to be in control. Encouraging people to share who haven't shared recently spreads the opportunity around. If anyone seems to want to share more than they ought to, it's reasonable to talk to them privately about limiting sharing so many get to experience the privilege. Occasionally, you will be surprised with a child or child-like sharing, but, over time, the benefits will always outweigh the surprises along the way! In fact, the surprises that God unwraps along the way through the body sharing will bring you great joy! Try it if you've never done it before. Whether you use live sharing or a pre-recorded video, do it! Let God bless your church family as they hear what God is doing in them and through them.

Announcements and Presentations- As most of us already know, announcements can be either the blessing or the curse of most church services. Announcements can excite our people to be part of something significant. Announcements can bore our people to death. Announcements can clearly reflect what's happening currently in our church family. Announcements can steal our time and drive both visitors and regulars away. There are so many pros and cons when it comes to announcements.

Many churches are solving the announcement problem by eliminating them completely. Instead of doing announcements, they are relying on the bulletin, media presentations and mailed and emailed flyers to get the word out about events and activities. They also depend on networks of personal contact or phone calls to get to people. All of those efforts need to be done, but here's the problem. My observation is that attendance at these events diminishes significantly over time when the public announcements stop. People simply don't attend. Most are not paying attention to the announcement screens, their mail or email. They aren't being sold on the activities or they simply don't care. If you don't promote it- they won't come! It's as simple as that. By the way, if you took a survey, a lot of people would tell you to skip the announcements. They don't want to be bothered with them. They like a one-hour-a-week Christian commitment, and they see no purpose in promoting things that they aren't interested in.

So let's go back and look at the original reason for announcements in a church service. We Are Fam-i-ly! (Sounds like a song.) Our weekly gathering isn't commercial. It's spiritual! We want to bring quality and excellence into our services but not at the expense of our original purpose. We realize that we can't do the things in a large gathering that we can do in a home with a smaller group of people. That's why so many of us are determined to help our people find a small group to be a part of. But, at the same time, we don't want to eliminate all the things that remind us that we are family. Announcements remind us that we are family. They interrupt the flow of our services to say, "There's something more than service attendance. There's something more than coming here once a week for an hour. In fact, this is only the beginning!" That's why I've placed announcements under the category of body life- believers from the body pointing the way to spiritual growth and service.

Now, as leaders, we create events, activities or ministries that we want our people to be involved in. We learn over time that they won't attend our classes or banquet or retreats or outreach barbecue or missions conference if we don't sell them on it. That's the truth! The average believer in the room is as busy as you and I are. They have no extra time for something that they don't really believe is important to them. So we have to help them decide that they want the product that we have created. We have to sell them if we really want them at that event. If we don't sell them, they won't buy! Media announcements before and after our services and printed flyers are useful reminders to people who are already sold on our activities. But most of them are not great sales tools. So all of our people who aren't already sold, including most of your visitors, won't understand the importance of the event and will not come.

> The leadership has to be very purposeful in deciding the critical components that will best move the body forward to maturity.

Now, here are some of the problems that we face. As the number of our ministries grows, we could end up using the entire service selling our people on our ministry opportunities. Besides, there are ministries that aren't relevant to the entire church. And some of our willing leaders aren't great salesman and they don't know how to limit their time. People get bored, visitors get turned off and we lose our entire purpose! Kem Meyers, Communications Director at Granger Community Church, talks all about the dilemma we face in her book, *Less Clutter. Less Noise.* (What a great title, Kem!) She talks about "Information obesity" and quotes from an article on ThinkSimpleNow.com on the cost of overfeeding. The consequences are productivity loss, mind clutter, lack of time, lack of personal reflection, and stress and anxiety. Good communication is not so much about sending the right message as it is releasing the right response. . .It's not what you say. It's what people hear. . .Your church or organization shouldn't be piling more on top of an already mounting problem, especially when people are looking for answers that will make a difference. If we're calling people to greater simplicity in their lives, we have to model it! [49]

Amen! So how do we solve this problem? Can we find balance to this dilemma? I believe we can. First of all, if you give time for announcements, celebrate them. See them as a critical part of our purpose. Do them on purpose. Believe that they serve your mission of building the body and drawing more and more people into a deeper commitment and service. Sell that concept to your people so they understand the great value of announcements. Design the announcements each week with quality and intentionality. Be creative with your announcements and not boring. Pick good communicators with practiced presentations. Use good media support. Show video announcements. Have mini-skits. As a body, if we have to sit through some commercials without our remote and mute button, we need to be entertained. We need to laugh. We need to see our need for this information and we need to be moved to action.

Look at all possible announcements over the next three months. Which ones need to be presented at what gathering? Map it out. Which announcements need to be repeated more than once for effectiveness? Which announcements are not relevant for the entire church family? This question is tough because every ministry leader believes their announcement is relevant for the entire church. Just ask them! Someone has to decide what needs to be announced and what doesn't. As churches get larger, fewer things should be announced in the gathering. The leadership has to be very purposeful in deciding the critical components that will best move the body forward to maturity.

Let's look at some examples. Regular women's and men's and youth and recovery events should be announced at those events and not in front of the entire church. But, on occasion, someone will need to talk about the regular women's Bible study or no new people will come. Personal contact is the ultimate tool to get people to attend an event. But the importance of the event will be clear when it's pitched from the platform. An occasional testimony and the pastor's strong endorsement will build credibility and interest in the body. Getting all of your men to an annual retreat is no easy task. Announcing it early and presenting it in a motivating way will get it on their minds. Doing several skits or videos over time will get the event on their calendars. Awana needs to be introduced when it starts up or only a few newer people will wander into its program. But most special events throughout the year focus on the families involved and don't need to be presented to the whole church. If a church group sends word home or returns from a mission opportunity, some sort of creative presentation needs to be made. If we want to capture the heart of our people for God's mission around the world, which we do, why would we pass an opportunity like this by? By the way, apply all of this advise to your website as well. Don't clutter your home page, or any page, for that matter. Clearly map out how people can find what they are looking for. Use your website as the support site for all of your activities and ministries in your church family. And again, make sure you keep it up to date.

Set clear and absolute limits on the time you give to announcements. For example, we have eight minutes total this week for announcements. That will be the 201 class intro video and set-up (2 mins.), an update from our missions team in Gabon (3 mins.), and a skit setting up the Fall Outreach Luau (3 mins.). Hold your presenters accountable to keep to their time limits. Train them to be responsible and to respect the plan for the whole service. Don't use them again if they can't learn to stay within the plan! Hold your presenters accountable for the quality and excellence in their announcements. Many churches that I visit have poorly-made videos and unprepared run-on announcements. No wonder a lot of people wouldn't mind getting rid of them altogether. If you have a message that needs to be presented, make that message so clear, interesting and compelling that people can't wait to see what happens next week.

Several years ago, I arrived for a visit to Andy Stanley's North Point Community Church near Atlanta. The parking lot was full and it was still fifteen minutes before the service! That wasn't the big surprise. I was blown away by what I saw when I walked into the auditorium. The room was absolutely packed, the lights were dim, and it was still eight minutes until the service started. What I didn't know was this- everyone had learned to come early for the Ten Minute Countdown. It felt like walking into the countdown at a movie theater. Every eye was glued to the screen. The announcements were playing, and 1000's of people had come early, just to see them and to get a seat! Can you believe it? The videos were so well done, so fun and entertaining. Everyone was eager to get out of bed, feed and pack up the kids, and drive to church early enough to unload their kids and get to the auditorium before the lights dimmed and the seats were gone! Amazing! It sounds like how we respond to a great new movie! North Point realized that if people will do it before a movie, they will do it before church. Of course, quality counts! The countdown was excellent. Not everyone can compete with Andy's media team. But recently I attended a much smaller church and was pleasantly surprised at the excellent video announcements in the middle

of the service. The pastor told me that two of their young adults put the whole thing together every week. Fantastic! Recruit that team! Get creative! Have fun! Get started!

What about seasonal presentations? Put them on that annual calendar and plan ahead. Structure some of your services around these opportunities. Get creative! We all shape our Christmas and Easter services around the season. But why not honor veterans and family members of our military near Memorial or Veteran's Day. Make it personal and memorable. Show a special video clip at the gathering before the Fourth of July. Build bridges to the current events that we see everyday, like September 11th. Use the gathering near Valentine's Day to celebrate romance and marriage. Have a couple share their personal struggles and current victory in the Lord.

> As our churches grow and we focus on precision and excellence, it's so easy to lose sight of the church in all her glory!

We need to be committed to excellence in everything we do. Away with sloppy, half-baked announcements that bore us to death! Away with repetitive information that everyone already knows and that takes away precious time from more important things. But, at the same time, away with cold and calculated professionalism that cares more about performance than the life of the body. As our churches grow and we focus on precision and excellence, it's so easy to lose sight of the church in all her glory. Our gatherings aren't a show! If that's what they become, I'm afraid that the Holy Spirit won't show! It's not simply about great worship and great preaching and go home. That doesn't cut it in the Kingdom! It's also about the life of the body and drawing **everyone** into that life! That **is** the goal of the church. It's not "Come and be entertained!" It's not even "Come and be challenged!" It's "Go and make disciples!" And it just makes sense that we take appropriate time to introduce the growing body to the significant events and activities that shape who we are as God's people. Sometimes it seems like we're bowing to a culture addicted to fast food and one hour TV shows. Let's get them in and out or they won't be back. That's simply not true! The same people that we're talking about will spend hours at dinner or at a movie or a friend's house. And they also will spend over an hour at the gathering of God's people, with excitement, if the presentations, the sharing, the singing and the message are alive and vibrant. Please listen to me! Don't simply agree or disagree with me. Wrestle together with this one and find the balance that God wants for your church.

The Offering- The offering is one of the most critical and yet under-valued components of the gathering. It's clear that many of us have forgotten the purpose of the offering. We often see it as the means to pay our bills and pastors and staff, like a tax. That perspective can make the offering an uncomfortable interruption in our service to ask everyone for money. How can we move past it as quickly and unnoticed as possible? Some churches have eliminated the offering and placed baskets or a box in the back of the auditorium. Although that move may be well-intentioned and compensated for with good preaching and clear instructions, I personally think it eliminates one of God's critical teaching tools for His people.

When I was a young pastor arriving at a new church, I was delighted to find that this baby church had adopted the plan of eliminating the offering for a basket at the back of the church. That took the pressure off of taking an offering and embarrassing those who didn't give. I was fine with that. I had always wondered what to do with the offering as a ministerial student. Raised in the church, I had watched the disrespect that takes place during most offerings. As soon as the prayer ended and the special music began,

people everywhere temporarily lost interest and began to whisper or fidget as the plates were being passed. The idea of a basket in the back solved that problem. What I didn't realize is it created another one.

On my father-in-law's third visit, Bill told me that he had forgotten to give all three times because we didn't pass a plate. He suggested that our offerings would probably be much larger if we returned to that traditional custom. His advice was invaluable insight. I tried it, and he was right! Our offerings were significantly larger and we never went back. That didn't solve the problem of what to do during the offering. But it did force me to assess and deal with the very purpose of an offering, from God's point of view.

In absolute contrast to a stagnant routine of collecting an offering, God had a gigantic reason for calling His children to give their offerings. First of all, it was a constant reminder to everyone that He was the Lord and Owner and that all of their wealth and possessions were His! In the Old Testament, the giving of all kinds of purposeful offerings and sacrifices refocused the Israelites on their relationship to God. Obedient and sacrificial giving was directly connected to God's blessing and strength. Giving was constantly intertwined with celebrative festivals and fasts and weeks of remembering who they were and where they had come from. They would tithe, and then, on top of that, they would give wave offerings, peace offerings, sin offerings, guilt offerings, grain offerings, and trespass offerings, just to name a few. None of this was optional! God obviously knew how much they needed to be reminded. As they lost their heart to give and obey, and as they became distracted by other things, they lost everything!

The New Testament call to giving is even more powerful! We are compelled to live a life that consistently reflects generosity and selfless sacrifice. Jesus makes our possessiveness over our money and things a pivotal issue for those who would choose to follow Him. Remember the rich young ruler? Randy Alcorn, in his book, *The Treasure Principle*, says that 15% of everything Jesus talked about was money and possessions! [50] Paul continually paints a picture of disciples giving freely and generously, with all of their heart. In II Corinthians 8 and 9, he calls God's people to be obedient, faithful, purposeful, and cheerful. That should be seen in everything we say and do, including our giving! There are patterns of regular giving both to the needs of the local church and to special needs as they emerge. Paul echoes God's heart throughout the Old Testament when, in I Corinthians 4, he says, "What do you have that God hasn't given you?" It's true! God not only wants us to remember His Lordship of All of our possessions; He wants us to consistently reflect His heart and life.

> We are compelled to live a life that consistently reflects generosity and selfless sacrifice.

Here's our dilemma as leaders. Giving is a Big Deal to God! It's foundational to a healthy Christian life! But giving is a little deal to most believers! It's true! Most believers today wouldn't even think of tipping God, let alone sacrificing with generosity. Something needs to be done to change the way we think and respond to God's call to give. And it's not taking away the plate and putting a basket in the back. Perhaps we need to make the offering more important, more honored and celebrated, more meaningful and exciting. Reminding and retraining our people over and over again probably is part of our solution. We've clearly lost the reminders of celebration and giving that God intends for us to have. Maybe we should be taught to write our checks during the service and then stand and wave them before the Lord. Maybe we should have "march" offerings. Maybe we should learn from the churches that have everyone bring their offerings to the front and lay them down before the Lord. Should we all kneel before the Lord as we present Him with our offerings? How can we help our people to gain an understanding of God's Majesty and Glory and the joy and privilege of surrendering our lives and possessions to Him? What will it take?

We can't do the same things every time we gather or they will become routine and predictable. That's part of our problem when we come to the time to receive an offering. If we want our people to learn to obey the Lord and experience the blessings of God, we've got to get creative. Just think about how creative God was under the Old Covenant when He tried to help His children remember His ownership and their need to give. Instead of seeing the offering as an obligation to get through, we need to see it as a great teaching opportunity to help our people move toward greater and deeper depths of maturity.

> Never assume that their level of maturity will help them overlook your lack of quality or unwillingness to be creative.

Communion, Baptism, Scripture Reading, and Prayer- These four worship components are fundamental to the Christian faith. They need to be a significant part of our liturgy as it fits into our church culture. But they also need to be alive and vibrant and relevant, both for our regulars and for our visitors. The rituals and traditions of our faith may change in form, but they must still be applied as Biblical mandates for all believers. Centuries have passed, but the symbols portrayed are and need to be as valid and relevant today as they were two thousand years ago. But here's our problem. We can't assume that our regular attendees will continue to catch the dynamic of prayer or communion if they are delivered in a boring or repetitious package. But do we have to constantly entertain our people to keep them happy? Well, let's remind ourselves that they are constantly being entertained in the rest of their world. Never assume that their level of maturity will help them overlook your lack of quality or unwillingness to be creative. There are plenty of other churches around who will work hard at building excellence into every aspect of their services. And they will be quick to welcome your people if they choose to look around. So be excellent and keep your family happy and excited about their church!

Let's also talk about communion, baptism, scripture reading and prayer in relationship to visitors. Assume that they either aren't believers or they don't understand your traditions. They have **no idea** what you're talking about! They really are newbies. Be clear, definitive, and instructive. Be brief and appealing. Explain what you're doing and win their minds and hearts. Let your explanations build on each other, week after week and month after month. What an opportunity! You have the privilege of strengthening the believers in their faith and moving nonbelievers closer and closer to their own relationship with Jesus.

The reading of scripture and prayer in services varies radically from church to church. I visit churches where it's obvious that their timing, structure and location in the service hasn't changed in fifty years. In other churches, it's clear that the limitations of time have restricted and dictated the placement and use of scripture and prayer. Some churches demonstrate that no one has thought at all about timing, structure or order. Don't just stick them in! Put them in the right places! Change it up! For example, scripture reading can be a powerful call to worship at the very beginning of the service. There's a time for scripture to be read to the sound of a quiet classical guitar or backed up by a loud orchestra or band. Create or use some of the great Scripture and prayer videos that are available or create your own! Try using two or three people taking turns reading a passage together. A special time of prayer for veterans around Veteran's Day or thankfulness for freedom around the Fourth of July is wonderful and moving. Rotate through different groups of people in your church family and pray for them. Bring them to the front with their friends or have them stand where they are and walk out to them. Have some of your leaders come and join with you in prayer. In other words, keep finding new and interesting ways to excite your people and visitors about prayer and God's Word. Pick the right people to read and pray. You want people who have ability and confidence. But you also want people who have heart and really demonstrate a connection with what they are doing. What they model the rest of the week and when they're back sitting with their friends should be an unquestionable commitment to Jesus Christ and His values. As you know, some people can pray up a storm, but there aren't many other signs that they are genuinely alive in Christ.

Picture this passionate psalm being proclaimed as a call to worship and as a demonstration of one of our purposes for gathering.

Shout with joy to the LORD, all the earth!
Worship the LORD with gladness;

Come before him with joyful songs.
Know that the LORD is God!

It is He who made us, and we are His;
We are His people, the sheep of His pasture.

Enter His gates with thanksgiving
and His His courts with praise;

give thanks to Him and praise His name.
For the LORD is good

and His love endures forever;
His faithfulness continues through all generations!

Psalm 100

Communion can be one of the most meaningful and provocative elements of our gathering. We vary in how we do it and how often we administer it, but, for all of us, it should be done with honor and majesty. It draws us back to the cross and reminds us of all of our inadequacies. It forces us, one more time, to examine ourselves. And it tells both non-believers and new believers that powerful story of God's redemptive grace. We need to be careful to use it as a teaching moment and to not trivialize it or normalize it. It is distinctive and we need to work to keep it distinctive. Some churches celebrate communion once a month to keep it special and to not let it get ordinary. Other churches celebrate it once a week because it is special. The key, I believe, is more about what you do when you do celebrate it. I don't want to be negative, but I personally struggle with the bread-and-cup popup-and-out combo pack that we occasionally use. It seems so commercial and easy. I understand the issue of convenience and ease and time, but come on, this is communion! I can see the need in a stadium with 50,000 attendees. And I guess, if you need to get it down to five minutes per service, you've gotta be quick with the juice and crackers. But what have we lost? What have we gained? And what have we told our congregation about the meaning of this moment? Sometimes I think God might say, "Don't even do it if you don't mean it! This represents my Body and Blood and you're treating it like Pop Tarts!" Listen, if you use or sell the little packages, please don't be offended. I know they have their place and purpose. But, as leaders, do give the moment dignity and don't let quickness and easiness lead to trivializing this precious sacrament. Enough of my ranting.

So what should we do each time we offer communion? Let's honor the Lord! Let's seize the moment and briefly tell the story again, one more time. " 'This is my body, which is given for you. Do this to remember me. . .this cup is the new covenant between God and his people- an agreement confirmed with my blood. Do this to remember me as often as you drink it.' For every time you eat this bread and drink this cup, you are announcing the Lord's death until he comes again." Paul points back to Jesus' words in I Corinthians. Look at the meaning. Look at the importance! Let's not miss that as we communicate to our people. Let's be creative. Let's make it different every time we do it. Let it be a fresh teaching moment. Let's plan our communion event, long or short, just like we plan our set of worship songs and our sermon. Sometimes communion can be part of a bigger picture in our gathering. It fits right in to the rest of our painting. Sometimes it fits perfectly at the end of our sermon. We've designed it that way. Other times we shape the entire service and sermon around communion and its importance. So let's make it meaningful. Let's figure out how to help our people truly get involved. Let's use testimonies. Let's use music and movie clips. Have everyone stand. Have everyone who's able to kneel. Have everyone walk forward to take the bread and cup. Have them dip the bread in a common cup. Now please don't do all of this the same Sunday!

I remember attending a communion service where they had placed six communion stations around the auditorium. We were asked to make our way to one of the stations. After taking the bread and cup, we were instructed to find someone else other than our spouse to pray with and have communion with. It was awkward and wonderful. I liked the idea, took it home and, over many years, did it with lots of variations. On some occasions I would encourage people to gather as families or friends and share communion together. Several times, I asked our people to look for someone they were thankful for and to then go to them after communion and share that thanks. Moments like those are unforgettable. Being creative in preparation with God allows God then to bring powerful life transformation and the dynamic building up of His body.

> We open the door of opportunity for true heart engagement, or we quickly move on because of a busy schedule. Don't do it!

Here are some things to remember. Communion is a special visual of what Jesus did on the cross. But it also invites us into His experience. It's meant to be a Divine moment with God. We are meeting with God. If nothing else in the service moves us to thought or action, communion should arrest our hearts and make us deal with our current reality. Am I alive in Christ? Am I living for Him or not? Do I have sin in my life that I need to deal with? Let a man examine himself and then eat and drink. Our preparation and communication at that moment makes all the difference in the world. We open the door of opportunity for true heart engagement, or we quickly move on because of a busy schedule. Don't do it! Use the moment the way God intended it to be used. Let people connect with God. Give them time. Lead them into it and through it. Don't get in their way. Often, a quiet song will allow them to pray or sing along. But sometimes that talking and singing actually prevents them from really getting quiet and doing business with God. Think about that! Sometimes we're afraid of silence. And that quietness actually can be very good for the soul. So be sensitive. Be sensitive to your people and to God. Don't let your time constraints prevent God from doing what He wants to do. Don't!

Let's take a moment to talk about pre-believers and communion. Communion provides non-believers with a perfect glance into the grace of God. It demonstrates this marvelous love relationship between God and everyone sitting in the gathering who has moved into relationship with Him. It can be powerful for those individuals as they watch and experience the moment. Communion clearly needs to be defined and explained for those who know nothing of its meaning or purpose. But God wants to use it to draw visitors who don't know Him closer to that miraculous encounter. Think about what He is doing in their hearts as they see this visual demonstration of God's immense love. Every time I've offered communion through my years of ministry, I've explained that communion is only for those who believe. I've given pre-believers the instruction to take a pass until they've placed their faith in Jesus. But I always encouraged them and told them how to go ahead and make that decision so they could immediately enjoy the privilege of taking communion for the first time. Many of our pre-believers have been born again right in the middle of a communion service. Some of us don't provide communion during our seeker-friendly gatherings because we don't want to turn off non-believing visitors. I personally believe we are hiding one of God's greatest evangelistic tools. We're not protecting non-believers! We're preventing them from seeing the wonderful glory of God and His church in communion together! Let's make communion all that it's meant to be every time we remember the Lord's death. And let's let our visitors see and experience the love of God as they watch His people remembering the cross.

Baptism is an outward acknowledgement and demonstration of the inner act of God that has already taken place in our lives. It's a personal declaration of our belief in and commitment to follow and obey Jesus. It's our choice to obey God's command! In Romans 6:4, Paul tells that we died and were buried with Christ in baptism. He goes on to say, in Galatians 3:27, that all of us who have been united in Christ in baptism have put on Christ. As we are immersed into the water and then come back out of it, baptism so clearly symbolizes our death to our old life and our newness of life in Christ. It also points back to our being baptized with the Holy Spirit at salvation and baptized into the family of God! The picture is amazing and the experience is unforgettable, both to the baptized and those watching! In Acts 10, we read about Peter's profound encounter with Cornelius. As Peter's eyes were opened to see God's love and redemptive grace, even for the Gentiles, he witnessed God undeniably saving them. And with immediate responsiveness, he said, "Can anyone object to their being baptized, now that they have received the Holy Spirit just as we did?"

Baptism isn't simply a parade of new converts so we can see who the new members are. It serves a much greater purpose, filled with opportunities that can significantly shape and impact lives for eternity. At the same time, baptism can radically impact those who are watching this beginning of life transformation. It's a testimony and a statement. It's a symbol and picture of death to an old way of life. As I've participated in countless baptisms, I've witnessed that amazing demonstration of God's transforming power in front of a watching world! New believers have wept with joy as non-believing friends and family have looked on with wonder. I've watched men, women, young people and children springing out of the water, laughing, crying, praising, hugging and feeling a sense of newness in this public acknowledgement of their faith and commitment.

Here's the point- God uses every baptism to SHOUT out His redemptive love to every listening ear within hearing distance! Don't hide this God-filled moment from anyone. Don't waste one baptism. Open wide the gates! Invite everyone! Celebrate and let the whole world see the mystery of His church. I've seen baptisms done with little to no preparation or fanfare, on Wednesday night or after church when most people have left. I've seen them done with lots of participation but with a handful of people watching. Don't tack baptisms on to an event, like they're not important. Every person counts. Every baptism counts. Don't let them be boring! How sad.

Some of us have sensed that baptisms, like communion, might make non-believers a little bit uncomfortable. Come on! Give me a break! What are we trying to do here? Make everyone comfortable? I thought we were trying to rescue lost people from a Christless eternity so they can come alive in Jesus! Our gatherings aren't about making everyone comfortable. And I would guess that for every ten people who are offended by baptisms, there are hundreds who are deeply moved and drawn one step closer to a life-changing encounter with a living God. I've witnessed it time and again.

I'll make some suggestions. Teach your believers so they clearly know what baptism is and what they are committing to. Make sure that they are old enough that they know what they are doing. On the other hand, loads of believers don't need another class. They just need to do it! Teach your people to bring all of their family and friends to their baptism. So many will come out of curiosity. Isn't that exciting? Do your baptisms LOUD! Do them on purpose. Celebrate them with as many people as possible. Plan them and announce them so your people have plenty of time to invite their people. Plan your baptisms like great outreach events. Celebrate with songs and testimonies and lots of good news. You want people leaving with something to talk about! Baptisms can be great at rivers and lakes, Easter services, backyard pools and regular gatherings of the family. Many larger churches, because of their size and multiple services, will do their baptisms at their designated times, shoot video and show testimonies and summary shots at the weekly gathering. Let's make every effort to use these for His glory! They are truly miraculous.

The Message

One of the greatest attractors to visitors is the message. Now, everyone who walks through the front door knows that they are going to get a message. What they don't know is if they'll have to endure it or if they'll actually enjoy it. The purpose of this book and assessment is for leaders to work together on issues that are holding them back from being all that they can be. But we have now arrived at untouchable territory, the sacred land of the sermon. If there's anything that most of us as pastors want avoided, it's the assessment of the message. Criticism of our sermons cuts right to the heart of many of us. We feel so violated, so misunderstood, so defeated. Isn't that true, my fellow preachers? It would be funnier if it weren't true. I can remember times when I'd get a hundred praises from exiting parishioners and I would be destroyed by one negative word.

Here's what I think the problem is. We know that there are churches on every corner that people can choose. Most of us realize we don't preach like Bill Hybels or Rick Warren. But we are doing the best we can! We worked hard to learn to communicate and prepare to the best of our ability. We know that we need to keep improving, but we're doing the best we can right know. We stand before the people and share what God has put on our hearts. And someone doesn't like it! Or several people don't like our preaching style. Ouch. Stab. Slice. We take it so personally. It feels like they are attacking us as individuals. And some of them are! Speaking of the great ones, John Maxwell, in his book, *Thinking for a Change*, talks about his own personal process and his struggle to learn to be a better communicator. John Maxwell! He admits that it took him eight years to learn to be himself. Can you believe it? Even the masters have had to learn and struggle! And he continues to learn.

I know that if I keep improving my thinking, it will impact my beliefs, which will change my expectations, which will affect my attitude, which changes my behavior, which improves my performance. And that will change my life! [51]

Now, there are all kinds of styles and there are styles for everyone. We can't please all of the people all the time. We can try, but it won't work! So we either have to come to grips with the fact that not everyone will love our sermons, or we'll continue to feel defeated and depressed every time the word comes back that someone doesn't like our preaching. Here's the truth- people will stay in your church and they won't like your preaching. There are people in Mark Driscoll's church and Andy Stanley's church and Ed Young's church who don't like their preaching either. Isn't that right, Mark? That's life in the pulpit. And here's worse news: they're not leaving- it's their church! They're staying for other reasons, God bless them, and they've decided to put up with your preaching. By the way, Andy Stanley, in his book, *Communicating for a Change*, challenges us to simply be ourselves. He quotes Chuck Swindoll, saying "Know who you are. Accept who you are. Be who you are!" And then he adds: "Be who you are. But be the very best communicator you can possibly be. To do that, you must be willing to sacrifice what's comfortable- what has become part of your style- for the sake of what is effective." [52]

I still remember that Sunday morning and it's been over thirty years. It was the end of the service and my friends came up to me to talk. My wife and I had enjoyed being with them as couples. They had great hearts and were quite involved in the church. "We've decided to leave the church. We love you guys, but your sermons just don't feed us. We're looking for someone who preaches like Charles Swindoll. We listen to him on the radio and love his preaching. We're hoping to find a pastor who preaches more like him." I picked myself off the floor, but I couldn't seem to get the five hundred pounds of pain and devastation off of me. As they walked away, no amount of success, accomplishment or spirituality could compensate for what I was feeling.

Four or five days later, I was walking through a grocery store when a young couple eagerly approached me. They were new to town and had visited our church four to five times. "Pastor Dale, we are so happy to finally meet you! We love your church and it's now our home. We also want you to know we picked it because you preach just like our last pastor- Charles Swindoll!" Can you believe it! I could hear God laughing from miles away!

What's a pastor to do? Here's what you do. Forgive them for their lack of good taste, love them, and get past it! You've got a church filled with sheep who love you and your preaching and they want and need to be fed. Feed them. Do your very best! Work to improve your speaking ability. Make sure you're spending enough time studying to know the Word well enough to deliver it well. Make sure you're spending enough time with God that you get His personal insight and heart on the passages and topics that you are teaching on. Some of us spend too much time studying and not enough time listening. And it shows. Don't over-study. There's more to pastoring than preaching a great sermon. On the other hand, I also attend churches where it's obvious that the pastor has spent very little time preparing for his sermon. Some of us have the gift of wing, but the wings don't always fly! I know there are rough weeks and difficult, weary seasons. What we have to make sure of is that we don't fall into the habit of preaching weak, ill-prepared sermons. There's no excuse for that. Our sermons need to have a standard of excellence, evidenced by our effort to do the very best we can. Let's do our best and God will do the rest!

Let me share a word for those of you who preach on rotation or only a few times a year. These same principles go for you. You need to do your very best! Don't settle for anything less. Your people may give you a break if you don't speak frequently, but you don't want a break. You want God's words flowing through you as His vessel. So work on these same issues and challenges. Prepare the very best you can and then get out of the way. God will use you and bless His people.

Some of you work full time at another job and have to also pastor your church. That must be so difficult. And it also must be difficult to find adequate time for good preparation before you preach at the gatherings. My heart goes out to you! I don't know how you do it. But I still believe that God wants you taking appropriate time in His Word as you prepare to preach each week. God's people deserve a sermon that has been well-prepared. And I know that God always wants to complement our circumstances with all the Power we need to do what He's called us to do. Some of you rotate with other pastors so there's not as much weekly pressure to prepare. That's a great plan if you can do it. But there are hundreds of thousands of you all around the world who have to work fulltime at other jobs and still need to preach God-anointed and well-prepared sermons each week. Do your best! Don't settle for anything less!

> Some of us have the gift of wing, but the wings don't always fly!

Here are a few more challenges on our preaching content.

- Our sermons need to be attention-grabbing. We don't want them sleeping if we can help it. We need good, relevant illustrations. Look for examples all the time. Open your eyes! Life is filled with

241

illustrations, but we're often not looking. Be creative. Buy some idea books. Think of ways to best illustrate the point that you are making. Recruit some friends to help you if they are more creative than you are. Pastors everywhere are using teams of people to help them think up good illustrations for sermons. And they're sharing those illustrations online. Don't be afraid to borrow. Do be afraid to impersonate! Use a testimony or a video clip or a song to make a point. We need to be enthusiastic. We need to connect with our people as we preach. We aren't giving speeches- we're winning hearts and minds. Walk out among the people as you preach if it helps them connect with what you're trying to say. Grab their hearts with the first illustration and hang on as you draw them in.

- Our sermons need to be Word-centered. The Word needs to be the main thing! There's great value in topical preaching. The problem with some topical preaching is some pastors forget to use the Bible. I've seen some pastors hold up a Bible, read a verse and talk for an hour. That's way too little Word and way too much preacher! Good topical preaching is filled with Scripture supporting that topic. Our people deserve to hear what God thinks about a subject and we can share some things too!

There's still great value in expositional preaching as well. Where else do most of our people learn the Word? Unfortunately, many of our people will only be taught the Scriptures if we teach them. If we never travel through a passage or a book in our preaching, many of our believers will never really understand the full riches of His Word. One reason we run from expositional preaching is we've all been bored by pastors who have mined every word to death. I'll bet even God wonders what in the world they are doing! Show me one example of that in Scripture. Good expositional preaching is alive and enjoyable and illustrated and topical and it doesn't have to cover every word or concept in a passage. Jesus' sermons were alive, vibrant and relevant. I personally love preaching topically and I love preaching expositionally. I think we get the job done when they are done together over the course of time.

> What a waste of a good sermon if our people don't do anything with it!

- Our sermons need to be practical and relevant. Whether we are preaching topical or expositional sermons, we need to bring the truth down to earth and home to our people. They need to understand with clarity what you and God are trying to say. In Psalm 119:105, David says, "Your Word is a lamp for my feet, a light for my path." We should use it like a light when we preach! Our people need to be able to relate the truths of the Word to their daily lives. We don't want to simply fill their minds with more and more facts. We want to change lives and better equip our people for living out the Mission! There's always something practical that you can send them home with. Think about the broad audience that you're preaching to. What are their needs? What struggles and issues are they facing right now? What are your young people and young adults struggling with? What spiritual truth do you need to provide your middle-aged or older adults with? Bring practical application. Help them meet God and His Word before they leave the gathering. What issue can they deal with right now that they will forget about if we don't provide the opportunity? What a waste of a good sermon if our people don't do anything with it!

- Our sermons need to be missional. We are all on a great mission, but many of our people don't know it. So many have been satisfied to sit and soak on Sunday for years and years and years. Their idea of being missional is doing an hour or two of activity each week or occasionally going or sending someone on a trip to somewhere else. Most new attendees arrive from other churches with decades of unmissional and unbiblical programming. We've got to use every opportunity to erase the wrong patterns and programming of the past and build a whole new way of thinking and living. Now, here's the truth. If you and I really get it, if we personally understand what the church should look like, it will come bursting out of us wherever we go- in meetings, at dinner, in gatherings, at home, at play and away! If we want to change the vision and the direction of our people, missional thinking needs to flow through the fiber of all of our sermons. There's very little that we preach about that doesn't ultimately impact the mission that we are all called to. So let it out-everywhere, all the time!

- Our sermons need to be visitor and non-believer-sensitive. We preach to the body, but we are sensitive to the crowd. Jesus frequently talked to the disciples with numbers of non-believers listening in. He was always sensitive to His listeners. In fact, he was often reading their minds! We want our auditoriums filled with visitors and non-believers. We want them to hear God's glorious Word with full application. We want to give the Holy Spirit opportunity to open their eyes to the truth and open their hearts to redemption. We know that ". . .the word of God is living and active, sharper than any two-edged sword, piercing. . .and able to judge the thoughts and intentions of the heart." Let it happen in church! So what is seeker-sensitive preaching? Is it a sermon minus anything difficult like hell or repentance or giving up sinful habits? Come on! Seeker-sensitive preaching is remembering that there are newbies in the house. They don't understand all the words or ideas. They need definition. They need compassion. They need to be helped through difficult concepts. They're hearts need to be won! Don't ignore them. Don't embarrass them. Don't preach over their heads. Speak right to them! Give them a reason to come back for more. Apply your truths to their lives. Give them hope. Give them Jesus. Give them the gospel before they leave and let them respond!

God draws people to church. He tenderizes and prepares their hearts. They don't see it coming! They often experience the power and conviction of the Holy Spirit as we sing and share during a gathering. I've watched so many people cry and not know why they were crying during a service. Then the message begins. Whatever the topic and text, God is ready to convict and convince these pre-believers that this is The Truth and this Truth will bring Life! "Pastor, you were speaking right to me. Did someone tell you what I'm going through?" We've heard that said countless times. Pastors- get out of the way and let the Holy Spirit do His work! As we end the message and bring final application to the believers, our pre-believers don't know what to do next. Tell them! **Don't rush this!** What could be more important? **Slow it down.** Tell them how to believe, repent, and surrender. Tell them how to come home. Make everything clear. **Open the door and let them in.** What could be more important right now? Ending on time? Getting to lunch? Prepping for third service? Staying with the schedule? Are you kidding? Listen to God! He's in charge! I'm not saying that schedules and timing aren't important. I am saying that sometimes the schedule becomes the Lord! I've seen it. So have you. Perhaps we need to reengineer our services to allow more margin for the Holy Spirit to do His work. Perhaps. Because isn't that one reason why we are here? Isn't it?

Purposeful Endings

How we end is often more important than how we begin. When visitors walk through our doors, we, as a family, usually stand waiting, looking our best. But where are we after the gathering ends? What's the end plan? I've already painted the picture of an entire team of ushers and greeters trained and actively serving before the gathering but nowhere to be found after the service. What sort of memories do we want visitors to take with them? Do you think they will remember what happens before more than what happens after the gathering? I think it all really matters! We need a plan and we need to make sure the plan happens.

A few years ago, I was visiting a church as the guest speaker. I had prayed carefully about the subject that I was going to preach on. That Sunday morning, I delivered the Word with passion and a strong call to commit and respond to God. I finished and handed the service back to the pastor. I expected him to give his people an opportunity to respond to God's Spirit. I believe their hearts

were prepared and ready. You can imagine my surprise when the pastor stepped up and called for a response. He asked his people who would bring food to the potluck the next Sunday. He broke it down and asked for hands to be raised. I couldn't believe it! What was he thinking? The moment was gone. Now, here's the question- from God's point of view, how often do we do that?

I've watched all kinds of endings to gatherings. Some have been glorious, and some haven't. Sometimes it's felt like everyone's just happy to get out of there. We've done our time and now we get to go home! If I can just finish this sermon, it will be over. And we say our Amens and it's every man for himself. Have I made my point? The service should end well. There needs to be an appropriate response to the message, whether it's a song, a time of silence, an altar call or a closing prayer. It needs to be planned and acted upon. Don't just throw in a song! I've seen that so many times. What a sorry way to end a great morning. What is the **right** application of the sermon? Should people respond? Do they need silence? Should music be quietly playing? What would be the right background song? Should everyone sing a response to God? What song would be perfect for this moment? Should people be asked to do something- kneel, stand, come forward. . .? God knows exactly how to end this sermon. Ask Him for help. He'd love to jump in.

That leads me to a question. Most of us would agree that God is as involved in the planning of the service as He is in service itself. Here's the question. Are we asking God to bless our plans or are we asking God to show us His plans for the service? We know that if we're walking with God, He guides us through our day, including the planning of events and gatherings. But are we listening as we plan, or are we making our plans and trusting Him with the results. What I'm challenging is how easy it is to become so professional in the planning and timing of our events that it would be difficult for even God to change or rearrange something in the service. Are we listening as we plan? Do we truly seek the mind of Christ as we put together the pieces of our event? Are we listening as we move through our gathering? Would we know it if God wanted a change? And would we change it, on the spot? Imagine the pastor talking with God and sensing His guidance and clear direction, on Saturday, after the schedule's been printed? Picture a worship leader, sensing a different song would be better to close the service, right near the end of the sermon? Now, these thoughts aren't throwing out the critical need for excellence in organizing and planning a great worship gathering. They're simply acknowledging that what we do is not natural- it's supernatural! It's empowered by the spirit of God. It's rational and logical, and yet it's not. It's invisible and surprising and not also clean and tidy and predictable. And if it is, God may not be as present as you and I would like Him to be. And none of us want to miss out on God, do we?

Let's come back to our ending. Many churches plan for visitors and regulars alike to respond at the end of the service. I like that. We need to provide every opportunity for people to move forward with God. If the Holy Spirit is convicting or convincing or teaching our people something new, let's let them deal with it- right here, right now. Many churches have a team of people at the side or front of the main room, ready to talk or pray with anyone who comes up. Sometimes a room is provided or a place is designated in the auditorium where people can go. Andy Stanley's family of churches has created "Starting Point," "a conversational environment, where people can explore faith and experience community." A wing of beautiful, smaller family rooms is dedicated to groups of people meeting for ten weeks during multiple services. With great advertising and signage, you can't miss the rooms or the strategy. These churches are clearly committed to walk with everyone who is ready for next steps. Of course, any strategy for follow-up at the end of the service requires the planning, recruitment, training and service of the right people. But the reward of being ready when people respond is indescribable!

Now, as the gathering ends, our visitors need to be told what to do next. What is the exit plan? Is there music playing after the service. That would be nice! Is there a room or location with refreshments for fellowship? Should they pick their children up now or later? Were they supposed to go to a visitor's information area? Where is that again? There need to be friendly, happy people everywhere, looking for lost guests wandering through your building. There need to be greeters greeting and pointing and giving hugs and saying goodbye. The church family needs to know what to do and the visitors need to know what to do.

Now to the mundane: what is the cleanup and breakdown plan? Have one! But **don't** do the plan until most of the people have left the room. Sometimes we are just so tired that we want to get packed and get home. But the gathering is about ministry and loving people and once-a-week opportunities that quickly fade away. Make a decision not to have anyone breaking down the stage or room until at least 15-20 minutes after the last song is played. Did you hear that? Some of our greatest ministry moments are missed because we're focused on getting to lunch. Are we too hungry to look for people who are hungry for Jesus? Train your musicians and worship leaders to go out and pet the sheep. In many churches, everyone on stage has more eye contact with visitors and the rest of the church than anyone else in the room. They can see what's happening in the auditorium. I've watched worship team members wander down after a service and find specific people to share with and minister to. It's wonderful! Train your leaders and maturing believers to be part of a purposeful ending. Train them to watch and pray and listen and serve. The cleanup can wait. That's the plan. But people and care and ministry have to come first! Don't they? Isn't that what we're here for?

Now it's time to pack. But don't leave it to whosoever will. Many churches have a paid crew who take over at this point. But lots of churches, and especially church plants and churches renting facilities, have a volunteer army doing all of the cleanup. I've also been at churches where the last people standing are the ones drafted to help clean up and put everything away. I've felt so guilty, even as the visitor, that I've jumped in to help. How disorganized can you get. Have a plan! I'm not talking about three hundred people taking two minutes to carry a chair to a chair tree. Maybe that's just practical. But there's lots more that needs to be done. Don't exhaust the people who have already been working if you can help it. Some come early and they need to go home. Some work hard throughout the gathering and they also need to be free to leave. Recruit one more team and let them do their job. I've been saddened to watch lead pastors packing and carrying out equipment after a long Sunday morning. I know it looks good to jump in and give a hand. And it probably should happen, occasionally. But there are usually far more strategic things for the pastors to be doing when they only see their sheep once a week. If you're renting a facility, get a team to set up the room and a different team to break it down. Get a team to help set up the band and sound and lights and, if necessary, a different breakdown team. And create alternate teams so most people don't have to help every week. That way, no one burns out and you can keep doing it year after year after year.

Has it been an excellent gathering? Did we stay with the plan? Did the plan work so well that no one really noticed it? Did we accomplish what we set out to do? Did we begin with strength and energy and finish well? Is everyone happy? Then let's go home!

Notes

PART THREE

Behind the CURTAIN!

THOUGHTS ON CHANGE

Lord, where we are wrong, make us willing to change; where we are right, make us easy to live with.
Peter Marshall

When it becomes more difficult to suffer than to change. . .you will change.
Robert Anthony

The only way to make sense out of change is to plunge into it, move with it, and join the dance.
Alan Watts

9. Follow-Up and Assimilation - Throw Out that Net the Very First Week!

We've worked hard to prepare our gathering for visitors. We've worked on all the details that make people want to come back. We've made them feel welcome from the moment they drove onto our property to the minute they drove away. They've seen the life of the body. They've met the family. They've experienced our worship and the passion and inspiration of the Word. But will they come back? What will bring them back? First of all, let's look at the God factor. God, as I've already said, is intimately involved in this whole process. Never forget that. He's the One who is already moving in the hearts of people and drawing them to the right church and, ultimately, to Himself! He certainly can put the want-to into the heart of our visitors. On top of that, a great experience and good memories will help people decide to come back for a second ride. It works at Disneyland, doesn't it?

Now, are you ready for a dose of reality? The moment most visitors walk out the door of your church and get home, something happens. The excitement of the moment wears off. Maybe it's the devil or maybe it's the flesh. But most visitors, as you probably know, do not come back! We are in a shopper's world with lots of options. People are used to trying many different stores and malls and restaurants and then picking their favorites. Nothing's wrong with that. They do need to find the right church. God may be guiding them to the church down the street! And there are visitors who you don't want to return. They're trouble and only God and their last church know it. So we don't want every visitor to stay. But we do want the visitors to stay who are supposed to stay! And what I've noticed is this: the more effort you put out to connect with your visitors, the more likely they will try your church again- just for that reason. In fact, I've had people tell me over and over again that the reason they came back and stayed was because we cared enough to keep reaching out to them. Let me say it again-we cared enough to keep reaching out to them! **So here's the question- do you care enough to keep reaching out to them?**

Immediate Contact

The first thing that you need to do is have a plan and a system of follow-up. Again, if you want to succeed, you have to plan to succeed! You can't wait for visitors to show up, and then say, "Duh, now what do we do?" Put someone in charge and create a system of immediate follow-up with every visitor. The smaller the church, the more personal you can be. The bigger the church, the more personal you need to be! Someone will need to be in charge of visitor follow-up or it won't get done! Someone needs to make sure that letters are sent, calls are made and invitations and events are followed through on.

> The more effort you put out to connect with your visitors, the more likely they will try your church again.

The Visitor Card- Have a clear plan for information collection. If you've created a welcome area, give your visitors a packet of info and ask them if they would fill out a visitor registration card and give it to you. Ask for it again during the gathering. Hand parents a registration card to be filled out when they hand you their children. If you ask for cards in 2-3 different ways, you'll probably get half of your visitors to register. Some of them really want to be anonymous. Most of them don't mind, but you need to make it easy for them. If you don't get a visitor card filled out with the right information, you will not be able to follow up on them! Some pastors tell me that they wait for the second or third visit before they follow up on visitors. They don't want to pounce on them. They want to give the visitors a chance to see if they really like the church. I say they've missed out on the most important opportunity to draw people in!

Most people will not come back for a second visit without some sort of follow-up. Don't miss that window in time!

The visitor card itself should give you enough information that you can intelligently communicate with the visitors. You can include all kinds of extras on that card, but make sure you get the basics- names, address, best phone numbers to call, email address, and age categories. Names and ages of children are always helpful. Who invited them gives you an excellent connection for further opportunities. There are great visitor cards to borrow from every-where, so take the best from everyone. They did!

An Immediate Follow-up Plan- Letters and emails should go out right away, welcoming the visitors, giving a brief overview of the church and encouraging them to come back again. One letter and email should come from the pastor. If it's a smaller church, the pastor might actually want to make that first contact. He'll win a thousand brownie points and the awe of the visitors. Trust me! In most settings, a secretary will call, send emails, welcome the visitors, give them some overview and invite them to come back. In large churches, an assimilation director, pastor, assistant or team member will make the calls. Another communication should come from a segment group. An email can come from a fellowship group leader, a small group leader, or an age segment leader. An example would be the leaders of the seniors or young married couples, welcoming them and inviting them to an activity. It is so impressive to be immediately invited to a small group or an event sponsored by your own age group or segment ministry. The children get a personal welcome from the children's pastor and the youth get one from the youth guy. Be sure to point them to your Facebook page and segment ministry pages on your website. Designed email communications are being used more and more as an immediate contact tool.

Some churches will send a gift or have a gift taken to the visitor's home. I've seen welcome baskets, a loaf of warm bread, a special CD, or a book hand-delivered right to their door. What a wonderful gesture of love! Now, many churches have done visitation programs where teams of people go out in pairs and visit the visitors in their home as soon as they can. A church secretary sets up those visits. Trained workers go out, welcome the newbies, share information about the church and look for opportunities to share spiritual truths as well. This plan worked well in the 50's to 80's. But, as people have become busier and more private, and as cities have become larger, it's become more and more difficult to set up and do visits like this! Most churches have stopped it and rely on the visitors to come to events. If visiting people still works in your community, then do it. It's always better to have the most contact with your new people. If that doesn't work for you, you'll just have to work harder to draw your visitors back.

Visitor Welcome Events- It's critical that you have a welcome event for your visitors during their first month. In fact, tell them about that event when you contact them the first week. It's an opportunity to meet the pastor and his wife and the staff! Most visitors would really like to meet the pastor and learn more about the church. Giving them this opportunity right away will often motivate them to continue to try the church out for a few more weeks before they keep shopping around. My observation is, the longer they visit, the more likely they will stay! A good welcome event will help with that process.

I've already shared that when our church was smaller, my wife and I would have groups of visitors over to our home two times a month. We would also invite some of our lead couples and singles to mix with these new people. We would do coffee and desserts for an hour and then we'd squeeze the 20-30 people into our living room for a second hour. We'd learn a little bit about everyone and why they had visited our church. Then we'd share some vision and values and our passion for the Kingdom. Several of our leaders would share their own experiences in small groups or ministry opportunities. Our visitors would hear life-changing testimonies as people briefly shared around the room. By the end of the evening, my wife and I had memorized everybody's names and felt like we had a good start getting to know them. The next Sunday, we could go up to them and immediately continue on with that initial friendship. The fact is, almost all of them kept coming back! And we grew and grew and grew. I'm convinced that a major factor in our growth can be attributed to the people making contact with and feeling cared about by the pastor and his wife, right from the get-go. We live in an impersonal society and we desperately want relationship. Sheep still would like to know their shepherds, even if that interaction is only occasionally.

As churches grow, events have to change, simply because of size. Flexibility is critical! There came a time where we had to move our welcoming event out of our home and into a larger space. We began to have newcomer luncheons once a month after church in a social hall. We obviously handled 4-5 times as many people meeting at the church. We lost some of the closeness and simply had to work harder to get to know people. We also now had more staff people and leaders involved in the process. It took a larger team of people calling, preparing for the monthly event, presenting the vision of the church, making personal contact with the people and following up with them afterwards. But we had the same result! People could see that we really cared about the Kingdom and that we really cared about them.

Here's another key to winning the hearts and minds of visitors. We invited them to partner with us at these welcome events. We invited them to be a vital part of us-part of a team. We told them that we didn't want them to simply fill a seat in the auditorium. We wanted them to be a part of a small group, where they could bond and grow and contribute to the lives of others. We encouraged them to catch our vision and values and to become an active part of one of our many ministries. We challenged them to jump in. And they did! I believe that most people want to be challenged. They don't want to live a mediocre life. Believers want to be part of a church that is going somewhere. And pre-believers are amazed at all that they have missed out on and are also drawn in by the testimonies and the vision of the Kingdom. So don't be afraid to lay it all out there. They don't have to jump in- you're not signing people up at the event. But they need to see your heart and vision. It will make a difference!

Next Steps

Follow-up has to continue now on a regular basis. Think about what it would feel like if the church looked like it cared about you for the first four weeks and then they moved on to their next targets. In a moment, we'll be talking about assimilating our visitors into the life of the church family. But, first, we need to do the administrative pieces that help make everything else work. The visitors need to be placed on the mailing and email list. Lots of churches are using designed emails for weekly announcements that include video greetings and doorways to leadership blogs. All of this is easily available all over the Internet, and it's quite reasonable in price. Visitors need a systematic check-up by phone or email, at least until they get connected and are a part of some sort of fellowship group. Someone, of course, needs to be over that process or it won't happen. It can't be random. There has to be a plan with names and a checklist and reminders from the last emails. There are some great software programs out there that make all of this easy and workable. That email or call lets the visitors know you haven't forgotten them and that you wonder how they are doing navigating their way through your different church opportunities. It also provides a chance to invite the visitors to special events that are coming up. Some churches have created a system with teams of people calling or emailing everyone in the church once a quarter. That contact is both to give encouragement and to receive any prayer requests for the body and church leadership. This certainly takes a lot of work, but the benefits are wonderful! People really feel they are cared about. And this amazes visitors when they are added to a plan of praying quarterly for the entire church personally.

Assimilation

Our ultimate goal is assimilating our visitors into our church family. It's O.K. for people to attend for a few weeks or even a few months as observers of the family. It often takes awhile to make sure that your church is the right home for them. People come with all kinds of issues. Some are afraid. Some have been significantly hurt, and it will take them time to trust again. Some are making sure that they really can fit in to this family. Non-believers will bring their own set of fears and questions and will need time to get involved.

With all that said, it's imperative that the visitors get connected. If they don't, most of them will eventually leave. It's a fact of life. Some people will attend simply for the music or sermon or the great program for their children or young people. All of these components are important. And they all work together to build a great church family. But the real glue in any church family is connection! People need friendships, and they want friendships. If they don't eventually find people like them to hang out with, they will leave. I believe this is why so many churches go through so many visitors. Large churches go through 1000's of visitors a year. And only a percentage of them stay. The turnover rate is staggering! And so much of that is because the visitors have made no real connection.

I remember the day they told me they were leaving the church. They were leaders and spiritually mature. They had been regular attenders and actively involved in various ministries and a small

group. Then it happened! They were no longer a part of a small group and, at the same time, they volunteered for an extended period of time in the children's department during our gathering. They felt that they were helping others by doing this ministry over a longer period of time. But, in the end, and without realizing it, they slowly isolated themselves from the entire church family. By the time they came back to the gathering, they felt like strangers in their own church. Everything felt wrong, and what they had loved somehow faded away. It was time to leave. I couldn't understand. It didn't make any sense. What I now know is that connection is critical and isolation is deadly!

By the way, I've observed that smaller churches have the very same problem when they don't intentionally work to help their visitors make that connection. Robert Logan reminds us of the God factor as we wrestle with the challenges of helping our visitors and our regulars become all that God intends for them to be.

> As leaders, we need to realize that our churches are stewards of the resources that God has given use. Those resources are people. To invest those people is to a take a risk by expending the energy to evangelize, assimilate and disciple them. If your church proves itself faithful with its resources- large or small- Christ will add more, and when he comes back from His journey, He will say to you. . . "Well done, good and faithful servant!" [53]

This issue of assimilation is really important. This isn't about trying to grow a big, fat church. This is an issue of keeping as many people as possible so we can invest in them and bring radical change in their lives. Most of the people visiting need a great church that will help them walk though the process of becoming fully devoted disciples of Jesus Christ! Your non-believing visitors may not visit anywhere else. This may be their last shot or one shot at Christianity. Draw them in. Be God's fishing rod. Be the tool that God uses to bring them into the family of God!

> Friendship is the great connector. Most people visit churches because of friendships and they stay because of friendships.

Leadership

I've already said that it's essential that we have a follow-up and assimilation plan. And a plan will only work with the right team of leaders. In a smaller church, you may find several administratively-gifted volunteers who will take this on as their ministry for the church. As your church grows in size, it will eventually take paid staff to make sure that all of the details of assimilation are cared for. So you need someone in charge, a long-term strategy and plan and a team of workers to call and follow-up. You need a distribution plan to get the names of your visitors out to the specific segment group leaders who need to make their contact. And you need to follow-up to get responses from your segment leaders so you know what's happening with your visitors. If you don't follow-up on your follow-up system, the cracks will begin and people will fall through- guaranteed!

Friendship

Don't miss out on one of the most valuable tools for drawing people into the life of the church family. Friendship is the great connector. Most people visit churches because of friendships and they stay because of friendships. It's so obvious, but let's not miss the point. Most people arrive at church because someone's either brought them or told them. They will probably come back if the same friends continue to invite them and continue that contact. Some of us will invite our friends to an event or a church service, and we'll immediately follow-up with a next step of friendship and interaction. But many of us invite our friends or acquaintances, and we don't know what to do next. Sometimes we as believers are quick to invite or hand out an event sheet, but we're slow to follow through and take that friendship to the next level. We don't want to look pushy or over-eager. Or we find it a lot easier to invite someone than to actually connect with them. Many of us are shy or too busy to make a consistent relationship with anyone outside our normal circle of friendships. We're even surprised that our "friend" has come to church. They may not really be the kind of person we want to hang out with. "They need Jesus and a church, but don't attach me to the deal!" " Heh, dude, it's cool that you showed up to check out my church. Hope you ready like it. The music is awesome. Check out the coffee bar. See ya later!" Imagine visiting a church because of an invite, seeing that person at church, and not getting a warm and committed response. I've seen it happen! So sad.

> Evangelism and making friends for Christ is a team effort and we all ultimately have to help each other in order to get the job done.

It's critical that we train our people to make friends like Jesus would and to keep those friendships going. This, of course, is a heart issue. We need to ask God for soft hearts toward the people whom God places in our path. But is also is an issue of understanding and training. If God gives us a friendship opportunity, we need to take it and use it for the Kingdom! Evangelism and making friends for Christ is a team effort and we all ultimately have to help each other in order to get the job done. It all starts with a life commitment to take as many people to heaven with us as we can, without prejudice or partiality. That **is** the Mission!

So here's a plan. Train your people to be responsible friends to those they invite to church. Train them to be hospitable and friendly to strangers as they show up at church. Teach them to open their homes and hearts to people who are new to church or new to town or perhaps have never been cared for by anyone before. Train them on how to make friendships and how to keep them going. Teach them how to follow-up on visitors they invite or meet. Teach them things like going out for dinner with their new friends, inviting these friends to sit with them at the next gathering and inviting the friends to their small group or the next outreach event. Have an "Invited By" line on your visitor cards so you know who invited the visitor. That can be very helpful as you make church contact and consider coming events.

Work like a team. Become the friendliest church in town. Isn't that what we're supposed to be? And this all should be second nature to everyone in leadership. Modeling is critical. Lead the way. Invite visitors out or home. Be intentional. Train all of your leaders to be intentional. Plan ahead for visitors. Create a plan where leaders actually adopt visitors. They call, they care, they invite and they don't let go! The larger church will necessitate a larger team of intentional "assimilators." Small group leaders and assistant leaders can grow and multiply their groups exponentially as they commit themselves to intentional friendships with visitors looking for connection. This goes way beyond personality. This is priority! This is commitment to the cause. By the way, there's no room for Prima Donnas in Biblical Christianity. When pastors and leaders and their wives are too "elite" to be truly friendly with the body or new attenders, it's time for them to take a leave of absence and remember the roots of their religion. Picture Jesus embracing the masses and loving the least of these. Now put yourselves as leaders in His shoes and you can see what we have to look like! There's no other way.

When I was fresh out of college, I wanted to travel the country and visit many of the churches

that I had read about before I jumped into church planting. So, for two months, I hit the road, drove about 8,000 miles and experienced God and His people everywhere! Some churches were friendly and others were cold. Some people talked to me and others had more important things to do. But here's the one I remember thirty-plus years later. I had read several of Ralph Neighbor's books about shepherding the sheep and cell ministries. So I arrived and visited his church one Sunday. My grand memory isn't anything about the pastor. It's about his people! They were so warm and friendly. They talked to me and cared about me! One couple, for no good reason, invited me home for dinner. And then they asked me to stay with them until I left town. I was a stranger, and they took me in. Why did they do that? I would guess that it was because they were either filled with God and His love, or they were trained and committed to act and look like Jesus, or both. Now, that's the type of church visitors are looking for!

Small Groups

Small groups can be one of the greatest resources for assimilation in your entire church. It's almost impossible to really get to know people at the gathering in most churches because of size. As friendly as you are, the natural limitations at a gathering necessitate the creation of smaller environments where real friendships can be developed.

Some churches will break larger congregations down into groups of fifty to a hundred people. These groups sometimes are geographical, and in other churches, they are focused on a segment of the congregation- young married couples, recovery ministry, seniors, middle-aged married couples, singles, parents with pre-schoolers, Awana workers, R.V. lovers, people who love dogs and the list goes on! You'd be amazed at what people will group around in a church. This organizational structure allows for significant growth with focused oversight over many groups within the body. A system like this can be used for care, assimilation, and oversight, as well as meeting social, ministry and outreach needs. Well-trained leaders can provide significant ministry to many more people than would otherwise be provided for in most large churches. I've done it. It works! The problem, like all organizational structures, lies in the recruiting, training, and maintaining of such a large system, with consistency and quality. What can start out great can fade into mediocrity without a strong commitment to high levels of accountability, on-going training and committed staff oversight. If you can do it, don't give up and settle for anything less than excellence!

I don't believe anything else can accomplish what small groups can do for you in your church. A small group provides the greatest opportunity to assimilate and grow believers of all stages and ages. Any group larger than thirty people becomes a small crowd where a majority can disappear and never really participate in spiritual maturity. But it's hard to hide in a purpose-driven small group with a well-trained leader. The right ingredients can create an atmosphere where spiritual growth and group accountability naturally happen. Andy Stanley and Bill Willits, in their book, *Creating Community*, add these thoughts: "That is what God called the church to be about: creating environments where authentic community can take place. Building relational, transforming communities where people are experiencing oneness with God and oneness with each other. Communities that are so compelling that they create a thirst in a watching world. " [54]

My wife and I built friendships with many of our neighbors in our subdivision when we were first married. Our children played with their children. If fact, my wife babysat for a number of them. So they would be in our home on a regular basis. It was very natural to begin to bring God into our conversations. As we invited these neighbors, who were now our friends, to various activities and special church events, they responded and began to visit. Some of our neighbors started coming every week. Others would come with us once a year on Easter Sunday or to a Christmas musical. My wife led one neighbor woman to the Lord. Then another young couple decided to give their lives to Jesus. As they began attending church, they were new and unfamiliar with everything we know as believers. So we adopted them out to one of our small groups. The group embraced them, showered them with love and walked them through all of their questions and issues. Years later, they love and serve God because a group of strangers took them in and cared for their souls!

Small groups can gather for all kinds of reasons. I've seen groups gather for social interaction and accomplish absolutely nothing of spiritual value. I'm all for social interaction, but there's too little time and opportunity to waste a good gathering without being more purposeful! A well-designed small group system in the church should plan to meet all the needs that people come with. The goal should be to offer social interaction, ministry and outreach opportunities, and, of course, spiritual growth and maturity. A balanced small group provides time for worship, time to study the Word, time for fellowship and time for prayer. A small group allows people to really get to know each other so they can encourage and stimulate each other in spiritual issues. They know each other's names and the names of their children. They learn to trust each other, care for each other, and pray for each other. Small groups learn to pray together and play together. They enjoy the eating and the fellowship as much as the meeting. Many small groups will become so bonded that they will hang out with each other and play together even when they're not told to.

> Every leader needs to be recruited, trained and released with a commitment to be part of a team that values the DNA of multiplication-disciples making disciples making disciples!

Small groups can become so bonded to each other that they become cliques in the larger church setting. That can be the downside. I've watched groups play together during the week and sit together on Sundays. They'll grow to love each other so much that they won't talk to anyone else. In fact, the idea of adding anyone new to their groups sounds intrusive. "We all know each other and trust each other. Why allow strangers in to wreck our time together?" And the idea of multiplying a growing group by splitting it in two is simply unthinkable! Now, I get it! I understand that. But all of these attitudes are exactly opposite to the purposes of reaching people for Christ and assimilating them into the family. That's why it's critical that we establish the guidelines and foundational principles for small groups right from the very beginning. Every leader needs to be recruited, trained and released with a commitment to be part of a team that values the DNA of multiplication- disciples making disciples making disciples! George Barna, in his book, *Growing True Disciples*, reflects on what happens when we don't establish the right foundations for our small group strategies. "Unless there is ample training for facilitators, a tight accountability process, strong relational connections, and a purposeful selection of materials to cover, the small groups will fail to produce disciples." [55] That's been proven over and over. But with that focus and intentionality, small groups can play a vital role both in maturing the body and assimilating new believers and attenders into the life of the body. So we have to train our small group members to love strangers and visitors. They need to be part of our team of dozens (100's, 1000's) of greeters and ambassadors for Jesus at our gatherings and all through the rest of the week, for that matter. And we need to teach them to invite new attenders to come visit their small group so they too can get connected and integrated into the church.

Small groups done on purpose can provide the catalyst for spiritual growth and maturity in all kinds of areas. For example, the entire group can study God's Word and wrestle through hard questions on dozens of topics both in areas of Biblical foundations and in practical living. If the leader and the group are functioning well together, each attender is challenged to deal with the issues being talked about instead of simply listening, leaving and forgetting. As the group talks about lifestyle evangelism, synergy happens, eyes are opened and hearts are softened. Training and prayer lead to outreach opportunities and the small group begins to bear fruit! Ministry ventures are picked. One small group goes to the rescue mission. Another takes on an inner city project. As the small group bonds together around ministry, most in the group experience new levels of spiritual growth and maturing like they never have simply as Sunday morning attenders! And that's what we want!

I've watched life transformation take place over and over again in small groups. I've seen pre-believers and new Christians embraced by the members of a small group. I've watched them grow and grow as questions have been answered and truths have been shared! I've watched older believers discover principles of living that they never had learned on their own. I've seen people learn to pray and learn to listen and learn to care. I've seen disconnected people finally become part of a bonded family. When one of our men was in a trucking accident and arrived at the hospital in a coma, I was called to come to be with the family. When I arrived, I discovered that his small group was already there! Phone calls were made and the hospital waiting room was quickly filled with their closest friends- their small group. Needs were fully met and I was rather unnecessary. It was beautiful! It was the body of Christ. Over the days that followed, the group was ever-present for encouragement, prayer and support. And the husband and wife visiting and caring the most were the youngest believers in the group- and perhaps the ones who had experienced the greatest amount of grace.

Lifestyle evangelism can become one of the greatest by-products of a purposeful small group experience. All of our small group leaders, assistant leaders and their husbands and wives were discipled and committed to modeling a lifestyle of building intentional bridges to non-believers in their neighborhoods and workplaces. They, in turn, discipled everyone in their small groups to pray for and make intentional, consistent, relational contacts with at least three non-believers. In fact, all of us in each small group turned in our three names so the entire group could have a list to pray through each week. We were partners in the Kingdom! We helped each other along in this strange, new area of Christianity that many of us were unfamiliar with.

The stronger members encouraged and helped the weaker members. What a novel thought! We helped each other through our fears and questions. We shared about having coffee at Starbucks and inviting our friends over for a barbecue. We talked about going for walks or fishing or skiing or hunting or seeing movies together. We shared about wonderful opportunities and awkward moments along the way. And our weekly prayer times included a focus on these friends and neighbors. Group synergy brought everyone on board. Tell me where else that can happen in the church? All of our groups actually cancelled our regular format every four to six weeks to have our own cultivating events with as many of our pre-believing friends as we could bring. So outreach picnics and barbecues and evenings at the lake and dinners were taking place everywhere, all the time because, **that** was the plan. People's lives were changed, and one by one, pre-believers entered the Kingdom.

You can see why it was our goal to get every visitor in a small group. Our director of assimilation would give our visitor's names to specific small group leaders for follow-up. We would either match types of people or ages or the location where they lived compared to the small group's location. Sometimes the contact simply didn't happen and we would then give the name to another small group leader. Sometimes the visitors visited and didn't like the small group. We needed to know that so we could refer them to a different small group. Small groups are like churches, and visitors need to be given the permission to move around until they find the group of people that they feel most comfortable with. Not every visitor fits with every small group in a church. It's really important to know that so you can help your new people maneuver until they find the right "family" and feel at home. There needs to be continued contact from a segment group or small group until your visitors either find the right group or it becomes obvious that they aren't interested. Everyone is busy and it takes time to draw people into a new group that they haven't been a part of. But being drawn into the right group is critical- it will make all the difference!

Small groups can be done successfully in a dozen different ways. You will find what seems like an endless list of excellent conferences, seminars and books on how to put together a small group structure in your church. While most of the ideas are similar, there are clear differences between churches and writers. Some prescribe very small groups, and others encourage very large groups, for a variety of reasons. Some recommend common content for the entire church, while others give various degrees of freedom to group leaders. Some will recommend attracting new members to on-going groups. These groups will keep dividing as they grow, releasing new leaders and a constant vision of multiplication. While that has been very effective for many churches, both Andy Stanley and Nelson Searcy point to closed groups with specific time limitations on their groups. For Nelson, it's twelve to fifteen people for twelve weeks. Multiplication comes through multiplying leaders with new groups. [56] For Andy, it's an eighteen to twenty-four month period of time, with a strong focus on accountability, belonging and care. These groups are encouraged to multiply at the end of their covenant time together. [57] Both have created dynamic systems that work. So there are many options out there for you. Not every system works in every church. Find one that works for you!

Let's talk about cell-based churches for a moment. Many of you reading this are part of or are planting a missional community of small groups. For those of us who are unfamiliar with this, cell-based churches set the highest priority on missional living and on having everyone attend a weekly cell gathering rather than on weekly attendance at a church facility. The gathering of the entire church plays a secondary role and sometimes is planned on a monthly or quarterly basis rather than a weekly basis. Any programming in the church is simplified so it doesn't conflict with the priority of the cell. A true cell church has everyone involved in a cell. While cell-based churches are found all around the world, there have been a smaller number of true cell churches in the United States. American culture seems to clash with the simplicity and focus of a church that places high value on small groups and lower value on larger gatherings and programs for children and youth and others. With busy lifestyles and often only a growing commitment to spiritual disciplines, it's a big challenge to get even half of our people involved in a weekly small group. Many churches have successfully combined and balanced the values of the cell-based ministry and the need for appropriate programming. If you're involved in a more traditional church and you're determined to draw everyone into a small group strategy, don't give up! It will be worth your every effort. As more and more of your people are involved, the word will spread. If you are a leader of a missional movement, and you're determined to make authentic disciples who multiply, don't give up! Don't lower the standard. Shift will happen, but so will movement if you keep yourself focused on His Mission.

Activities and Events

Church and ministry activities and events can be one of the easiest ways to both attract and assimilate visitors into the church family. As new attenders hear about and are invited to various opportunities that come at them, they will begin to see the life of the body, outside of the weekly gathering. Attending a church filled with activity and excitement and energy will make people feel like they're part of something that's alive and going somewhere! Visiting those events will almost immediately tie them in and make them some friends. I've watched it over and over again. Visitors will go to that picnic or roller-skating night or that Awana evening with their children or a women's Bible study or a recovery meeting. They'll be amazed at the fun and fellowship and pure enjoyment of the activity. Needs will be met! They'll leave with new friends and a growing bond to the church as a whole. And they'll be back. Now, this isn't magic. It doesn't happen to everyone. But most people who get to the right, well-planned events and activities will like them and will come back for more. You can see why it's invaluable to get them there so friendships can develop. You can also see why it's critical that those events are well-planned and attractive.

A young pre-Christian family had heard about our Awana program at the church. When their children were invited to attend with some friends, the whole family showed up to check it out. They were amazed at the sea of people and the dynamic energy of that weekly event. They allowed their

children to come back week after week, and it wasn't long before the children gave their hearts to Jesus. Now, the children had to memorize scripture every week to pass each of the sections in their manuals. So their parents worked with them to learn God's Word. How cool!

It didn't take long for the parents to decide to start bringing their children to our gathering on Sunday mornings. Well, you guessed it! Soon they gave their lives to Christ and became an active part of our church family. They grow in the Lord and developed a heart to serve. In fact, you could count on them being at the church every Thursday night serving as leaders and working with children in our Awana program. Isn't that incredible? Now, as amazing and wonderful as that is, stories like this happen everywhere, all the time, by God's divine plan.

So how do we get them to events and activities? We invite them! We invite them through bulletins and announcements and flyers and emailings and tweets and media presentations. We invite them through phone calls and church leadership contacts. We train our people to invite their friends and new acquaintances to the right events and activities. We train them to invite their friends and then bring them so there's personal ownership in the contact. We train our segment group leaders to model the core value of outreach and assimilation in everything they do. And we train them to continually pass those values down to everyone involved in their activity or ministry. We teach them how to market their activities and how to always use their ministries to draw newer people into the life of the body. We teach our leaders to help their participants always create an inviting atmosphere of love and acceptance. These are core values to die for! All of our growth and energy and activity will become wasted effort the moment we surrender these core values of always modeling and multiplying a lifestyle of love and intentional outreach.

Imagine this- let's be a visitor and walk into three different men's groups at the same church. Let's make them the same size with the same basic make-up. But that's all they have in common. The first group is distant and disconnected. It's a room full of lonely guys with no leadership. No one's figured out how to help them begin to trust each other and how to begin opening up with each other. Anyone new walking into the room will only increase the loneliness and emptiness of the group. How sad! The second set of guys is totally cliquish and walled-in. They love each other and think they're the friendliest guys in the world. They're laughing and having the greatest time. But no one can break in! They think so much of themselves and their inside stories that they're completely thoughtless about anyone else. Here's the sad truth- they don't even know it. Anyone visiting will arrive a stranger and leave with no intention of returning. The third group is completely different. They're happy, they're having a great time, and they love drawing newer men into their circle. They're sensitive to outsiders, they've taught themselves to reach out to strangers quickly and with absolute sincerity. They bring their own friends to activities and they love meeting other new guys as they show up. These men really function as a team, working together to grow a strong, multiplying group that they enjoy and that the new guys also enjoy.

I've visited all three of these types of groups in many different churches. Some of them have been women's groups, some are youth groups, some have been church boards, and others have been various segments groups. Can you think of any groups in your church that sound like the first two? What helped create the difference in the third group? And how can we help all of our activities and ministries become like Group Number Three? Let's be honest. Some people are more naturally embracing and warmer to strangers than others are. Some leaders multiply groups like this more easily than others do. But then there's the God factor. We become more loving and whole as we are filled with the Spirit and draw from God's strength. As groups grow in the Lord, these qualities will show up.

A critical key to creating the difference in the third group is leadership- value-driven leadership. These are leaders who are committed to building ministries around God-dependence and Christ-like character. First of all, we **have** to decide that these are values that we will not surrender. Secondly, we **have** to model these values as leaders or we need to step down from leadership. Thirdly, we **have** to train and recruit and possibly remove leaders throughout our church structure so that these character and lifestyle values are at the foundation of everything we are building. As **All** of your leaders learn to train and model and multiply these values in **All** of their activities and ministries, your consistency will create that wonderful atmosphere of love that God actually commands us to have.

You will find so many resources available that will help you in this area of assimilation and so much more. Search the web. Check out the resources pages of our larger churches. Look up books on Amazon and our Christian discounters. One of the authors you'll find is Nelson Searcy. Nelson is a pastor and a gifted and prolific writer on a wide variety of strategies aimed at growing strong, healthy churches. These books, which are must-reads, include *Activate, Connect, Healthy Systems, Healthy Church, Ignite, Revolve, Launch and Maximize*. His book, *Fusion*, attacks the subject of "turning first-time guests into fully-engaged members of your church," the book's subtitle. Searcy asks the critical question: "Why assimilate? Assimilation leads to transformation by giving people the means and opportunity to become maturing followers of Christ. In broad terms, 'assimilation' can be defined as the process used to encourage your first-time guests to continue coming back until they see and understand God's power, accept Jesus as their Saviour and commit themselves to the local church through church membership. . .Encouraging people to stick around our churches is not about making our auditoriums look full and our numbers impressive; it's about leading them to faith in Jesus, through the Spirit's prompting." [58] That **is** what it's all about, isn't it?

Let's ask some questions about this critical area of follow-up and assimilation. Are we making those immediate contacts? Do we have a plan? Is someone in charge of that plan and is it being done? Is it the right plan? Is it working? Are we collecting information from a good percentage of our visitors each week? Is our collection system working? Have we designed a path that draws our visitors into those first steps of connection with our church family? Is the plan clear and visible for everyone to see, does it connect with every visitor and is it done on a regular basis? Is it the right plan? Is it working? How do we know if it is working? Do we have the accountability in our system that shows us that the plan is getting done? Are visitors coming back because of our process? Are they telling us that? What is our process of follow-up on each visitor?

Are we assimilating visitors into the life of our church? How do we help them connect with our people? Who are specifically responsible for and involved in assimilating visitors into our ministries and family? Do they have a clear plan? Are they working their plan and is it working? Are we teaching our people how to love and respond to visitors? Are our people learning to be warm and caring to visitors each time we gather? Are we hearing that from visitors? Are we teaching our people how to follow-thru with their own friends as they invite them to events and gatherings? Are they doing it? How are we using events and ministries to connect and assimilate new people? Are our ministry leaders using their full potential to draw new people into their groups and into the life of Christ? Do we have a plan and process to draw people into a small group? Is it working? Are our groups intentionally connecting people to each other, to God and His mission to reach the lost? Are we seeing the majority of our people connecting to others through small groups or other ministries?

Go deeper! I've just asked some starting questions needed to help us begin to assess how we are really doing in this critical area of follow-up and assimilation.

Serving and Ministry

Serving in the Kingdom can be one of the most attractive ways to draw new people into the life of the church and family! We've talked about how appealing it can be to have ministries that meet needs as people arrive at your church. But now, we're talking about how exciting it can be to new attenders to see ministry opportunities that they can step into. Usually they have to like the people, the preacher and the music first. But once they've migrated through those initial steps, ministry can jump out as a significant opportunity and attracter. "Look at these incredible ministries that we can get involved in! " People who have never lifted a finger to serve in past church settings will brag proudly about the chance they have to serve in your church, or at the Rescue Mission, or with the youth or children's ministries. Why? Because they've found their place! They've found something that they believe in. Perhaps nothing clicked in their past church experiences. Perhaps no one excited them about serving and ministry. Or maybe they're pre-Christians or new Christians and this is something completely new to them altogether.

> We were made to serve! Find the right ministry, use your gifts and look out! Great things will happen.

Now, many people aren't looking for a place to serve. They haven't been attracted to church by the idea of doing some sort of ministry. For some, that's the last thing that they're thinking about. They're arriving to take, not to give! But that's often because they haven't been introduced to something that really grabs their hearts. Several years ago, my wife and I traveled for a week in China. Nothing in the adventure could compensate my wife for the difficulties of being away from the normal comforts of home. Nothing, that is, until we came to the orphaned children. Suddenly, the world changed and my wife's heart was connected and committed. Sometimes our visitors and our regulars, for that matter, are just like that. They need to be helped in the journey of discovering that serving can be wonderful. We were made to serve. Find the right ministry, use your gifts and look out! Great things will happen.

Let's admit it- ministry may not only look boring; it actually can be boring! Anything can be boring if it's not done well or if the wrong people are doing it. Many people see serving at churches like it's a job that has to be done. "Someone has to do it. It might as well be You!" So we recruit unexcited, minimally-willing people to fill jobs in the church that they should not be doing. Or we have willing people who really aren't right for those jobs. Like the grumpy usher who feels that it's his duty to hand out bulletins and to show people to their seats, whether they like it or not! Heh, is he still serving in your church? No wonder visitors don't come back! And no wonder we often have a problem with recruitment and exciting people about serving.

Ministry should be and can be very exciting in any church family. But there are keys to building a lifestyle of serving in your church.

1) Leaders have to proclaim and reaffirm their commitment that serving with joy is a core value for every believer. We're all made to serve! In Ephesians 4, Paul compares all of us to all of the parts of the human body. "He makes the whole body fit together perfectly. As each part does its own special work, it helps the other parts grow, so that the whole body is healthy and growing and full of love."[59] Every part is necessary. And every person is made to serve. Service is a privilege. We're actually serving the Lord in everything that we do, all week long. Look at all that He's done for us. How can I do less than give Him my best? There's a song in there somewhere. That message has to be trumpeted everywhere by everyone all the time. It's core. **Everybody serves. Service isn't optional. It's our lifestyle. 500 attenders = 500 servers! Children serve. Retirees serve. Newbies serve. Everybody serves. That's who we are!** It's got to come through in sermons and training sessions and small groups and one-on-one conversations on a regular basis.

As this concept is repeatedly clarified as a core value throughout the church, it will motivate and encourage everyone to get on board.

2) That core value of serving with joy has to be modeled. And modeling, of course, starts from the top down. If we can't demonstrate this characteristic, we shouldn't be a leader. That's bad modeling and it will hurt the entire church! A central part of modeling a servant's heart is being filled with God's love and character. We can't just **do** it! We have to **be** it! **Being supersedes doing!** We again have to draw close and stay close to God to be filled with His power and character. One natural overflow is a servant's heart! Then we don't have to try to be filled with joy over the task that we need to do. The joy comes naturally! As we truly model joyous servanthood, **it will spread**! There's no doubt about it!

> Asking people to serve in ways that don't match their capabilities sets everyone up for stress and failure.

3) We've got to help people serve in the areas that they are gifted to serve in. Believers find the greatest joy serving the Lord in the right ministry using the right set of spiritual gifts and talents. They often sense God's call and His blessing on them as they function right where they're supposed to be serving. Eric Rees, in his book S.H.A.P.E., writes on how God has shaped us to serve! He defines what he calls Kingdom Purpose as:

> . . .your specific contribution to the body of Christ, within your generation; that causes you to totally depend on God and authentically display his love toward others- all through the expression of your unique S.H.A.P.E. . .Your Kingdom Purpose is way more than a career. It's a special commissioning from God to make a difference on this earth. [60]

I love that! The acronym addresses these five characteristics:

Spiritual Gifts- special abilities from God
Heart- special passions from God
Abilities- special talents from God
Personality- the special way God has wired you
Experiences- parts of the past God intends to use in you

Eric goes on to talk about activating your serving sweet spot, that alignment that comes as we walk in God's power and as we find God's center of service for our lives. [61] Buy the book! This gives us one more reason for why it's so important to help people discover their spiritual gifts and then find the right place to help. Asking people to serve in ways that don't match their capabilities sets everyone up for stress and failure. And nobody wants that! So it just makes sense that quiet people should not be greeters and, by the way, they usually don't really want to be greeters. If they do greet and usher, it's probably because they're simply trying to do their part to help. Now, sometimes, with a limited number of people, we all do have to jump in. If you're in a small church, everyone has to help. If you're part of a church plant or in a rented facility, everyone has to do his or her part to get the job done or it won't happen! That's life! Get a grip! Ask God for a servant's heart so you have His strength and heart to do what you have to do.

If we don't change that paradigm and begin matching people to their appropriate ministries, we'll eventually discover why people don't like to serve and why some of them begin to leave. Let people who like to do something with their hands work with their hands. And help the gifted leaders find positions to lead. Recruit capable organizers to help get ministries on track and running smoothly. We often have a room full of capable people at our gatherings who would serve the Lord if they could just discover that right place of ministry. Let's help them find it. Now, there will always be finicky people who'll whine and complain and will never be happy serving anywhere. Deal with them. Ignore them. Placate them. Do whatever you have to do with them. But don't let them drain you or handicap you! Remember- they're only a handful of people. Let's focus on mobilizing the majority! Gary McIntosh and Glen Martin, in their book, *Finding Them, Keeping Them,* say a lot to this issue of volunteerism. 1) People will volunteer if they see a real need. 2) People will volunteer when asked to commit in writing. 3) People will volunteer to values and goals and not guilt and shame. 4) People will volunteer if you talk with them personally. [62] Add those thoughts to your bank as you pray and think about recruiting.

4) We need to do everything we can to keep our people from getting overloaded and burned out. We can work hard to match people to the right jobs. But if they get exhausted and lose heart, **everyone loses.** I've watched it happen over and over again. People volunteer and are excited about helping in a ministry. They commit themselves and work hard to serve and they get the job done. The problem is, many of them over-commit and don't realize that at the beginning. They may take on several jobs without seeing the big picture. Here's the problem- our systems often provide no means of relief. So our dear people work and work and work. And when they want off, it's tough or impossible for that to happen. So they keep working or they feel guilty. That can't go on forever. Get ready for burnout or drop out.

How do we prevent this scenario from happening? We create systems of relief. We recruit two workers for every job. Or we recruit our worker and have them recruit assistant workers. We train all of them with excellence. We provide clear policy instructions, including the issues of relief and overload. We provide for time off. We stay on top of what's happening in the lives of our ministry teams so relief comes before it's critical. We don't expand our ministries or start new ones until we build this level of quality and care into present ministries. Did you hear that? If necessary, we cut back to a size that is manageable.

Now, as many of you know, this doesn't always seem to work out. For example, when you're planting a new church or beginning a ministry, it always seems that more effort has to be put out by fewer workers to get everything going. Isn't that usually true? The secret is constantly recruiting and training for tomorrow. "Everybody serves! Sign up today for training!" We have the tendency to do what needs to be done now, and we'll think about systems and better recruitment tomorrow. Tomorrow arrives, people are burning out and there are no replacements. So prepare today and have a great tomorrow. And if you've done everything and you can't get enough workers to provide a ministry with excellence, then cut it back or shut it down. It's not working. The timing must be wrong. Admit it, deal with it and move on!

Let's assume that service is celebrated as a core value in your church, all of your leaders are modeling it beautifully, your workers are serving in their gifts and your systems are in place to protect everyone from overload. Now, I know that that's a daydream for many of our churches. But let's set that as the goal, and let's dream of the day that that will be the current reality of your church. If you don't ever set and shoot at the goal, you'll never hit the target. Let me tell you how that focus and goal will impact your ministry recruitment. There are churches today across our continent where service is second nature to the body. There's excitement everywhere about ministry! People love being a part of serving the Kingdom. They tell everyone about the people they are serving. Their ministries flow out of their buildings, throughout their cities and all around the world. Servanthood is truly a lifestyle. It happens all week long- at home, at work, in the community and at church. Training is continually being offered to help people serve to the best of their ability. There is a constant flow of people signing up to serve. There are wait lists of people wanting be involved in ministry.

Can you guess what reaction visitors have as they arrive to a church like that? They are completely drawn in. They feel the excitement. They see the joy in the leaders and workers in the various ministries of the church. They see the happy faces everywhere. They hear the testimonies and announcements about ministry opportunities and levels of training to help people know what they are doing. They get multiple invitations to learn about and to become a part of the ministry team. And they accept. They sign up. They join the team. And they too begin to feel the thrill of serving God. They tell their friends. And they sign up. And it multiplies. Again and again. Now, that's what I'm talking about! Can you feel it? Can you feel that excitement that wells up when the Kingdom is shining in all its glory? And it's shining when we are all working together in harmony within His will! Isn't that what we want? And that's what He wants! So let's get there together.

We will talk more about serving as one of the greatest ways to touch lives and reach communities. But let's take a moment now to ask some questions about ministry in your church:

> Is serving with joy a core value throughout the leadership in your church? Does everyone understand it? Does everyone believe it? Does everyone know it's a foundational component of everything else in the church? Is it written down and quoted and taught and preached about like everyone really believes it? Do all of your leaders and I mean **all** your leaders model servanthood for all the body to see? What do you need to do to bring everyone on board? How do you celebrate the ministries that flow out of your church? How do you market ministries to the body in general? How well do you do? How do you introduce people to ministry? Do you train and present personality testing and spiritual gifts? How do you recruit people to move to the next step? Do you make general invitations? Do you invite them personally or do you expect them to come to you? How do you screen your people and then train them to serve in each area of ministry? Do you have advance training for maturing workers and leaders? These are a few of the critical questions that need to be asked about this important area of Christian living. Be diligent and unafraid and you will succeed and see your dreams come true!

Notes

THOUGHTS ON CHANGE

True life is lived when tiny changes occur.
Leo Tolstoy

Our dilemma is that we hate change and love it at the same time; what we really want is for things to remain the same but get better.
Sydney J. Harris

Always remember that the future comes one day at a time.
Dean Acheson

10. Programs and Facility-Focus On Excellence and Watch Them Keep Coming!

We've spent countless hours assessing and improving and preparing for our visitors. We've worked on all of the basics, from property appearance to people skills and attitudes. We've focused on our gathering and our follow-up. But now it's time to walk down the hallway and look at everything else that we're doing. We've looked generically at activities and ministries. But, now, we want to go into far more detail.

My goal is to help you look at what you are doing and how well you are doing in every area of ministry throughout your church. Again, I want to make you think. I won't ask all of the questions. I want to get you started. I want to be as broad with my strokes as possible in this section, and then I want you to be as specific as possible as you work together and think of your individual ministries. I'll point at a lot of detail and I want you to go beyond me and sift through your specific area of ministry to think of things I don't address. We'll start with your facility and then move on to the programs that function inside or outside your buildings. Please grab a pen and some paper. Let my thoughts fuel your own ideas and imagination. You can't do everything now. But if you start dreaming today, just wait until you see what you can achieve tomorrow. So write those ideas down. Take notes. Create a list of the things that need to be improved, eliminated or added to your own ministry. And when you come together as a ministry team, you'll have a wealth of ideas to share together. Let's get started!

Facilities

Adequate Room Space

Let's begin by looking at your room for ministry. Unfortunately, your rooms do make a difference. Churches with limited space are handicapped in their ability to do all the ministries that they would like to do. And limited ministry will often deter visitors from returning and churches from growing. It's a common problem, and it needs to be solved! Church plants constantly wrestle with this issue and will solve it by renting additional space in order to do what they need to do. Some churches will grow quite extensively based on the energy and enthusiasm of the gathering. But there will come a time when that no longer works. The rest of the program also has to move into place. If that doesn't happen, the whole ship will slow down and begin to sink. And space makes a huge difference.

So solving the space problem is a big deal for many churches. That's where you have to get creative. Find an answer. Be relentless in your process. Don't give up! If you can't find the room to effectively do the ministry, you're killing your potential. Rent another room. Recruit and use someone's house. Rent an office facility and use it for multiple ministries. Rent some rooms in another church that's sitting empty most of the week. Don't be so fussy that you arrive at a dead-end.

We moved into our new facility and immediately ran out of space. It was wonderful having our own building, but we had no place for our children! Now, that's a problem! We searched for a solution and found the answer. There was a pre-school building about a mile away from our church property. And it was empty on Sundays. What an opportunity! We met with the owners and negotiated a rental plan that worked for both of us. We

recruited more workers and established a good plan of communication with our church whenever there was a need to contact the parents. Of course, we kept the babies and children under two onsite in our nursery. Families began dropping their children off at the pre-school instead of bringing them to church. I'm sure there was reluctance by some at first. But any fears vanished quickly. It didn't take long for us to pack out the pre-school. Fortunately, it wasn't long before we finished the second phase of our building and moved our children over to our own property. Some churches will never take the risk of trying an off-campus pre-school for their children. And that's why some churches will never grow!

***

Now, some ministries don't need traditional space. Go meet in the park or in the back room of a restaurant. A high school class takes over a corner of Burger King on Sunday mornings. A youth group rents out space in a strip mall during the week. A young church rents meeting rooms at a nearby hotel for special events. The ladies Bible study meets in a living room each week. People in the church offer space at their businesses for church ministries. Most of these ideas should be no-brainers.

Often the greater difficulty is figuring out how to pay for the space and everything else, for that matter! Most good ideas come with a price tag. Many churches feel so limited financially that they simply can't see how they can get the space that they need. Here are the two questions that you need to always ask.

> **1) Is this a real need that we have?**
> **2) Do we believe that it's God's will?**

If the answers are both YES, Then do it! Step out by faith and do the next step! During the course of many years, our church hit the financial wall over and over again. The first reaction to many discussions on our board was, "We can't afford it!" From a natural perspective, we couldn't. But we always went back to those two questions. If the answers were "Yes", we would step out by faith and move forward. God never failed us. Not once! Now, God has given us each a brain to use. If everything logical is saying that you can't do one more thing, that's probably what God is saying too. But many church leaders become so afraid to step out by faith and trust God that they miss out on the very miracles that God was planning for them. How sad. Step out!

Creating the Right Room Space

Having the right space and the right amount of space is almost as important as having the room in the first place. Sometimes we have to take what we can get. "We're planting in this school facility and this is what we have to work with." "This is our present church building and we're stuck with it." "This is the building that I got when I was called to pastor here." "These rooms are all we have." "There is no other solution. We've tried everything!" I'm heard them all and I understand. I've even said a few of them. There are times when we **are** stuck. But that's not the end. That's simply the now! We have to do what we have to do right now. But, tomorrow, we'll find something better. Don't give up! And don't give in to mediocrity. Use what you have to the best of your ability. Think hard about how to make it better. Change it Up! Get creative. Think outside the box.

Do whatever you can to provide the right space and the right amount of space to each ministry as soon as possible. There is a price to be paid. It's unavoidable! Loads of people are immature and insensitive to the issues that you face as a church. They'll visit and see that small, inadequate room that you're going to stuff their kid into. Now, it seems to work for everyone else at the church. That doesn't mean it works for them. They may give their son to you, or they may just keep him in the service. But they may not be back! You'll never know why, but it was that room. Don't just look through your eyes. That won't work. Step back and look through the eyes of visitors. What do they see? Would they be turned off by the size and uses of our rooms? Would they want to come and join us to do that in this room? For example, put ten to twelve junior high young people in a boring, little room for an hour and see how long their attention span lasts. Listen to what they tell their parents when church is over. Yet I've seen it done over and over again.

Rooms need to match ministries. Ask the question, how large a room do we need for this function? How many people of this age **would be happy** in this room? I've watched church leadership step back from old patterns and ways of thinking and arrive at great, new ideas. I've seen programs moved completely around for the absolute best. I've seen walls knocked down and buildings remodeled with brilliance, using old space in an entirely new way. I've heard conservative thinkers complain and whine, but life goes on! And change has to take place. Old spaces have become new, and far better. So think! Don't be afraid. Look at the big picture. Ask the hard questions. What do we really need? How can we make this better?

Start dreaming about your next steps. What sort of spaces will we need to do what we really would like to do? Start planning for tomorrow. Visit lots of churches. Get a sense of how spaces should work in your area of ministry. Don't let the journey frustrate you. Let it motivate you toward excellence now and a great future tomorrow.

The Right Stuff- Equipping Our Rooms

Next, we need to look at having the right stuff in the right space. We can't expect people to come and join us in our ministries and activities if we haven't worked hard to appropriately equip our rooms. Let's start with a standard of excellence. We need to be excellent in everything we do. So our rooms and spaces need to look excellent. Our rooms need to be attractive, well lit, nicely painted and trimmed, with quality floor coverings. Those are the basics. Why would visitors think that we care if we haven't done the basics?

> Equipping our rooms properly means that we've created an environment that will do the very best to aid us in our specific ministry.

Now, I've visited many churches that have worked hard to create very attractive rooms. And I've also walked through many churches where no one seems to care about the quality and condition of the secondary rooms that they are using. Some rooms are poorly carpeted while others have ancient paint jobs with poorly painted patches. Doesn't anybody care? Now, money is always the issue. But I think apathy has become the greater issue. I believe that many of us become blind to our buildings and get used to mediocrity. If we really cared, we'd find the money to take care of the basics. Please, open your eyes! If you want anyone new to come back again, fix it up!

Our rooms need to be well-equipped for the specific ministry that we are doing. If you want to know what the right stuff is, you will need to visit lots of churches. I learned the most down through the years by traveling around and visiting as many different churches as I possibly could. I'd drive for hours to look at rooms and layouts and equipment and decorations and lighting and trim and much more. Through the years, I've taken my wife and friends and teams and staff and boards to look at church after church after church. I've personally learned so much, and I've been continually stretched to move our buildings and spaces to the next level of purpose and excellence. Things are always changing and there's so much to learn! I'm not talking about necessarily finding the latest new way of doing things. I am talking about being smart with our space. What is working for others in ministry today? Some of us have plenty of space, but we're not using it to our best advantage. Some of us have the right space, but it's poorly equipped. It looks exactly like it looked ten or twenty or forty years ago. It wasn't very creative then and nothing's changed.

I had heard of their plans to build a new gym-like room for their youth ministry. But was I shocked when I walked in and saw what they had done! It was an amazing, purpose-driven ministry facility totally designed to meet the real desires and needs of young people. It's like they built what the kids really wanted. It was filled with music and screens with videos, all kinds of recreational options and games, loads of couches, a food and beverage area and lots more. And it was packed with young people! In fact, it was packed all the time. By the way, the leadership has changed the equipment in the space several times to stay on top of the real needs and opportunities that they are facing. Now, think about this one. There are churches everywhere with large rooms that are sitting empty all week long. They simply haven't put together the right stuff to make it happen. What a waste!

Equipping our rooms properly means that we've created an environment that will do the very best to aid us in our specific ministry. Sometimes that means we need to buy the right chairs for the group that we are working with. Sometimes the wall decorations make all the difference in the world. Having appropriate cabinets and tables and shelves is so important. Buying the right equipment for our children is critical. Sometimes the need is for a different set of lights or a different color for the room or floor. For many of us, the cost hasn't been the factor that has kept us from moving forward. It's been more of an issue of time. It takes time and effort to figure out next steps. Hopefully, reading this book and going through this assessment will help you move forward on your process.

Others of us are truly handicapped by finances. We can't go out and buy everything that other churches are able to buy to equip our rooms. Listen- don't let that stop you! You need to dream and get creative with the space you have and the resources that you do have. Most churches that have all the great stuff today didn't have it when they were your size. But they decided to be excellent with what they did have. And they worked hard to find appropriate resources so they could grow and move to the next level of quality and effectiveness! So do your best to find the resources you need to equip your rooms to the very best of your ability. Search for resources. Some churches are throwing away equipment that other churches would call treasure. Don't throw that stuff away. Give it away. Keep looking. Don't give up. Go find that treasure!

Going the Extra Mile

Sometimes we have the ability and the resources to go beyond what is good and acceptable in ministry. We can move into that next step of excellence. And why not? I'm thrilled as I walk into facilities where the leaders and their workers have teamed up to do some extraordinary things. I love walking down hallways filled with the scenes and sounds of jungles and animals and fish and worlds beyond. Sometimes that happens when the right people land in your church or it dawns on you how you can use that talent that's already there. Sometimes it happens because we pay to have it done.

> Here's a principle: when people really get excited about their church, they tell their friends and bring them too!

I love it when I find rooms that look like I've arrived at Disneyland. By the way, the kids love it too! It's wonderful to discover beautiful rooms that adults love meeting in for their various ministries. I enjoy walking into youth rooms that look enticing and alive and attractive to young people. Here's the principle: when people really get excited about their church, they tell their friends and bring them too. I've watched it over and over again in churches everywhere.

It was their first Sunday and they were meeting in a school gym. Every church plant is different, so I had no idea what to expect. I didn't know about the quality or size of the leadership team. And no one had any idea how many people would show up the first Sunday. Now, first Sundays are often filled with all kinds of glitches- that's life. No matter how many preview gatherings you do, you can't deal with every detail. Using school classrooms, they had every reason to be frustrated and to get it wrong. But what I saw was amazing! Excellent signage was everywhere. School classrooms were transformed and extensively equipped for children of every age. A marvelous number of happy, eager workers had been recruited. And they were waiting, early, in each room for families to arrive. The rooms looked great and appealing. Hundreds of brand new visitors arrived, and the staff was ready. People loved what they found, and they came back, with their friends. The leadership made the most of their opportunity, and it worked!

I visited yet another church this past Sunday where every room filled with children over the age of three had its own theme with fabulous equipment and lights and stages and happy personnel. I saw thatched huts and strange creatures of every kind. And I'm not just talking about the children! It may sound extravagant and extreme to work that hard at creativity for ministry events. But we want to reach people. We want to help them transform from immature believers into fully devoted disciples of Jesus Christ. If this is one of the hooks that it takes to get them away from their flat screens and weekend alternatives, then let's do it! We are competing with a world that is very creative. It certainly doesn't hurt our spirituality to go the extra mile in creativity. And it makes it interesting and enjoyable for our children as well. If you have a big budget, go for it! If you have a tiny budget, do the very best you can with the talent and resources that God's given you.

Programs

The programs in your church- what you do and how you do what you do- will play a significant role in attracting visitors and keeping them as members of your church family. Programming a church ministry is a big deal. You can do all the wrong things and do them well, but few will come or stay. You can do all the right things with the wrong personnel. You can do too much or too little. All of this is so important. Let's look at some of the basics of programming in the church.

<u>Programming Foundations 101</u>

1) All of your programs need to be done on purpose.

2) If an existing program doesn't match your purpose and direction, it needs to be modified or put to rest.

3) You can't do everything! Focus on a few things and do them well!

4) Programs should exist for the people and not the people for the programs.

---

5) Do too many programs and you'll exhaust your workers! Do too few programs and you'll never gain the habit! The lifestyle simply won't appear!

6) When churches find balance in their programming, their people are able to serve with excitement, energy and excellence!

Programs, Space and Resources

Let's look again at the relationship between our space and our programs. Churches without the right space are handicapped in their ability to do all the things that they'd like to do. And limited ministry will often deter visitors from returning and churches from growing. Space is a big deal. If you have limited resources and space, do a few things and do them well! Some churches look at their limited space and they immediately give up. And they lose. Listen to this! Leaders everywhere have turned impossible situations into opportunities. They've started with what they've had and they've done their very best. They've attracted a crowd and they've moved to the next level. You can't move to the next level if you don't try.

> Leaders everywhere have turned impossible situations into opportunities. They started with what they've had and they've done their very best.

Now, other churches try too hard. They try to do everything at once. They want to be like the big church, but they're the little church. You can't do it all with limited space and resources. You'll burn through your people and your money and you'll end up with nothing. If you want to move to the next level, do a few things and do them well. Look at the space and resources that you have or that you can get. Evaluate what you can do well, with passion, and what people want and need. If it takes everything you have to do a great gathering, then focus on that and do whatever it takes to make that all that it can be. Go for it! Pace yourself. Have a plan that you can succeed at. And then watch the people come.

> It's not a failure to do something that doesn't work. It's a failure if we keep doing it over and over again. And it's a greater failure to not even try!

Having the Right Programs

One of the keys to attracting and keeping visitors is doing the right things. We've looked extensively at hundreds of details that count. Now let's talk about our programming. The activities and events that we do will make all the difference in the world. There are churches that work very hard on their programs and yet no one comes. They come up with good ideas, they plan, they organize and they advertise. Unfortunately, they're the wrong ideas. Nobody's interested in doing what they've planned. Now let's be honest. All of us have planned things that haven't worked. It's not a failure to do something that doesn't work. It's a failure if we keep doing it over and over again. And it's a greater failure to not even try! It's part of God's great plan that we learn from our mistakes. So let's make this commitment together. "I will not be afraid to try many things, but I will try to learn from my mistakes as quickly as possible. I will not be afraid to change it up!"

So how do we learn to do the right things with our programming in our church? First of all, learn to ask lots of questions. And learn to ask the right questions! What do people really want? That's the big question! What needs are really waiting to be met? It seems like some churches specialize in doing things that nobody's asking for! Don't be one of those churches! Start by looking at your own ministries. Which ones are working? Which ones aren't working? Which ones do you have to drag people to? Why aren't they working? Why do you keep doing things that aren't working?

Most people are looking for a church that will meet all of their needs. Of course, that will never happen. But they will often look and look and, then, finally, they'll settle somewhere. It might as well be at your church. Here's my story. When I was a young pastor beginning in a church with 75-100 people, the numbers obviously weren't attractive. We had limited space and resources. We had few programs. We had few leaders. We had very few young people. But we did our best with what we had. We had a great children's ministry. Almost everyone in the church was in a small group. And we did have a good gathering. Most of our people were friendly. We quickly hired a part-time youth pastor so we would be prepared, as families would come to visit.

Now, visitors would say, "We really like your church. If only you were larger, if only you had a larger youth group, if only blah, blah, blah, blah, blah!" I would say, "If only you'd stay, we'd have a bigger church and youth group!" They would leave, but many of those same people came back when our church was much larger. That's when I felt like saying. "Sorry! There's no room in the inn!" Of course, I was a good boy and I kept my mouth shut.

Fortunately, lots of other people did like who we were and what we were offering. They stayed, they brought their friends, and we grow and kept on growing. Doing our best with what we had helped us to move to the next level. And so can you!

Sometimes we keep doing ministries because we don't want to hurt the people running the programs. We certainly don't want to hurt people, but we also don't want to leave them doing something that's going nowhere. We need to be filled with kindness and grace and patience as we walk people through this process. We need to help them see that we love them and we care about what they are doing. We need to help them see how exciting it will be to involve them in a different ministry that will truly be effective. As we go through this process, we've always got to remember that people are more important than programs. The ultimate goal is to have happy people serving effectively in life-changing ministries. We can't settle for anything less.

Other times we keep doing ministries because we've always done them. Like a great sage once said, if the horse is dead, dismount! Don't be held hostage by an ineffective ministry. Evaluate it, fix it, or put it out of its misery. Remember, it's draining your time and resources. It's robbing you of the opportunity of doing the right things with the same people and resources. Don't wait too long. Time is a 'passing!

Now, let's be real. Some people will be hurt. You can't help that. And other people will get angry and will create a storm or quit. It will happen. Guaranteed! Love them. Pray for them. Be as gentle as you can be. Do your best. Be patient. Win hearts and minds. Bring as many people along as you can. But, just remember, not everyone will get on board. Never has happened and it never will! It's always more important to do what's right than to do what we've always done. So make sure it's right, before God, and then do it.

Why don't we talk for a moment about what people need and want? And let's use children's ministry as our example. First of all, parents need childcare. If you want parents to come to your church and if you want them to come back again, you have to provide child-care. Why would any parent ever come back if you didn't provide childcare? Now, not every parent will use that childcare when they first attend your church. They don't trust you. And their children don't trust you. But they're still going to look and see what childcare you are providing for when they do trust you. If they don't think that you will really care for their children, they won't be back. Secondly, children need healthy childcare. They need to feel loved and cared about. They need to feel safe. They're visiting a place that they've never been to before. They need to like it, and they need to want to come back. If they don't want to come back, they'll make that clear to their parents. You can see why it's so important that you create an atmosphere and a program that is attractive both to visiting parents and their children.

Childcare comes in all shapes and sizes. Some churches think that childcare is babysitting. So they either ask for a volunteer or they hire a teenager to babysit any children that show up for the more important ministry, like the Sunday morning service. I've visited too many churches that have forced unhappy teenagers to babysit whenever children show up for the service. It's obvious. As you walk into the church, you'll notice a sad teenager in a side room sitting either alone or with one or two children. I wouldn't want to be that teenager or that child, and I wouldn't bring my child back if I were the parent. If you're going to have childcare, then you're going to need to do better than that.

Other churches think the childcare is children's ministry. They think that children are very important. They want every child that shows up to have an absolutely excellent experience. They want those children to be happy, cared for and stimulated with biblical truth. These churches want those children leaving their ministries excited and anxious to come back next week. So they plan, program and recruit workers with that in mind. What will make that child excited about walking through our door? What will make her so happy and distracted that she forgets all about her parents? What sort of games, songs, activities and environment will make him love this room? How can we help these children learn to like each other and get along as quickly as possible?

How often do we need to change their environment? How many workers do we need to do this ministry effectively? How many rooms do we need to use? What activities can we do outside? How should we use music and drama and puppets and art and recreation and videos with these children? What's the best curriculum and teaching style to help them learn about the character and priorities of Jesus? Now, that's what I'm talking about! That's the kind of thinking that will lead to the right programming. And we can't wait to do all of this after we have loads of children. We've got to think this way and plan this way before they come. And then, they will come, and they'll bring all of their friends.

A young pastor and his wife arrived at their new church. They discovered ministries that were taking place and ministries that needed to be started. Within a short period of time, the pastor's wife was asked her opinion about the current women's ministry. She had discovered that a small group of women gathered one morning a week to crochet, and that was their only women's program. The pastor's wife, knowing that she was new, decided to encourage them and not share her opinion.

A year later, the same women leading the ministry again asked her what she thought of what they were doing. This time, she decided to be honest with them. She shared with them that some of the younger women in the church were showing an interest in Bible study. She asked these leaders what they thought about doing a ladies Bible study one morning a week, either with or instead of crocheting. These elder's wives were so offended by this challenge to their ministry that, within weeks, they had pulled their husbands and

quit the church. Can you believe that? Sometimes speaking the truth comes at a very high price. But not speaking the truth comes at an even higher price!

⟨━━━━━━━━━━━━━━━━━━━━━━━━⟩

So let's look at all of our ministries. What are people really looking for? What do they really need and want? They want to be cared about. They want to be valued. They want to be listened to. They want to make friends. They want to have a good time. They want to feel good when they leave. Don't you? As we assess our ministries and evaluate our plans and programming, we always need to have people in mind. Sometimes we create programs and hope that people will like them. Sometimes we've created programs that we like, but no one else may want them. What do people really want? And, what do visitors really want? Why would they ever come to this ministry or program or event? And why would they ever come back? Those are critical questions that must be answered if we want our programs to truly be effective.

We need to ask lots of questions inside our church, but we also need to ask lots of questions outside the walls of our church building. What are the needs in our specific community? What do single mom's need? What types of activities are parents asking for? What types of children's activities and family activities would visitors be excited about? What programs and events would make young people not only want to come- what would make them want to bring all their friends? What do singles like to do? What do young married couples like to do? Are you offering the programs and activities that are matching their interests and desires? What about seniors? What about men? What about women? Are we doing the same things that we've done for the last fifty years? Then it probably isn't working! How do we know that what we're doing is what people want? Have we asked them? Are visitors coming? And are they bringing their friends? Here's a reality check- if our ministries are growing, people must like them. If they're not growing, probably something is wrong.

Are we willing to implement necessary change? By the way, great programming can often be done off of our church property. Many churches are handicapping their growth potential by restricting most of their programming to their own campus or within the walls of their own buildings.

How, again, do we learn to do the right things with our programming in our church? We need to learn everything we can from others! What are other churches doing? Where have they succeeded? Where have they failed? Most of us have limited time and resources. We don't have the luxury of making too many mistakes. So let's let others make them for us! Some churches work hard and set up good ministries, but they fail within a given period of time. They run out of resources, so they either quit or they keep trying to do the ministry that isn't working. So sad. Let's take the time to learn from other people's mistakes. And let's also find out where those churches are succeeding in our areas of ministry.

> **Most of us have limited time and resources. We don't have the luxury of making too many mistakes. So let's let others make them for us!**

Many of us have churches within our own community that we can learn from. It's always valuable to check around and find out what has worked and hasn't worked in our own local community. There are things that may work here that won't work in another city. And there are things that may work there that won't work here. Now, don't necessarily let someone else's failure keep you from trying a new venture in a particular area of ministry. Another church in town may have tried and failed in a ministry that you'll succeed at simply because you'll do it differently than they did. In other words, listen, learn everything you can, ask God for his wisdom on what to do, and then do it! Don't be afraid to make a call and set up an appointment to check out another church's ministry. Or find out when they're specific ministries are taking place, and go and visit them. Most churches are proud to show you what they're doing.

There are churches all over the country that have become models that we can learn from in our areas of programming and ministry. Their reputations have leaked out! Let's learn everything we can from them. Don't be afraid to drive a few hours. Leaders will fly across the nation to churches like Saddleback Church in Southern California and Willow Creek Church in Chicago to learn everything they can about why these churches have succeeded in their programming. I've personally flown to countless conferences across the country so I could grab as many ideas as possible to take home with me. I've learned and learned and learned in dozens and dozens of churches. I've gained so much simply walking around and asking a lot of questions on Sunday mornings in many churches. Churches and ministries love to put on conferences when they feel that they have really dialed in their area of ministry. There are conferences on women's ministries, men's ministries, singles ministries, couples ministries, youth ministries, children's ministries, senior's ministries, recovery ministries, and the list of conferences goes on and on! All of these conferences offer a wealth of resources. Learn everything you can, and then take the parts that seem most appropriate for what you're trying to accomplish.

You can also find loads of programming material on the Internet. Churches by the thousands are putting their ideas and resources online. Type your ministry name into any search engine and you'll find endless pages of information. You will find that certain pages will pop out like a gold mine! Many larger churches market their ministry programs so other churches can use them as well. Churches all over the country are using children's ministry programs, small group programs, and youth ministry programs that were created by some other church. Isn't it incredible to realize that people all around the world could use your great idea? It's not always necessary nor is it expedient to reinvent the wheel. On the other hand, invent that new wheel if you have the talent and insight. Go for it!

Don't be afraid to buy packaged programming from other churches. It's usually worth spending the money and letting someone else do all the work. Creative individuals and teams have spent literally thousands of hours working on training manuals and curriculum for you and me. Some of that material can be used just the way it is. And some of it needs to be modified to fit your particular church and ministry needs. For example, I've attended many conferences and seminars on small group ministry. I've grabbed the best ideas and material from each of those churches and conferences. Then I've created a strategy and a training manual that has worked best for us. Grab the best and chuck the rest!

Here's one more thought on doing the right programming. Don't be afraid to fail! Some people never succeed because they're too afraid to fail. Can you believe it? Perhaps they've failed before, or they've watched others try and fail. It's like shooting a basket. Some people can, some of us can't and most people are in-between. But we'll never know until we try! Most of us who have been around for a while have tried many programs on the road to finding the right ones that work. We try, we learn, we improve, we change it up, we make it better, or we try something completely different. That's just the way it is! So listen lots, do your homework, assess your opportunities, create your plan and then do it.

Having the Right Personnel

I'm sure it's already clear that it's very essential that you have the right people serving in the right ministries. It's important to have enough people and it's important to have the right people. It's amazing to me that we find so many people serving in the wrong ministries in the church. I think a lot of it has to do with how we recruit. It seems that we often recruit out of desperation. We need our ministry positions filled, so we recruit based more on our needs then on the personalities and spiritual giftedness of those whom we are recruiting. We politely push people to sign up, and many people end up feeling so guilty that they sign up for a ministry that they should never be a part of. They're not equipped for it. They're not gifted for it. It doesn't make them happy and they don't make anyone happy in the ministry either. Now everybody's stuck. They don't know how to get out of the ministry and we don't know how to get them out of the ministry. They'll feel like a failure if they quit, and they'll feel hurt if we make them quit.

There is a way to get the right people doing the right ministries. But it means that we have to start by focusing on our people before we focus on our ministries. We start with an assessment system. We ask all of our people to do a personal assessment of their interests, talents, and spiritual gifts. They do the assessment and we set up interviews to walk them through the results. This helps our people discover the areas of ministry where they would best serve and find the greatest joy. And this helps us discover how to match our people to our ministries! This assessment and interview process can be very eye opening to our people who are serving in the wrong ministry. It can help them see why they're not finding joy serving where they are, and it can help them see other ministry opportunities where they could better serve. A properly trained interviewer can coach people toward appropriate ministries without making them feel guilty or embarrassed.

> **We need to give them an easy way in and an easy way out. We want them to succeed! We want them to love ministry- for life!**

An ongoing church-wide assessment system helps everyone remember that all ministry flows out of the talents and spiritual giftedness that God has created in each of us. If everyone goes through the assessment, everyone knows how he or she can best serve, even if they don't volunteer. The process trumpets the core value that everyone has been created to serve! As new people visit and decide to stay, the assessment process will help them discover how they can best serve in their new church. A live interview can provide a very natural opportunity to let people know about all the different ministry opportunities where people can serve. It can be very exciting as people identify their own interests, talents and giftedness and begin to match them with ministry. Classes are often offered, like SHAPE classes out of Willow Creek. Many online assessments are now available over the Internet. A normal assessment system would notify ministry leaders so they would be able to contact the right people to consider serving in their ministries. Be sure to let people know at the end of your interview process that they will be contacted by ministry leaders so they are not surprised. And then make sure they are contacted!

Some people are simply afraid to do ministry. They've never done it before, or they've had a bad experience. They either weren't properly trained, or they were serving outside of their giftedness and talents. We need to have a process in our churches that allows people to take baby steps when it comes to ministry. We need to train them. We need to give them opportunities to "test drive" different ministries. We need to give them an easy way in and an easy way out. We want them to succeed! We want them to love ministry- for life. If we can coach them and walk them through the right process at the beginning, they'll be our best recruiters to bring others on board.

Programs for ALL?

One of the great temptations that many churches bow to is the pressure to try to do programs for everyone. That's not only impossible; it's not smart. Most churches simply cannot do programs for everyone, and they shouldn't do everyone's program. Many churches will try to do so many different things in ministry that they run out of workers and resources. Think about it. All ministries compete over workers and resources. If there was a never-ending supply of volunteers and money, we could do everything that we want to do. But that isn't reality! All of us are limited in what we can do. It's much smarter to do a few things and do them well than to try to do many things and do some of them poorly.

It's critical that we decide which programs are most important to us. Which programs and ministries will enable us to reach our goals? Of course, this means that we have to be purpose-driven. We have to know where we are going. We have to have a plan. We have to know what we're trying to produce. Many churches don't know where they're going. They're simply doing what they've done for the last 20-40 years. They may be canceling programs because they don't work and adding programs because people want them. But they're not intentional.

> One of the purposes of the local church is to help turn self-serving people into fully devoted disciples of Jesus! Christ.

It's so important that we slow down, step back and evaluate our programming from God's point of view. Are we really accomplishing God's purposes? Dann Spader of Sonlife Ministries has addressed the issue of purposeless programming for years. What was God's original purpose for the church? And are we working together to accomplish that purpose? God commands us to make disciples. Are we making disciples? What do real disciples looked like? As we design our programs, do we actually have goals in mind that come out of biblical core values that we have established? What is the end product that God has in mind for each of the ministries that we have operating in our church? Dann says that one of the purposes of the local church is to help turn self-serving people into fully devoted disciples of Jesus Christ. That means that every believer needs to learn how to reflect the mind, character and priorities of Christ. We need to live it, share it and multiply it! That's what the Christian life is all about.

Now, let's look at our programming. Everything that we do in our church programming needs to be a product of the goals that we've established for our church. And our goals need to flow out of our core values. And our core values need to reflect the heart of God and His purposes. As we evaluate our programming and various ministries, we need to stop doing things that aren't helping us achieve our goals. Again, there's too little time and too few resources to do things that aren't purposeful. We can't do everything. So we've got to decide what ministries and events and activities are really making a difference in the lives of our people and our outreach.

Sometimes we're doing a lot of good things, but we're not focusing on the best things. Sometimes we're just doing too many things. Some churches have to end ministries that aren't doing well to free up room and resources and personnel for new opportunities they are focused on. It has to be done! It needs to be done with grace and love and patience and wisdom, but it needs to be done. Thom Rainer and Eric Geiger, in their book, *Simple Church*, talk about the need for just that- a simple church: simple on purpose, simple on programming, and simple on process.

> You must eliminate nonessential programs, limit adding more programs, reduce special events, and ensure that the process is easy to communicate and simple to understand. Eliminating is simply good stewardship. It matters to God! [63]

It's so important that we look at every area of ministry in our church through the magnifying glass of purpose-driven programming. For example, look at your youth ministry. Is it purposeful? Is it intentional? Do you have a plan? You know where you're going? Are all of the activities and events tied together under a specific strategy? What are you trying to accomplish in your young people? What is the end product? What is your process of moving them from self-centeredness to spiritual maturity? Are your leaders trained and equipped? Do they know where you as a team are going? Do you have a clear plan of what you want to accomplish in those three to four years in the lives of young people coming to your youth ministry? Is there a commitment to balanced programming? Are your young people being built up in knowledge and in character? Are they being equipped to serve and to share? Are they actively involved in outreach personally and corporately? Are some of them being developed into leaders? And, are they having fun? We want our young people to love the Lord, to love our church and to love the kingdom! Youth ministry should be passionate, intentional, purpose-driven and loads of fun!

What about great ministry ideas coming from the congregation? Should we be encouraging our people to do the dreams and ministries that God has put in their hearts? Absolutely! We want all of our people discovering their spiritual gifts and using them along with their talents to serve the Lord. We want to mobilize the body. God has placed ministry dreams in the hearts and minds of our people that we might never think of ourselves. God wants to use us collectively to accomplish His will. There are people with great ideas, people who can engineer the obstacles, those who can organize those ideas, and then people who can work the plan. That's why we need to team up to get the job done. Here's the problem. We can't do everybody's Great idea. We just can't! There certainly aren't enough people and they're clearly aren't enough resources. We also wouldn't be purpose-driven. We would be doing everything that everybody wants us to do and missing what God wants us to do.

We certainly want to encourage people to do the dreams and ministries that God has placed on their hearts. But we also need to realize that there are times that people will dream their own dreams that have nothing to do with God's plan for them! Just because you can dream it doesn't mean that you can or should do it! For example, there are people who want to sing for the Lord. They're passionate about singing for the Lord. Unfortunately, God clearly hasn't given them that talent. And all of us know it! So what do we do? We need to help them discover other areas where they are better able to serve the Lord. There are other people who want to organize a new ministry. But they don't have the gift of organization, and that's evident to all. Then there are people who want to be part of a new ministry. They don't want to start it. They don't want to organize it. But they want to be part of it. And they're determined to get someone else to start it and organize it and lead it so they can be in it. Now, there's a ministry dream that forces other people to do things that they don't really want to do. Examples like this take place all the time in our churches. We could conclude that the conflict isn't worth it. We could decide that it's easier to set up all the ministries ourselves and then encourage everybody to do our ministries. But that would stifle creativity, and it wouldn't allow for God to use other people as part of his creative process.

It seemed that, as the pastor, I always had people coming to me with new ideas for ministry in our church. They had ideas about food pantries and jail ministry and clothing outlets and activities for young moms and the ideas went on and on! I would either sit down with them and listen to their ideas, or I would send them to the pastor or person in charge of a specific area of ministry. Now, most of the ideas were great. But some of them just did not fit with the things that we were trying to accomplish. And almost all of them depended upon someone organizing the plan and recruiting people to do the ministry. If I person-ally was evaluating the idea and it looked like it was good, I would often let them know that there were no leaders available to help them and no money to do their dream. If they were willing to lead, organize and recruit for their own ministry idea, I was willing to release them to go for it. Some people had a good idea, but they wanted me or someone else to make the whole thing happen. Those ideas usually died quickly. But many ideas were organized into highly effective, disciple-making programs that significantly impacted our church!

Many of our most effective ministries were born out of the dreams of ordinary people in our

church and not the leaders. They became the leaders! We had exciting children's ministries and youth ministries and women's ministries and men's ministries and recovery ministries that did not come from the top down. In fact, many of our ministries arrived on the hearts and minds of our visitors! I believe that God actually sent people to us with ministry dreams that He had put on their hearts. And they arrived with the gifts and talents to establish and lead those ministries. One young couple arrived with a passion to start an Awana program. They organized it, recruited their leaders and started this powerful outreach and disciple-making children's ministry. As time went by, that program grew to minister to 400 children a week, served by 80 workers! Children were getting saved and were learning God's Word. And parents were beginning to attend church. Another couple arrived, and the wife had a great idea for a women's outreach program. We released her to organize and recruit for this bimonthly event. Within a short period of time, 40 women were setting these events up and 150 women were showing up. Women found the Lord every time one of these events took place! These are just a few of so many examples of what happens when we release people to do ministry.

Here are some ways to find balance in this arena of personal and corporate ministry. Encourage your people to do their dreams. Fan that flame throughout the church. Encourage everybody to discover and then use the talents and gifts God has given to them. We each have seven days a week during which we can continually serve the Lord. We don't need the church to give us a platform to do our dreams. But we also need to encourage our people to be part of the corporate ministries that God has already put on our hearts. There are so many things that we can do together as a team. Many of the ministries that we have organized in our churches need lots of people to do them well. If we try to do too many things, we won't do as well as we would if we focus on a few good things. If someone does have an idea for a new church ministry or event or activity, bring that idea to the pastor or the person in charge. Talk it through. It may be exactly what God has in mind!

Let's talk one more time about excellence in ministry. Why should our ministries fall short of excellence? In most of our careers, we are expected to do our jobs well. Isn't that true? Many of our jobs call for excellence, or we'll be moved on! When businesses lose their drive for excellence, they also begin to lose their business. Over time, employees become sloppy and less caring about the needs of the customer, and those customers begin to disappear. Businesses that remain excellent, even in difficult times, stay that way because excellence is a core value. Assessment is essential! Employee behavior and customer satisfaction are both guarded and held in high regard. If we expect to have excellence in our secular world, why wouldn't we want to be even more excellent in the kingdom of God? Why not? Look at Whom we represent. But here are the excuses that we use:

1) We have limited personnel.
2) We have limited resources.
3) We have limited space.
4) We have limited energy.
5) We have limited creativity.

That list can go on and on, but these five excuses usually cover them all. Here's the answer to all five excuses:

1) **Stop it!** - Stop making excuses for doing less than your best. Stop feeling sorry that you're not the church down the street. Stop whining and complaining about the church down the street.

Stop trying to compete with the church down the street. You'll never compete. Be yourself!

2) **Do less!** – Do what you can do well. Decide what ministry will look like if you refocus and only do what you can do well.

3) **Do your best!** – Be as creative as you can be with what you have. Do the team thing so you have your best pool of dreamers, analyzers, planners and doers.

So it often seems like we don't want to really work as hard on excellence in our ministry as we do in our secular work. The pay and benefits, of course, aren't the same, for now. We often spend and expend ourselves in our careers and have leftovers for ministry. Maybe we need to remind ourselves why we're doing ministry in the first place. If we could see the incredible, eternal value coming out of effective, purposeful ministry, I believe it would change everything!

Every ministry proposal must be run through the grid of purpose-driven thinking. Does this idea fit within our purposes? Does it help us achieve our goals? Will it help us do a better job of making disciples or caring for the body or reaching lost people for Christ? Who would create the plan? Who would oversee this ministry? How much will it cost? How many people will it involve? Does this really serve the purposes that God has placed before us? These are just a few of many questions that need to be asked before we add a new ministry to the things that we are already doing.

Let's take another moment to talk about all of the ministries that we already have established in our church. I hope that it's clear that they too must be run through the grid of purpose-driven thinking. Let's not skip that. Why are we doing the ministries that we are doing? Are they accomplishing the goals that we have established? If not, then we either need to fix them or drop them. Personally, I would much rather fix the ministry and make it better than end it. But sometimes you have to do what you have to do.

Jim Collins, in his book, "Good to Great", talks about the qualities that are essential in businesses that choose to excel. One of those qualities is having the tenacity to bring about appropriate change, no matter how difficult that is. Collins talks about the willingness to do brutally honest evaluations of our current areas of service in order to accomplish the goals that we want to achieve. [64] That sort of thinking is essential in our churches if we want to be all that God wants us to be! So let's look honestly at ourselves. Let's look at the effectiveness of our ministries. Let's look at them inside and out. Let's not be afraid to discover weaknesses. Let's ask the hard questions. Let's be sure to assess our commitment to excellence in each part of our ministry model. Let's come up with reasonable solutions to the issues that we discover. And let's work together to make our ministries the very best that they can be!

We've done a sweeping overview of programming in your church. I hope that it has stirred up lots of questions, ideas and forward thinking. I will want you to take the time to look at all the details of your particular ministry. But let's wait until we get through the next two chapters. In chapter 11, we'll talk about our commitment as a leadership team to the same end product in our disciplemaking strategies. And in chapter 12, we'll see how critical an outreach mindset and plan is in every one of our ministries. Then we'll have a holistic picture against which we can clearly assess where we are and where we want to be.

Notes

THOUGHTS ON CHANGE

For changes to be of any true value, they've got to be lasting and consistent.
Tony Robbins

We live in a moment of history where change is so speeded up that we begin to see the present only when it is already disappearing.
R. D. Laing

Change, like sunshine, can be a friend or a foe, a blessing or a curse, a dawn or a dusk.
William Arthur Ward

11. The Roadmap to Maturity- The Disciplemaking Process from 0 to 100!

We've spent a great deal of time looking at all of the technical details that will help us do well in our various ministries. It's critical that we dial in the detail! If we don't, our lack of care will certainly come around to bite us. When details aren't taken care of, they become distractions to visitors that have to be overcome. Why lose visitors or waste energy making up for distractions when you don't have to. But now, let's talk about our End Product. We've finally arrived at the Main Thing. The Big Idea!

There always is an **END PRODUCT**,
whether it's a good one or a bad one.

And if we don't do the right things, it will be a bad product- guaranteed.

Here's a God thought.
We want to be disciples who make disciples.

That **Is His** End Product!

And the **right** Biblical core values set us up for the
Journey toward that **correct** End Product.

Now, if that is God's will, then we can't be content with any-thing less! Why do you think many churches and pastors end up maintaining and sustaining programs that aren't achieving targeted end-goals and end products? I believe that most of us as pastors arrive at our churches with vision and values and a desire to make disciples. But I think that, over time, many of us get tired of trying and running up against walls, and we either get burned out or we give up, or both. And we end up going nowhere. But if we don't keep our focus on God's End Product, then we might as well pack our bags, quit, or shut it down. That **is** what we are here for. There is no other purpose! So we begin with a Biblical set of core values that we will not surrender. We establish our vision and mission based on those core values. We then develop the right purposes and objectives, which in turn lead to the right plan and goals. That's the way we reach God's End Product!

The Right Core Values		The Right Vision & Mission		The Right Purposes & Objectives		The Right Goals & Plans		**The Right End-Product**
	→		→		→		→	

We've already said that we want to help turn self-serving people into fully devoted disciples of Jesus Christ. We want to help every believer, in every age group and ministry, learn how to reflect the mind, character and priorities of Christ. That's our ultimate goal. So where do we begin? There's got to be a plan. There has to be a general church-wide plan, and there's also got to be a plan in every ministry department. Let's begin by talking about the process.

The Disciple-Making Process

Visitors arrive as a hundred different packages, of every shape, size and variation. You have younger and older visitors, and you have younger believers, older believers and seekers. You have junior-highers and single moms, widowers and women in recovery. You have visitors who are apprehensive and visitors who are eager and hungry for truth. And you somehow have to meet each of them just where they are. They won't fit into one mold. We realize that. But it would be helpful if we had one common plan for the whole church that then diversifies into each of our segment groups. It's important that all of us are on the same page and have the same goals and process in mind.

Every church has to establish its own set of goals in the disciple-making process. What are we trying to accomplish in the lives of our visitors and our own people? What are the bigger goals? And what are the details that will help us accomplish each of those goals? Many churches will borrow ideas and process concepts from each other or from national ministries as they work on their vision, values and goals. For example, Dann Spader helps churches establish the process of building up believers, equipping workers, winning the lost, multiplying and sending leaders. Rick Warren helps churches see the need to walk people through the process of learning to worship God, connect with His people, become disciples, serve, and evangelize the lost. Bill Hybels talks about focusing on the purposes of exaltation, evangelism, edification and extension in each of our lives. Many churches take one of these examples of our purposes and they establish an entire process that they use to walk people to maturity in Christ. It doesn't matter if you borrow one or create your own. You need a plan that you can enact in the life of every person who walks through your doors.

As a senior pastor, I attended an endless number of training events and seminars across the country from which I grabbed concepts in programming and disciplemaking. I learned and contextualized and applied so many great ideas that I picked up from others. I also created many systems of my own along the way. But why reinvent the wheel? If it works, use it. If it needs to be changed up to work in your own setting, change it up!

Here's an example of a perfect marriage of ideas. I was passionate about evangelism and disciplemaking. We had already established many productive systems for training and ministry through the years. But my youth pastors pushed me to attend Sonlife's training events. I was reluctant to go because I felt it would be the same thing that I was already doing. The fact is, it was. But adding

the Sonlife training and strategies to our ministry, it significantly moved us to a whole new level of transforming lives and multiplying disciples. That investment of time and resources radically impacted our church!

So your plan needs to be created, clarified and mapped out in a way that everyone understands where you are going. It needs to be so clear that everyone knows what the process is and what needs to be done to help people walk through that process. Did you hear that? Let me repeat myself. **Your plan needs to be so clear to everyone that they know what the process is and then what needs to be done to help people walk through that process.** They need to know the pathway. How will we walk this seeker through a process to faith in Jesus Christ? And then, how will we help him learn what it means to be a practicing disciple? How will we set her up with a disciplemaker? How will we help them grow in their knowledge of God's Word and His principles for living? How will we get them meaningfully and purposefully connected with other believers in the body? Will we help them get adopted by a small group? How will we help them discover the joy of serving and the joy of giving? And what about learning to reach out to their friends? What's our plan to teach them about lifestyle evangelism? So do **you** have a plan? Have you put it on paper? Is it clear? Do all of your leaders agree, understand and own it? If not, you have work to do!

Disciplemaking in North America

Disciplemaking isn't a new topic that's just arrived on the scene. It's been written about, taught and practiced around the globe since Jesus' day. And we can find an endless flow of books on the subject for centuries that have significantly impacted our continent. Think of the influence of John Wesley and his disciplemaking movement and strategies from three hundred years ago! Go back to the spiritual movement of the nineteenth and early twentieth centuries and you'll see a passion to make disciples who grow and go. Think back on the challenges toward a disciplemaking life from men and women like Dwight L. Moody, Martin Lloyd Jones, A.B. Simpson, A.W.Tozer, Henrietta Mears, and C.S. Lewis, to just name a few. And we can't ignore the great work arriving from a young, thirty-one year old pastor by the name of Bonheoffer: *The Cost of Discipleship*. [65] You can find hundreds of books written on the subject during the last fifty years. At the same time, Dawson Trotman, transformed by disciplemaking in his own life, began to impact others through a 2nd Timothy 2:2 strategy. Discipling adults and young people around him, a movement began sweeping the nation. At the same time, Dawson discipled a sailor, who discipled a sailor, who discipled a sailor. By the end of World War II, thousands of men on ships and bases around the world had been discipled. What an amazing story! The Navigators has continued to wave the banner of multiplying disciplemakers all around the world, writing loads of books and manuals on the subject. In the early 70's, Dwight Pentecost, a professor and prolific writer, addressed the urgent need of his day. In his foreword, Pentecost wrote these words in his book, *Design for Discipleship*: "The subject of Discipleship is frequently discussed today. Men are called to become disciples without any definition of the concept, and without any clarification of the requirements the Lord makes of those who are His disciples. Hence no intelligent decision can be made concerning this important question. Discipleship is frequently equated with salvation and often erroneously made a condition for becoming a Christian." [66] In 1974, Robert Coleman wrote *The Master Plan of Evangelism*. That simple, single book has influenced so many leaders, pastors, writers, believers and movements. Dan Spader took the principles from Coleman's book and began a movement called Sonlife. Its Christ-centered and Christ-modeled principles and strategies have influenced tens of thousands of youth and lead pastors.

Disciplemaking content has overflowed throughout the last fifty years in North America. Local churches have written manuals and hosted conferences. Denominations have created and then encouraged complete disciplemaking strategies. Thousands of churches have taught disciplemaking classes and tried so many discipleship strategies. There's been a noticeable increase in the number of books on the subject since the beginning of this new millennium. It seems like an intensity is building, like a fresh wave. It could be the latest thing, the newest fad for Christian communicators. But I believe it's actually happening because God Himself is trying so patiently to get our attention. The urgency is so great. He's shouting louder and louder! It's now or never! This is the day! This is the Moment!

Our Problem

Here's the problem- we're not making disciples! We're barely making believers! We're a fast-paced, easily distracted people, both as sheep and as shepherds, constantly looking for easy successes and quick fixes. Isn't that right? We lecture people and expect them to change. We train them and expect them to go. We move them into classrooms or homes and through a process of learning content, and we expect them to get it, grow and actually become disciples. They don't and they won't. It hasn't happened and it won't happen. Not that way! They listen and learn a little. A few will respond, without much help. But the rest really do need help or they won't ever grow up. And, as time passes, pastors move on, or people move, or programs die. And so does passion! The vision for disciplemaking hasn't been widespread. We've been more focused on Christian education than Christian transformation. Education is so much easier for all of us. We've largely left it up to the student to grow or not to grow. There's been limited accountability. There's been little emphasis on self-leadership. Making disciples has aimed at knowledge and perhaps character, but it's missed the entire command to multiply- go and make disciples! Most believers in North America aren't obeying God's command to make disciples. Most leaders aren't and most pastors aren't either.

Most believers have no idea what a real disciple is! In fact, many of us will debate over the definition of a disciple or what it means to make a disciple. Francis Chan and Mark Beuving address the issue in their book, *Multiply*. "If you were to ask individual Christians today what it means to make disciples, you would likely get jumbled thoughts, ambiguous answers, and probably even some blank stares. In all our activity as Christians and with all our resources in the church, we are in danger of practically ignoring the commission of Christ. We view evangelism as a dreaded topic, we reduce disciple-ship to a canned program, and so many in the church end up sidelined in a spectator mentality that delegates disciple making to pastors and professionals, ministers and missionaries." [67] That's a **Big** problem. Our solution isn't simply changing the programming in our church. We're talking about a complete reprogramming of everything- the way we think and what we do. Think about it! He commanded us to go and make disciples and to make disciples who Go! We're not doing very well at being disciples, we're not doing well at making disciples, and we're certainly not making disciples who Go. While we've worked hard at educating believers and perfecting our do's and don'ts, we've missed the mark on the most important things. We've forgotten why we are here. We've forgotten what He died for. Jesus didn't die so we could build great buildings filled with well-educated believers and feel happy about our accomplishments. **He died to set us free so we could spend a lifetime setting as many other people free as possible!** He died and rose again to start a movement that would radically impact and change the world. Unfortunately, as we've moved to aggressively change the rest of the world, the church has fallen asleep on our own continent.

Let's be honest. How many believers do you know who are making disciples who go? Most of our church-based disciple-making programs are making believers who know, not disciples to go. How many of our disciples are truly making other disciples? Francis and Mark go on to say: "So what does disciple-making look like? We have to be careful about how we answer this question. For some of us, our church experience has been so focused on pro-grams that we immediately think about Jesus's command to make disciples in programmatic terms. We expect our church leaders to create some sort of disciple-maker campaign where we sign up, commit to participating for a few months, and then get to cross the Great Commission off our list. But making disciples is far more than a program. It is the mission of our lives. It defines us. A disciple is a disciple maker." [68] An authentic, developing disciple reflects the mind, the character and the priorities of Christ more and more as he or she grows up. Certainly, we're growing believers in their knowledge and practice through our growth–level programs in our church. But it's obvious that most of them are not coming out the other side living out the character and priorities of Christ. We don't see our congregations filled with life–style evangelists and disciple-makers. Isn't that true? Just look at the numbers. We're failing with the majority of our people. Ervin McManus, in *An Unstoppable Force*, writes this: "We made a mistake of making heroes out of those who were simply living a normal Christian life. . .It is not the extraordinary standard but the minimum standard that is the critical boundary in shaping a culture. To unleash an apostolic ethos, it is essential to establish a radical minimum. It is essential to call people to a radical minimum standard. It's easy to confuse the minimum with the extraordinary. . . . We keep lowering the bar until we clear it." [69] It's so sad, but it's true! And what happens next? Dietrich Bonhoeffer penned these startling words in his classic work, *The Cost Of Discipleship:* "Christianity without discipleship is always Christianity without Christ." [70] That's what happens next.

Several years ago, I attended an event where Dan Spader of Sonlife Classic launched "Live 2:6", a new disciple–making leadership product for the church. [71] In his day with us, Dan spoke about years of disciplemaking training with thousands of men and women all around the world. As he shared story after story, he told us about a leadership training event that he had just taught in India. Dan detailed the list of requirements necessary to attend that particular training. One requirement was that the attenders had to have already made four generations of disciples. **Four generations!** And six hundred Indian men and women came to the training. I almost fell over. What an amazing thought! Imagine strategically discipling someone with an actual plan that they would do the same thing. And imagine purposefully parenting that process out four or five or even more generations. I think that's almost unheard of in our part of the world. It's revolutionary. And it's right! Why wouldn't we love our disciples and their purposeful multiplication so much that we would want to help them do it too? John Piper points back to the Word as he looks at the same issue in the book, *Finish the Mission:*

> This sounds like what Paul is getting at in 2 Timothy 2:2, when he instructs his disciple Timothy: "What you have heard from me in the presence of many witnesses entrust to faithful men who will be able to teach others also." "Timothy, my disciple, disciple others to disciple others." Four spiritual generations get explicit mention here: Paul, Timothy, "faithful men," and "others also"- with the implication that further generations are to follow. Discipling, seen in this light, means not merely the pursuit of our own spiritual maturity but getting outside ourselves for personal connection and substantial, intentional investment of time in a few others—the kind of investment for which there must be going to accomplish among the nations. [72]

> Why would anyone want our religion and its rules without its life-changing power?

People all around us are applying this principle of multiplication every day- to make money. It's called Multi–Level Marketing. The only way that they can ensure that they will actually make money is to carefully build structures of buyers- for seven generations. And they do work hard at it. Our churches are filled with people who have tried multi–level marketing. You may be one of them. Here's the question. Why wouldn't we care even more about strong, healthy multiplication in the kingdom of God? It just makes sense! I do think that most of us have never thought about it. I know the

Navigators have been pressing this for years. But obviously, most of us haven't adopted this mindset or we would have a completely different church here in North America. When we have been making disciples, it's been far more random, and multiplication has generally been providential and not planned. Why not grab onto this biblical concept with all our hearts and begin fathering movements to change our churches, communities and our world? Why not?

In reality, we're seeing more people leaving the "Christian" faith than there are people coming to the faith across our land. Our gospel has become impotent, as it's lost the support of our lifestyles. Why would anyone want our religion and its rules without its life-changing power? Now, we know it still has its power. We see it everywhere. But with the majority of believers not truly living out their Christianity the way that God intended it to be lived out, you can see why people aren't flocking to church today.

So when we talk about the disciple-making process and what needs to change, this is when our subject becomes radical. In so many ways, everything needs to change- the way we think, the way we lead, the way we process and what we do. Many churches change a few things and expect different results. If we really want to reach people for Christ in this 21st century, and if we want our churches filled with fully devoted, multiplying disciples, we'll have to do radical remodeling. Mike Breen, in *Building a Discipling Culture*, says: "Effective discipleship builds the church, not the other way around. We need to understand the church as the effect of discipleship and not the cause. If you set out to build the church, there is no guarantee you will make disciples. It is far more likely that you will create consumers who depend on the spiritual services that religious professionals provide." [73] As we go through this chapter, carefully think through what you're doing now in each of these areas. Then begin to think through what will need to change to bring your church into alignment with God's strategy.

Entry Points and the Pathway

Every disciplemaking process has to clearly mark out the pathway and then provide entry points along the path. Gary McIntosh, in his book, *Beyond the First Visit*, says: "Pathways of belonging are strategically designed ministries that assist new people in gaining a sense of being part of the church. . .Recognizing that people are living without salvation in Jesus Christ and outside the church, we want to help them walk along a pathway that leads to Christ. The pathway began when they first became aware of your church, which led to their initial visit, then to their feeling well served through your various ministries and finally to their involvement in your church. . .Effective churches spend more time caring about others than for themselves." [74] That's a key point. The entire focus of the church has to shift to a greater care for getting others onto this pathway than a care for personal comfort and satisfaction. As you, as a church family, become passionate about getting everyone on the road to disciplemaking, a new purpose and excitement will develop throughout the church. Let's look at your entry points- doors through which people can begin their process of discipleship. You need entry points for all of your visitors and you need entry points for the rest of your attenders. You need clearly identifiable entry points for seekers, young believers, growing believers and mature believers. Some people will begin because you've taken them by the hand and walked them through that door. Some people will walk in with their friends. Others will come in their own time, but they need to see where that door is when they are ready. Entry points can be identified during a service or ministry, on a brochure or a bulletin, or on a flyer, letter or email sent out to visitors or regulars.

We've already talked about all kinds of entry points. Let's review a few of them- a visitors' dessert, a new attenders' class or picnic, a new believers' or new members' class, a small group or segment group or a class social, a visitors' night at a recovery ministry or a youth group event or a children's party. Opportunities like these can then be used to help people both map out their next step and the rest of their journey. We want people to clearly see what they need to do next. And we also want them to see what it involves to grow in the Lord. So these events are simply the catalysts that provide the way to share the next steps. We share the process of discipleship. We hand out maps. These brochures or flyers should give the big picture as well as the segment ministries that are being presented. The point is, there have to be initial and on-going ways that people can either walk into or be invited into the process of growing as a disciple. It has to be simple. It has to be understandable.

So take a look at your disciplemaking process. How have you succeeded with your entry points? Look at your church as a whole. How do you draw your visitor or regulars into entry points? Do you have a system? Do you send out letters or emails or flyers? Is it your goal to get all of your visitors and regulars to our various entry points so they can see their own need to go through the process? Are you achieving your goals? How do you know? If not, what do you need to do to improve your plan? Do your people know how to walk their friends through the process of becoming a maturing disciple? Do you have people assigned to oversee each of these objectives in each of your segment groups? How do you assess their process and progress? Is there a church-wide strategy where leaders come together for accountability and focus together on this critical effort?

Look at some individual segment groups. What are your entry points for seeking adults and seeking young people? What about new believers of various ages? Do your people clearly see and understand those entry points? What about your entry point for someone transferring from another church? How do they discover where they are on the journey and where you think they need to go next? What about entry points for people who've been attending for years but they desperately need to be part of a process? Do you approach them or do you wait for them to show interest? You may wait a lifetime! How aggressive will you be to help people walk though one of your entry points? What will you do? These are a few of the questions you need to ask yourselves as you assess and plan for effective disciplemaking.

Growth Level Plans

The next thing we have to look at is the actual plan that we have in place to grow our people and make disciples. We can set up a very effective entry plan for people of all kinds, but what do we have waiting for them on the other side of **Door Number One**? Sometimes our worst nightmare is what we've already got established for spiritual growth in our churches. Some of us haven't put a great deal of thought into why we do what we do in areas of ministry like Sunday School or other teaching or training opportunities. We have programs operating that have been going for decades.

> If we want people who are truly growing in their understanding of God's Word and learning to live like Jesus lived, we've got to have a plan that takes them there.

They may have been effective years ago, but they're not doing anything of significant value today! Some of us have a smorgasbord of ministries, activities and events for our people. But there's no overall strategy or plan on how they work together. For example, I've seen churches with three or four great childrens' ministries, all functioning quite well, but with no unifying focus or cohesive plan. Are they competing or complementing each other? Are they working together to accomplish an intentional set of goals? Or are they simply doing their own thing? These issues must be addressed if we want to accomplish more than simply doing programs and filling rooms and being busy. There's got to be a better reason.

Please don't presume that what you are doing is effective. Willow Creek Community Church landed on the map as one of the pivotal centers of innovation and church leadership expertise for the North American church. Yet, in studies of the last ten years, found in their books, *Reveal and Move*[75], their leaders declared that their ministry process was creating more attenders than disciples! Their surveys proved that busyness and activity at church weren't creating spiritual growth and maturity. They concluded that the only way to actually help believers grow up spiritually is to walk them through a process that will lead them to becoming Christ-centered. Now, that's discipleship! That's what we're talking about! And if Willow Creek can admit that they have been missing their target, we would be pretty foolish not to assess ourselves to see what our own End Product is. So step back. Start by brainstorming over what you really need in each of your segment groups to effectively make fully devoted disciples. Don't worry about the programs that you already have. Evaluate them later. As you begin to dream together, set your mind on the End Product. If we want people who are truly growing in their understanding of God's Word and learning to live like Jesus lived, we've got to have a plan that takes them there. You'll have to look at each segment group separately. What you do with your children and young people will be completely different from what you do with your adults. But you'll have the same goal.

It's great to be able to tell you that Willow Creek has come up with an excellent conclusion to years of extensive research. In the book, *Move*, they share, again, that the key is the right leaders doing the right things! The four practices that are successfully leading people to spiritual maturity are these. 1) They get people actually moving toward a Christ-centered life. 2) They embed the Bible in everything. They breathe the scripture. 3) They create ownership-congregants don't just belong to church: they are the church. 4) As a church, they pastor their community. They serve their community. They jump in and get involved. [76] Buy the book. It has great insight.

By the way, there are churches all across our continent that are really working on this issue of disciplemaking. George Barna, in his research, crossed the nation and found many churches that were actually making disciples. In his book, *Growing Healthy Disciples*, he says, ". . .we quickly learned that a church engaged in effective disciplemaking is a church that will grow steadily and solidly." [77] So we won't sacrifice growth in our churches if we're really about making disciples who make disciples. In fact, many of us will see our churches actually start to grow. That's good news!

As we return to assess our own ministry, we need to look at how much time we have to work with each group and what we need to do with that time. For example, depending on your school system, you have two years with juniors, two years with junior-highers, and four years with high-schoolers. The leaders over each of these segment groups must decide what they want to accomplish in their limited time. And they also need to work together, complementing each other. They need to plan what they will build into these kids and young people. Let's look at an example. The junior high leadership needs to know what's been poured into the juniors. What doctrine, what character principles, what Bible history, and what practical lifestyle issues have been addressed and how were they taught and instilled in these children? Then there needs to be some sort of partnered handoff between departments so no one gets dropped and continuity continues in this critical process of making disciples.

> Disciplemaking is far more than presenting truth. It's about forming hearts and minds and changing lives!

Each ministry needs to build on the foundations that have been already laid. It's not enough to simply buy the easiest Sunday School curriculum to teach in a class. It's even worse to throw together a half-baked lesson plan the night before a class meets. Where are we going? Where do we want to take these young people or children? What Biblical topics and issues do we want to cover with this particular age group? How many hours and settings a month will it take to accomplish our goals over these next few years? Will we meet on Sunday morning or add a weeknight or Saturday morning? Do we need some sort of smaller group setting? What about one-on-one training? And will we need other activities or events to complement the training that we're doing? What will it take to get the job done? If that's what it takes, that's what we have to aim for.

Here are some even bigger ideas as we think through the various ministries in our church. Let's say that you either create or find the right curriculum to use within your specific ministry. You may present it, but will anyone really listen and learn and apply those truths to their lives? Disciplemaking is far more than presenting truth. It's about forming hearts and minds and changing lives. I'm afraid that we often end up succumbing to the easiest possible method of making disciples, and then we wonder why it doesn't work. If we want someone to truly understand the truth, we have to present the truth, we have to dialogue with them personally to see if they understand it, and we need to walk them through to practical application. That's the truth! That, of course, takes time and commitment. That means that the teachers and workers involved in each ministry are disciples committed to the process of making disciples. They personally have to get it! They have to realize that the goal isn't to do a good lesson or to have a great program. And the goal isn't to fill minds with as much information as possible. The goal is to bring on-going transformation to every individual person in that room. This also means that what you have been doing may not work anymore. You may have to add small groups, more meetings or one-on-one discussions to achieve your goals.

We're discovering all around the world that classroom and curriculum-driven learning isn't working like it used to. Or at least we thought it used to. So many in our world today still don't know how to read or write. The only way to teach them is through stories and oral learning. And much of our post-modern world also prefers to learn through story. Out goes traditional methodology and in comes a whole new opportunity to reach, teach and disciple people, here and all around the world. It takes us back to Biblical times. And it forces us to rely less on the number count in a room and far more on what we are actually developing in the lives of those we are passing the story on to. Do they really understand? Can they pass it on to others with clarity? And are they living it out for everyone to see? That's the greatest story!

I believe this kind of thinking changes everything! Our purpose now focuses on truly making maturing disciples, and that purpose now guides how we plan and whom we recruit and why we do what we do. In "normal" settings, we set up a program, recruit willing workers, do the curriculum, work our plan, and clap if everything goes well. And everything goes well if we reach our numbers and everyone's happy. **But we usually aren't making real disciples!** We may be providing Christian education, but is anyone really listening and learning and applying truth?

Making Authentic Disciples

If we really want to make disciples, we have to build our entire church programming around that goal. We create or find curriculum that will aid these goals. We recruit workers who actually see their role as disciple makers. Worker training focuses as much on being disciples and making disciples as it does on technique and quality in teaching and programming. The quality of the programming and the numbers reached are important. But the goal, at the end of the day, is to make sure that each individual really gets it and wants to live it. Ultimately, we're using our programs to change and shape lives. When the programs disappear or when people move, and they will, we want lives that will continue to reflect the life of Jesus.

Imagine this. Our workers take personal ownership in the process of making disciples of those under their charge! They eagerly invest time and prayer and resources with that end goal in mind. Picture a junior high ministry worker adopting five students in her small group for two years like they are her own. Envision her getting to know their families and taking the girls, one-on-one, out to McDonalds, earning the right to go deeper into their lives. Picture her caring dearly that each of these girls grows stronger and stronger in the Lord and clearly understands what it means to be a true follower of Christ. That discipling relationship might be so wonderful and powerful and effective that our worker decides to move right on up into the high school ministry with her five students. Now, **that** would be a completely different paradigm from what we're often used to. It would necessitate a whole new approach in recruiting. So what? Are we looking for effectiveness or the same-old same-old? That's what I'm talking about!

Disciplemaking Basics

In order to create authentic disciples in our ministry programs, we have to build a strong foundation with these three components:

1) The Right Content
2) The Right Delivery System
3) The Right People Modeling Leadership

The Right Content

Let's talk some more about what we want to teach and develop in our people in order to build authentic disciples in our ministries. First, we have to decide what ingredients we need to put in to get the right End Product out. What is the content of our disciplemaking? What are the subjects that every disciple needs to master? What topics are essential for every Christian? Either create that list or find a source that will help you with that content.

Next, we need to decide how deep we want to go and how long we want to take to cover that material. Do we want to create a system that moves people through a process every four years? Do we want a one-year rotation for basics? Will people have to wait for two or four more years to get the same content if they miss a class, or will classes be offered more often? What about advanced learning? We're building disciples who are brand new Christians. We're working with ones who've been around for a while, but they haven't really grown up in their character and lifestyle. So we provide baby food and then the foundations of our faith. But what about helping our people who need to be taken into deeper levels of understanding in Biblical truth and practical application? Will we create several different tracks to work with different levels of learning and maturity? Doesn't that just make sense? For example, a sermon or an hour in a class on spiritual warfare will provide the basics for believers. But what's the next step? Where will they get advanced training on how to really stand against the Enemy? Those questions have to be answered! By the way, here are some of the topics that I personally think everyone needs to understand and apply to their lives.

Key Topics for Spiritual Growth- Basic and Advanced

Who we are in Christ

Assurance of Salvation

Worship and Dependence

First Steps- Baptism, Church, . . .

The Bible and How to Read It

The Purpose and Power of Prayer

Spirit-Filled Living and the Flesh

Spiritual Disciplines

Holiness and Purity

A Lifestyle of Evangelism

Dependence on God

Financial Stewardship and Giving

Christian Values

Christian Character

Spiritual Gifts

Spiritual Fruit

Spiritual Discernment

Discovering the Will of God

Spiritual Warfare

Biblical Foundations

   -Doctrine and History

   -Lifestyle- ex: Compassion- The Least. . .

The Family-Loving One Another	-Issues- ex: Abortion, Homosexuality. . .
Obedience and Christian Living	-Relationships- ex: Marriage, Family. . .
Stewards of our Resources	World Evangelism
Service and Servanthood	Modeling and Leadership
Equipping Others	Discipling Others for Multiplication

It's important to be aware that most people arriving to your church know little to nothing about many of the topics that I've listed. And what they have been taught may be the opposite of what the Bible teaches. How and when will your new believers and other visitors learn these critical and foundational concepts for living? Again, how will your children, young people, and young adults go through this process of discipleship? Finding answers to these questions is truly critical!

Don't assume that many will be mature enough or motivated to move through this journey on their own. In fact, left on their own, most believers will stay in diapers for decades! And your church will suffer because of it. How has that worked so far? Most of us are overdue for significant change. How will you help your people go through this process toward spiritual maturity? And how will you help them catch up if they have missed important Biblical truths along the way? How can you motivate them to take the ride? What's the plan?

Let's Count the Ways!

Look at our actual process of making disciples. Will our process be content and classroom-driven? And is that effective in your culture? We don't want to do what's easiest, and we don't want to do what we've always done. We want to do what's most effective in bringing life transformation, don't we? So here's a thought: Jesus' model for making disciples was first relationship-driven and then content-driven. Over time, He identified people who were after more. He built a relationship with each of them. His technique was to walk with them and then talk with them about the subjects that were on His heart. He perhaps taught more from His life than from His words! He often would use the circumstances of the moment to centerpiece His teaching and application. Yes, He would sit and teach groups of all sizes. But, as He was taking His actual disciples deeper, He would meet with them in small groups and one-on-one. They would go for long walks, field trips, weekend and all-week campouts and retreats. This was truly life-on-life disciplemaking, and look at the results. Now, Jesus was the Master Disciplemaker. Wouldn't it make sense that we learn from His process and try our best to apply it to our own circumstances?

It seems to me that we need all kinds of ways to work with our people to turn them into genuine disciples. We need the weekly gathering with its life and energy and modeling and its sermon. We need some classroom-like settings and small groups, and we clearly need one-on-one disciplemakers. Again, the goal isn't to get everyone through a program or a set of classes. That hasn't proven to do a whole lot for the church. Our goal is to help our visitors and our people become fully devoted disciples of Jesus! That goal demands an entirely different way of looking at this process.

> The real secret is unwrapping the value and purpose for becoming a genuine, knowledge-able, practicing disciple of Jesus.

We've said that there are three components that we need to create our disciple-making strategy. We need the right content, we need the right delivery system and we need the right people to help us make disciples. Excellent training and teaching material is everywhere. Buy it, borrow it or write it, but it's perhaps the easiest

338

piece of this pie. The major decisions need to be made around having the right delivery system that will work in your church and then having the right people to do the discipling. Let's look at some examples. Many churches have given up on what we used to call the "Sunday School" hour. You may not have heard of that. But it's still there! Loads of people will still come to an event alongside the gathering if it's worth it. I see it happening everywhere. I believe adult Sunday School died from boredom! Many of our churches were simply plugging in teachers and providing classes with little sense of purpose or reason. People won't do that anymore. Our time is too valuable. Most of us won't just attend something because it's there. But almost all of us do attend something if we think it's important to us. The real secret is unwrapping the value and purpose **for** becoming a genuine, knowledgeable, practicing disciple of Jesus. That's the real issue here!

Before I move on, let's look at some sources for good content that you can dig through. By the way, be sure to look at the excellent books that I've been quoting from throughout this book. Here are just a few helpful resources for disciplemaking.

Books on Disciplemaking

The Master Plan of Evangelism by Robert Coleman

The Lost Art of Disciple Making by Leroy Eims

Personal Disciplemaking by Christopher Adsit

Books, Workbooks and Websites as Resources to Make Disciples

Basics-

JesusWalk.com/beginning

Core Discipleship- coregroups.com

Discipleship Tools- discipleshiptools.org

Group- *The Growing Others* Series

NavPress-The Navigator's 2:7 Series

Multiplication Ministries International- One-on-One Discipleship

Advanced-

Not a Fan by Kyle Idleman

Multiply by Francis Chan & Mark Beuving

Real Life Discipleship Training Manual by Willis, Putnam, Krause and Guindon

Discipleship Essentials by Greg Ogden

Disciplemaking Content on the Internet

Weare3DM.com- Multiplying Missional Leaders

Verge.com

LifewayResources.com- ex.: LifeSpan- A Lifelong Plan for Spiritual Transformation

Pastors.com

The Orange Conference.com

David C. Cook- tru.davidccook.com- Discipleship

Navpress.com-Discipleship Inside Out, Discipleship Journal, Real-life Discipleship

IVPChurchlink.com- Discipleship

Small Group Ministry Resources

Small Group- *Growing Out* Series- Group

Christianity Today- smallgroups.com

Willow Creek Resources willowcreek.com

Lifeway- Adult Small Group Resources

General Church Ministry Resources

ChurchLeaders.com

Outreach Magazine

Church Source- Zondervan.com

Church Ministry Resource Catalog- Group group.com

Building Church Leaders- Christianity Today- building-churchleaders.com

Ministry Today- ministrytodaymag.com

Church Leaders- Churchleaders.com

Relevant Magazine- relevantmagazine.com

Church Volunteer Central by Group- churchvolunteercentral.com

Children's Ministry Magazine by Group- childrensministry.com

Youth Leaders Only- interlinc-online.com

Group Magazine for Youth Workers- youthministry.com

The Right Delivery System

Let's look again at how we can deliver our content in the most effective and attractive way. And let's begin with our events and gatherings. We have to find the right times to provide that learning experience. Our content is worthless if no one will come when we want to present it! I think it still could be alongside our weekly gathering. Or it could be Sunday night. We personally discovered that a lot of people liked the idea of being part of a disciplemaking process on Sunday nights. For many people, it's more about what we're doing and less about when we're doing it! Rick Warren originally found that, in his community, people would come for three to four hours once a quarter on a Saturday morning. So that's when he began his C.L.A.S.S. 101 to 501 discipleship training at Saddleback. Now you'll find those classes scheduled on various weeknight evenings and Sunday afternoons. Things change!

Some churches will do weekend retreats focused on particular areas of spiritual growth. Another great way to grow our people is to periodically create special events and seminars with speakers who will target the specific areas that we are focusing on. For example, there are great speakers and seminars available to teach on marriage, raising children God's way, creationism, men struggling with moral issues, Biblical stewardship and lifestyle evangelism, to name a few.

I believe one of the best tools for the delivery of systematic training and disciplemaking is the small group. We've already talked about the great value of believers coming together on a regular basis in a small group setting. There is worship and prayer and modeling and authenticity. Believers interact and they have to get real. Flaws are exposed and hearts and needs are revealed. The strategy of leaders walking their group through the right content with open discussion and careful application is fantastic. Significant numbers of people can be moved through critical content and lifestyle application in small groups. Of course, relationship commitment and some level of accountability is key to truly making disciples in any training environment. By the way, the size of the groups will make a difference if you want to make disciples. Neil Cole, in his book, *Church 3.0*, looks at the ingredients needed to get the right results. "Trying to accomplish comparable results with the wrong-sized grouping wastes energy and resources and leaves nothing to show for it. For instance, when churches try to make disciples using groups of twenty-five to seventy-five and skip the size of two or three, then much of the true power of relational accountability and obedience is traded for a sort of group exercise that may train people in skills but not in holistic discipleship." [78]

Let's take a few more moments to look at using smaller groups for disciplemaking. There are many invaluable purposes for using small groups. And they each can accomplish significant goals and life changes for the people attending. But this issue of the size and function of the groups is critical if you want to make authentic disciples. You just can't do it if you can't build accountable relationships. It simply won't happen! By the way, it's intriguing to me that, in the late 1700's, John Wesley used several kinds of small group settings to create a disciplemaking movement that swept the world. One of his requirements was complete transparency and accountability in each of these small groups of four to eight people. Now, successful small group structures that work will vary from triads to a dozen or more people. So much of it depends on the leader and the structure. Mike Breen, in his book, *Building a Discipling Culture*, believes that the right small group concept can significantly impact the growing believer, simply by being surrounded by other growing Christians. He describes what can happen in what he has defined as a "huddle." "Huddles work because they expose people to the learning of a group rather than only one-on-one mentoring. What a member gets to see is not only how the leader is discipling them, but also how the leader is discipling other people as well. Because each person is different, different skills and practices are needed to disciple various personality types. Discipleship in a committed group of people allows people to learn how they will disciple other people in the future who aren't like them. Such committed discipleship also allows what is being spoken into the life of another person to possibly be true of you as well." [79] It's a great case for using groups as one excellent means of making disciples.

By the way, technology is clearly bringing us closer together. The ease of immediate communication will only improve. This current reality can truly aid us in our effort to spend quality time together. We really don't have to always be in the same room! We have easy access to sharing online content. We can quickly dictate our thoughts and text, tweet, Facebook or email them to a friend or our group. The options of cellphone audio and video calling allow a dozen people to talk at any time of the day! A small group leader, perhaps on his way to work, can call his guys two or three mornings a week at a pre-determined time to check in and to pray. A disciplemaker can "Facetime" or text the woman she's discipling to keep the relationship and journey current, even when they're both out of town. The only thing that will hold us back will be our own lack of creativity or unwillingness to try new things. Let's return to the main subject.

Authentic Disciplemaking

The missing link in most of our disciplemaking strategies is the absence of a plan of having everyone in some sort of a disciplemaking relationship. The church isn't called to make disciples. We are! As the church leadership, it's our job to train and mobilize the body to make disciples. We certainly need to help. We need to set up classes to help them. We need to set up small groups and offer curriculum. But it's the responsibility of every believer to personally be involved both in the harvest fields and in the disciplemaking process! We can help get the engine started, but a lifestyle of evangelizing and making disciples has to eventually stand on its own. That **has** to be the goal of any disciplemaking program and process initiated by the church. Now, what in the world do we do? How do we begin? Let's take the time to walk through this critical concept and lifestyle.

Go and make disciples! Jesus's last words started a revolution that was intended to include every believer until He returns. Go and make disciples! Reach your family. Reach your neighbor. Reach your community. Reach your nation. Reach your world, one person at a time! And then help them become disciples who live out the life of Jesus the same way you're living out the life of Jesus. We've already learned what a disciple is. A fully devoted disciple reflects the mind, the character and the priorities of Christ. It's clearly a priority of God that we make disciples.

Disciples can be made in so many ways. We grow and learn to both be and make disciples in the context of community. Reading the Word, gathering with God's people, going to Bible studies and other training activities all are intended to help shape us into authentic disciples. The problem is most of us become more and more knowledgeable about the things of God. We can learn and learn for decades. But it often stops there! Paul talks about people having the knowledge of truth but having no power! That's just one of our problems.

Disciplemaking that begins and ends with the classroom almost always falls short. That's part of why we're in crisis in the North American church. It just doesn't seem to create very many fully-formed disciples. It creates educated believers and a handful of self-disciplined disciples. In contrast with educated attenders, real disciples walk with God. As they draw close to God, they think more and more like Him. They demonstrate His character because the power of the Holy Spirit is at work in them! Real disciples love the church and the lost, with all their heart, because that's God's love flowing out of them. And real disciples make disciples, because that's what He commanded us to do.

> We can help get the engine started, but a lifestyle of evangelizing and making disciples has to eventually stand on its own.

So how do we make real disciples? We walk with them, one person at a time. That's the missing ingredient in the church. We assume that believers will discipline themselves to grow up and become all that we and God want them to be. But, for most believers, it doesn't work that way! There's great value in our people sitting under good preaching and instruction, but there has to be more. There has to be some plan for walking together. There has to be some sort of volunteered accountability for most believers to really grow up and become a disciplemaker themselves.

How does that work? Here are some steps:

1) **Be a Disciplemaker**. Pick one, two or three people and begin to walk with them. Ask God to help you select who you should disciple. He has an opinion! Pray as you think through the people in your life that God might want you to invest in. Make a list of those people. It should include anyone you've led to the Lord. In fact, they should be at the top of your list. Who else will disciple them? Look at new believers around you, at work, home or church. Think about believers around you who need to grow up in the Lord and they're demonstrating some hunger to do just that. What about a younger person in the church or an older person? Leroy Eims has been one of the great warriors of the Kingdom, modeling and pressing disciplemaking as a critical part of the normal Christian life. Here's what he says in his classic work, *The Lost Art of Disciple Making*. "The first step in forming a band of people who are eager for discipleship training is motivation. They must be motivated in two directions- inward and outward. Inwardly they must be motivated to have fellowship with Jesus Christ, and outwardly they must become witnesses for Jesus Christ." [80] Later on, Eims calls this "hunger"- a hunger for God and a hunger to serve God in His Mission, whatever the

cost! Whether we're discipling a small group or an individual, we start with the hungry ones, and then we watch it spread! Narrow that list down to the one to three people that you would like to disciple. Set up an appointment and meet with them for coffee. Tell them what God has put on your heart. By the way, you will find so many good books that will help you through these details of beginning and walking through a disciplemaking relationship. I'm simply giving you an overview to get going!

Now, as you begin to meet with them, you want them to reflect the mind, the character and the priorities of Jesus! Make sure you're looking like Him too. Howard Hendricks has repeatedly said, " more is caught than taught!" and it's true! Your words, your attitudes, character and actions will have far more power to shape your disciples than what you try to teach them. Walking with them involves time and commitment for the long run. Think of it as an apprenticeship. Plan to spend the next 10-20 years shaping each disciple and then walking together shaping the lives of others! The early years will be more intensive. This is where the foundations are poured. Talk together about sermons and studies and classes and conversations with others.

Robert Coleman unpacks Jesus's disciplemaking strategy at great length in his classic book "Master Plan of Evangelism." As he assesses the eight components that are critical to the disciplemaking process, one of them is Time! What an invaluable commodity! Coleman observes, "Contrary to what one might expect, as the ministry of Christ lengthened into the second and third years, he gave increasingly more time to the chosen disciples, not less." [81] Listen to that! Most of us shorten the time we spend with someone we are discipling as they grow and mature. We assume that they will stand on their own. But Jesus invested more time and look at His results! Time. We all have it, but we don't seem to have enough of it, do we? It passes so quickly, and there seems to be little left for the things that count the most. But if we want to really make disciples who make disciples, we've got to figure this one out.

2) **Have a Plan.** Walking in a disciplemaking relationship should be both spontaneous and intentional. We should plan to spend intentional time on a regular basis. Sometimes you will spend your time just talking about what's happening in the normal flow of life. Crisis happens and it needs to be unpacked. Walking together through life is far more important than getting through a systematic disciplemaking plan. On the other hand, it's important to have that plan so you're actually building a healthy, reproducing believer. So find something to guide you through the concepts that you want to pour into your disciple. That may be a book or content from the Internet.

Have a plan of what you would like to cover over several years. I've already said that there are thirty-plus topics often found in disciplemaking books that we want our disciples to walk in and to multiply. We want to talk about everything from spiritual disciplines, spiritual warfare and walking in the power of the Spirit to generosity, obedience and discernment, to name a few. We want living, walking, multiplying disciples who will live Christ out loud long after we are gone. Think about that! Barna, in his research, found these tools among the methods that proved to be most effective in making disciples today: Bible memorization, online curriculum, two to three year classes on worldview foundations, daily Bible reading plans, book discussion groups, life plan development, spiritual gift assessment and activation, group disciplemaking and one-on-one disciplemaking! [82] These just make sense. Let's do them!

3) **Work in Community to Make Disciples.** God never intended on us doing all the heavy lifting by ourselves. We were born into the family of God. We are made to live, to work and to make disciples together. We should bring our friends to small groups and classes and other gatherings so they are exposed to good Christian friendship and modeling and teaching. As a family, we should all be helping each other to grow strong in the Lord. Many new or less mature believers actually start to grow up as they are surrounded by stronger believers in settings like a small growth

group. We should work together as stronger believers to get all the less mature believers into a community that will challenge them and help them grow. Disciples are made, not born!

4) **Real Disciplemaking requires Accountability.** The majority of believers are not growing up and making disciples themselves. Most have attended many classes and most have been in small groups. They've learned and learned and learned, but most do not grow up and multiply. While some of disciplemaking must be done in community, ultimately, for most people, it requires a one-on-one relationship that includes some level of accountability. Someone has to be disciplemaking and someone has to be growing into a disciplemaker. **Decide to be a disciplemaker. Then go and make disciples who make disciples!**

Multiplying Disciples

Go and multiply disciples! Is that what He meant? It has to be what He meant. If we make an authentic disciple, he or she too will make a disciple, who will make a disciple, who will make a disciple. And, if everyone obeys Jesus, that will go on and on and on! Francis Chan and Mark Beuving lay this concept down as one of the purposes of their disciplemaking book, *Multiply*. They say, "The goal is that once you've walked through the material, you can turn around and guide someone else through it. In fact, you are encouraged to guide others as you are learning. Don't wait until you have completed it all before teaching others what you learn. God wants us to be talking about Him all throughout the week. Discipleship is all about living life together. . ." [83] I like it! They've made it so clear. The book isn't to be read. It's to be lived and passed on, right away. That, again, brings us back to the problem. We have focused largely on passing on knowledge and we've overlooked passing on a repeating lifestyle. We've worked to make sure that our believers have learned their lesson, but we've ignored the need for them to actually go and make another disciple. So our process has ended with limited addition instead of unstoppable multiplication.

What would happen if we actually multiplied disciples? Often we "disciple" someone and then we leave them to their own future. We go and "disciple" someone else and do the same thing! That's addition at best. With no long-term relationship with their disciple-maker, many believers drop back into a mediocre Christian life at best. They don't continue to grow and they clearly don't go.

Let's learn something from the experience of others. AA teaches that alcoholics need accountability for life! They always will need a sponsor to walk with them and, when they get well, they need to sponsor others for life. It's the only way to make sure they don't go backwards as alcoholics. We know that without accountability most Christians also slide! Maybe we can learn something here.

What if we focused on actually making multiplying disciples? What would that look like? Here's an example:

	We	Disciple 3-		the 1st	Generation
The	3	Disciple 3-	$3 \times 3 = 9$	the 2nd	Generation
The	9	Disciple 3-	$9 \times 3 = 27$	the 3rd	Generation
The	27	Disciple 3-	$27 \times 3 = 81$	the 4th	Generation

That's **120** Disciples in

Four Generations of DISCIPLEMAKING!

Look at this example carefully. We disciple three, and we help them disciple three, and then we help them help their disciples disciple three and we repeat that one more time. We are actually focusing on the depth of our disciplemaking. We are really making multiplying disciples. We will probably disciple more than three people ourselves in a lifetime. But if we only disciple three and we help them reproduce our modeling out for four generations, we would have 120 disciples! **120 disciples, who are all committed to multiply!**

Imagine discipling three disciples each with a focus on repro-ducing for four generations. That would be amazing! Doing this would revolutionize our churches! Now, here's our reality check-not everyone would become a disciple, not everyone would become a multiplying disciple, and not everyone would multiply for four generations. **But, if this became our standard, our baseline, our disciplemaking strategy in our churches, it would change every-thing! Are you listening?**

We've already talked about Multi-Level Marketing. People sell products and then find others to sell those same products with them. The goal is to get as many people selling your products as possible, so you can make as much money as possible. It's the American way! People recruit friends, family and others and teach them to recruit people who recruit more people. The real money is made if you get a "down-line" 7 generations deep. People work very hard to do well in this business. But think about using this concept for the Kingdom of God.

Think about making Disciples FOUR Generations Deep!

There's something to get excited about!

Before we move on too quickly and completely forget this new way of thinking, I'm going to repeat myself and review this concept so we don't miss it. This is the main thing! This is the cen-terpiece of the book. If we miss this, we miss everything! Disciple someone. Take the time to actually develop in them the mind of Christ, Spirit-empowered character, and God-focused life priorities. That will take time. It may take years. Walk with that person. Spend close, consistent time, helping them deepen their walk with the Lord. Help them build in the fiber that will stay in place when you may be gone. As you invest in that person, help him or her begin to disciple someone else. Don't wait too long for this next step. As your disciple develops and grows beyond the basics, it will be time for them to make a disciple. This action will play a significant role helping your disciple to grow up and depend even more on the power of God.

Walk with them as they now begin to pass the same life principles on to their disciple. You've been functioning as a father or mother; now, you're helping like a grandparent. Your disciple will need to build the mind of Christ, Spirit-empowered character, and God-focused life priorities into his or her disciple. That will take time. It may take years. They need to walk with that person, spending close, consistent time, helping them deepen their walk with the Lord. They'll need to help them build in the inner strength that will stay in place when your disciple may be gone. As they invest in that person, they'll need to help him or her begin to disciple someone else. They shouldn't wait too long for this next step. Look at how your role has changed. You still care for and are mentoring your disciple, but now your focus is on helping them reproduce and multiply. You're helping them father a disciple and now grandfather a disciple, just like you have. Get ready to be a great-grandpa! And it can go on and on and on.

Let's clarify that our posture of fathering or mothering generations of disciples shouldn't create an unhealthy co-dependence on us as disciplemakers. That would simply create the same End Product that we see today. Many believers will submit to a set of disciplines as long as they attend a structured environment that keeps them accountable. But as soon as they leave the ministry or small group or church, or as soon as distress or distractions arrive, the lifestyle goes to the wind! We've all seen that over and over again, haven't we? It's like many of our weight-loss programs. Until we own our self-discipline, we'll keep doing seasonal swings. Now I'm getting personal. Our absolute goal in discipling has to include helping our disciples to live it out and pass it on, from a lifestyle of self-leadership and not simply from our presence and prodding! We have to grow them and then wean them while we're still discipling them. Doesn't that make sense? We move, they move, everything keeps changing. As we father and mother movements the rest of our lives, we'll have to learn to hang on and let go. That's what parenting is!

This truly is a whole new way of thinking, isn't it! If we, as men, all were discipled to father and grandfather and great-grandfather and great-great-grandfather, we'd be doing this right here, right now. And ladies, you'd be doing the same thing. But we weren't, were we? It can start with you and me! Let's continue on with this picture. We're focusing on depth and not breadth. We want deeply rooted disciples who make disciples who make disciples. That will only happen if you stay with your disciple and help him to disciple a disciplemaker. Isn't that true? We've proven historically that without this kind of care and accountability, disciplemaking will be mediocre at best.

So let's pick one or two people to disciple if we're not already in an intentional disciplemaking relationship. Let's ask God to guide us to just the right individuals. Some of us can disciple several people at once. Others of us will disciple one person at a time. Again, we're making a disciple and helping him make a disciple and helping him make a disciple and helping him make a disciple.

-This will only happen if we commit ourselves to multi-generational disciplemaking.

-We have to decide that we will invest our lives in building many generations of disciples.

Look at the incredible fruit of this way of thinking. If I only disciple three people in my lifetime, but if I help them each to do the same thing for four generations of disciples, one hundred and twenty disciples is just the starting number. This **is** actually fathering or mothering a movement! Here's the amazing truth. So many of us as mature leaders in the church could be fathering and mothering movements of disciplemakers. Think about how this would change your church in the next ten to twenty years. It would truly change everything!

This would change our communities.

This would change the church in North America.

This, I believe, is the KEY to our future as God's people.

And, ironically, this would be returning to the very command

that He gave to us in the first place! Go and Make Disciples!

Let's do a reality check again. Not everyone will make disciples. Not everyone will make disciples who make disciples. Not everyone who's discipled will make a disciple. Not everyone will father or mother a movement of multiplication. Have we thought of all of the excuses? There's one more and it's the biggest one. Many senior pastors won't do this! You may not be willing to do this. As a senior leader, you truly are the gatekeeper for the future of your church. My question is: Why would you not begin a multiplication movement in your church, starting it yourself? I can think of some reasons:

I don't believe it will work.

I don't want to do it myself.

I don't know whom to begin with.

I think other changes will work more easily.

I think other changes will bring the results we are after.

I don't believe our people will do it.

I don't believe our leaders will do it.

I don't want to change what we're doing.

I have no time to add one more thing.

I'm really tired and running as fast as I can.

I'm really tired and just hanging on.

I'll look at it again, next year. There's too much going on.

I think it will take too long.

I've tried it before.

Have I forgotten anything?

I'm not trying to pick on us as pastors and leaders. But I've met with far too many of us to ignore this side of our corner. There are many reasons why we don't do something, even when it's mission-critical! I'm writing it out just to ask this question: How else are we going to turn our churches and our nation and our world around? I don't think there is another way. Mega-churches aren't the answer. Cell churches aren't the answer. Traditional methods of doing church aren't working. We are going backwards! I don't believe the real answer is new methodology or new forms or structures. I believe the answer is new hearts and minds- hearts and minds, filled with the Spirit, devoted, obedient, and on mission! How will we get there if we're not making disciples differently than we have in the past?

Before I end these thoughts, I've got to ask this: Will you father a disciplemaking movement? As senior pastor, will you step up to the plate and lead the way? As board members and fellow leaders in the church, will you join with your pastor and make this a fresh start? I won't presume that you aren't already doing this. But I do know that what many of us are doing is not adequate. We'll have to do a whole lot of changes to get an effective result. Are you willing to begin the necessary steps as leaders to get the end results that we so desperately need? I pray that you will!

The Pathway

Let's pull back and look at how all of this must fit together in our local church programming. Most churches will need to put together a combination of these methods to help their believers become mature and devoted followers. Look at it like the pieces of a puzzle that need to all come together. Let's make up one example:

> Here's what we want to cover in our small groups over the next two years. Then we'll continue on to new material with existing groups but rotate back through this same content with new groups. Let's complement that training with basic and advanced training on specific subjects on Saturday mornings once a month. Let's also provide a number of weekend retreats that will take our people deeper in specialized areas of growth and need. Let's create a new believer track and another growth track that people can get through on a two-year rotation. That way, people can go through most of this content and experience without killing themselves. Let's keep training and then continue resourcing our disciple-makers so they have everything they need to multiply the life of Christ. And let's provide a map for them. Let's let them see where we're taking them and what needs to be poured into a developing disciple.

The use of a discipleship Journey Map can be extremely helpful. Your people need to know where they are going if you want to get them there. And we've got to help them understand our goal. We don't simply want them to pick out an interesting class or two. And we don't want them in a small group or at a weekend retreat simply because it's fun or a great way to learn or make friends. We have an End Product in mind. We want everyone to grow up. And we want them helping others to grow up the rest of their lives. We want them on a journey with some sort of written checklist that helps everyone see where they have come and where they still need to go. My observation is that our churches are filled with people who haven't finished the journey, and they don't know it. But their lives show it! For example, if you asked many of them to help someone else understand the basic principles of spiritual warfare, they plead ignorance! Or if you asked them to be involved in training younger believers on how to build friendships with nonbelievers or how to begin to share their faith, they'd have to say no. And that's because they wouldn't know what to do!!

A Journey Map can help believers see their areas of weakness and opportunities to grow. One type of journey map can point out all the areas of spiritual development that we need to grow in. That can be extremely helpful so we can actually see where we have developed and where we still need to grow. Another type of journey map actually shows the classes and event opportunities that will get you to the end-goal. For example, Saddleback has its baseball field diagram showing the five areas of spiritual growth that every believer needs to develop. Everyone who attends Saddleback knows that they, at some point, need to get all the way around the bases. They can't escape that goal! It's printed everywhere! Church attenders would have to work really hard to ignore the need to go through Classes 101 to 501! Every church needs some sort of journey map that will help everyone, from visitors to regulars, to know where they are being taken. And there needs to be an entry point where the map is clearly defined. Many churches will use an introductory class for that specific purpose. It also can be so helpful if the there is an opportunity provided for a one-on-one discussion about the purpose of completing the journey.

Saddleback's Baseball Diamond Strategy [84]

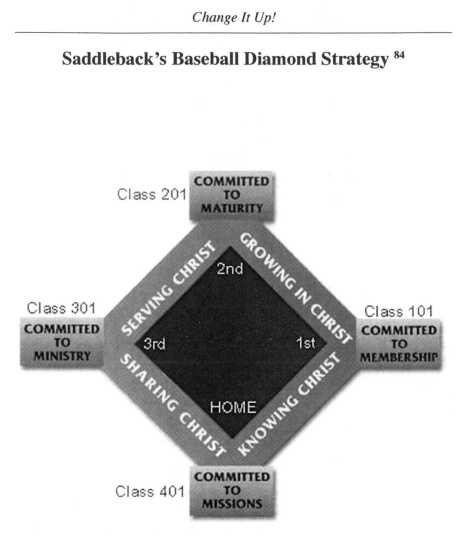

" Go therefore and MAKE DISCIPLES ... "

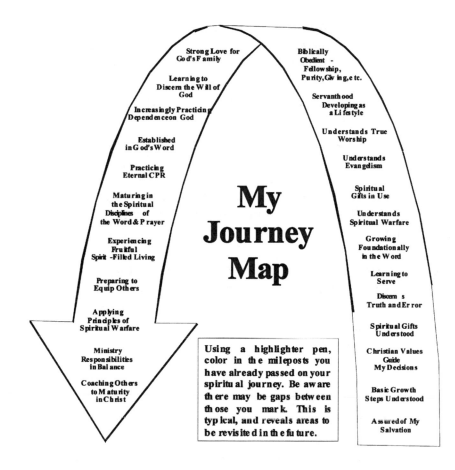

Strong Love for
God's Family

Learning to
Discern the Will of
God

Increasingly Practicing
Dependence on God

Established
in God's Word

Practicing
Eternal CPR

Maturing in
the Spiritual
Disciplines of
the Word & Prayer

Experiencing
Fruitful
Spirit -Filled Living

Preparing to
Equip Others

Applying
Principles of
Spiritual Warfare

Ministry
Responsibilities
in Balance

Coaching Others
to Maturity
in Christ

Biblically
Obedient -
Fellowship,
Purity, Giving, etc.

Servanthood
Developing as
a Lifestyle

Understands True
Worship

Understands
Evangelism

Spiritual
Gifts in Use

Understands
Spiritual Warfare

Growing
Foundationally
in the Word

Learning to
Serve

Discerns
Truth and Error

Spiritual Gifts
Understood

Christian Values
Guide
My Decisions

Basic Growth
Steps Understood

Assured of My
Salvation

My Journey Map

Using a highlighter pen, color in the mileposts you have already passed on your spiritual journey. Be aware there may be gaps between those you mark. This is typical, and reveals areas to be revisited in the future.

...Who Make Disciples Who Make..."

Here's a map that gets more specific on the detail of where we need to grow in order to be a maturing disciple of Christ.

The Right People

Now we add disciplemakers to our content and venues. My observation, again, is that classes and events often fill minds with information but don't necessarily change lives. Isn't that true? Don't we see this as one of the great dilemmas of the 21st century church? It seems like many of our people become professional students of the Word, they show up for everything, but they don't grow up! And many others just show up and they don't grow up either. Why is that? I think it's because we're not calling them to personal responsibility. We're not giving them a lifestyle to live up to. There's no personal guidance, and there's certainly no personal accountability. Believers can catch a class, but they don't have to learn. They can attend a growth group, but they don't have to grow. Attendance doesn't guarantee anything but a body count. How, then, do we help people truly grow? I believe we have to get personal. We have to build one-on-one relationships, like Jesus did. And, as we go deeper, we have to call for greater commitment. We have to hold each other accountable.

As I became more and more convinced of the need for disciplemaking in our church, I had a strange revelation. I saw that our church was filled with unemployed disciplemakers and a multitude of people who needed to be discipled! How had I missed that opportunity? They were all sitting there right in front of me! I created a plan, recruited and trained an army of mature believers and then released them on one or two other church attenders at a time. We used a system of teaching and small groups and one-on-one disciplemaking with wonderful results. Mature believers were mobilized and were able to use their gifts and experience in the Lord. And less mature believers were developed and walked toward a life of maturity in Christ. Now, that's God's plan for His church.

We need to recruit, train and release a multiplying team of disciplemakers if we want to truly raise up an army of disciples who make disciples in our churches. I believe that many people won't leave an equipping session really understanding and applying its truths without personal help from another believer. If that's true, then that becomes the next challenge in programming. We have our content and our events and venues for delivery. But now, this changes everything when it comes to personnel. Instead of simply recruiting teachers and presenters, small group leaders and hosts, we're also looking for a kind of person. We have to recruit people who are willing to learn how to pass it on and make disciples of others! That means that they have to be a developing disciple to help make developing disciples.

You can see how the focus changes. One question could be, "Where in the world could we find enough mature believers in our church to recruit that kind of worker?" But the correct questions really should be, "How do we need to change our recruiting and training strategies so we actually have disciples making disciples in our church? What do we need to do? Where do we begin?" And you probably need to begin with your current leaders and workers. If you turn your workers and leaders into authentic disciples and disciple-makers, everything else will be easy! Begin with the few and you'll end up multiplying until a majority of our people are making disciples. Now, as you can see, this way of thinking could change everything! And it will take a number of years of steady, intentional hard work to produce this kind of transformation in your ministry. But think of the long-lasting fruit that will come from this. And think about the fruit of **not** changing anything.

One of the great obstacles that we face today seems to be a low commitment level by many of our church attenders to any time outside of the main gathering. Our people are extremely busy. Between jobs, sports, other recreation, hobbies and family activities, it's hard to help them find any time to really grow as disciples. Sunday School has almost disappeared, and training, small groups and evening Bible studies are attended by a minority of our people.

Some of us have given up and surrendered to this sad reality. In fact, many of our church plants will determine that the gathering and small groups **are** their strategy for disciplemaking. Unfortunately, many small groups are making friends, but they aren't making disciples. There's no clear plan. There's no overall strategy to walk people through a process to maturity in Christ. Listen- we can't give up! Weekend sermons can never be expected to take a congregation on this critical journey. It just doesn't work. It's a great beginning and they certainly contribute, but there's got to be so much more. It would take seven to ten years of strategic, systematic preaching with no one missing and everyone listening. Show me that church.

This problem is not going to go away. But this is not the time to give up. This is the time for change!

First, we've got to find or create the disciple-making plan that will work in our setting, with our people. Francis Chan's book or Bill Hybel's program may not work in your church. But something will work. Grab on to that. Find it!

Next, we need to sell the plan. The goal is making authentic disciples who Go! I believe that a lot of church attenders aren't committed because they see no real purpose for their lives. The goal they see is attendance and numbers, not making disciples and multiplication. History proves that great vision attracts followers. We need to raise the standard and not give in to declining commitment. The sale starts with our leaders. If our leaders get it, believe it and will live it, we can strategically begin to change our entire church.

Finally, we need to work the plan. We've got to go for it. We need to make this issue of making disciples one of those values that we are willing to die for. It will take that sort of tenacity to have victory and fruitfulness. But who said it would be easy?

Training for Ministry

Making authentic disciples must combine the prerequisite of learning God's truth with the necessity of practicing those principles and serving the Lord. As I've said over and over again, our churches are filled with believers who are filled with information that they're not applying to their lives. How tragic! They've been born again into the greatest movement of all time and they're sitting on the sidelines. They'd find the greatest joy and fulfillment as participants, but they somehow haven't gotten there. It's our great opportunity and challenge to help them find their way. God's created and equipped us all to serve. He's given us gifts and abilities and He's called us to use them for His glory.

As leaders, it's our responsibility to create an environment where believers know they need to be built up and equipped as workers to do what God has called them to do. We need a plan for growing our people. But we also need a strategy for training our people. We've already talked about an assessment process that helps us find the right people to serve in the right ministries in our church. That assessment would include matching our interests, experiences and spiritual gifts to ministry opportunities.

But training our people has to go far beyond the jobs that we have available within the confines of our church ministries. Every believer needs to be mobilized to serve God on a daily basis. Most churches will activate 10-30 % of their church attenders and will fill the majority of their ministry needs. Even at our creative best, we'll never mobilize the church through in-house ministry. That's not good enough! God wants all of us actively serving Him every day. If we simply focus on filling our ministry positions, then that's all we'll do. But if we focus on mobilizing the entire body, we'll significantly impact our world.

> We've got to get way out of the box to see the heart of God on this issue of ministry. We can't begin with ministry positions. We have to begin with people!

What ministries do we need to train our people to do? When we think of serving, we often land on things like ushering, child-care, teaching a class, leading a group, cleaning the kitchen and serving on the board. These and a hundred ministries like them are all very important. And all of these in-house ministry servers need valuable training to help them do their jobs with excellence. But that's only the beginning. We've got to get way out of the box to see the heart of God on this issue of ministry. We can't begin with ministry positions. We have to begin with people! We have to see that all of us are called to bring transformation to a lost and dying world. We all have been called and equipped to make a significant difference in our world. As we discover our gifts and talents for service, we need to see our potential in serving the Lord, wherever He wants to use us.

Our ministry begins in our home and neighborhood and at our work or school. We need to train our people to see themselves as servants looking for ways to touch lives and impact their world with the love of God. Ministry should be happening everyday with neighbors and friends and fellow-employees. All we have to do is open our eyes to see the needs that are all around us! Then, on top of that, many of our people will discover a ministry that's tied to an organization, like helping at a rescue mission, a crisis pregnancy center, a missionary hospital or in an after-school program. Others will use their gifts to minister to people in need, like making meals for the sick, providing rides for the elderly, or praying with people in crisis. Some ministry is planned, but a lot of ministry can be spontaneous and God-inspired. We need to train our people to use their talents and gifts to serve God with all their heart! Some workers in our churches put in an hour or two of ministry one day a week, and they feel like they've done their time. That's a good beginning, but now, they need to discover how to serve the Lord the rest of the week. We need to train our people how to get a life that really has meaning and purpose.

Jesus had even more in mind when He talked about workers in the Kingdom. In Matthew 9:36-37, Jesus looked out on a desperate and needy world. Here's what He said:

> *When he saw the crowds, he had compassion on them, because they were harassed and helpless, like sheep without a shepherd. Then he said to his disciples, "The harvest is plentiful but the workers are few.*

> *Ask the Lord of the harvest, therefore to send out workers into his harvest field.*

When Jesus talked about workers, He was referring to believers reaching out to lost people in the harvest fields of everyday life. Most believers, unfortunately, don't intentionally reach out to make friends with people who need Jesus. That's why Jesus could say the same thing today. The harvest here and around the world is absolutely plentiful, but the workers are few! It's not that we don't have the workers. We sit next to them every Sunday. They're just not doing their job. That **is** the work and ministry of every believer. And that's what we need to be trained to do! We'll talk a lot more about this in our next chapter.

There are also many specialized areas of in-house ministry that we need to be training our people for or we'll have train wrecks. There need to be various levels of leadership training in our churches. Do we have to all learn the hard way? Why can't we train our leaders how to lead with godly character and excellence? We need to train our teachers and department heads. We need to train our small group leaders. We need to train all of our servers in our various ministries how to deal with people like a servant and not like a lord. We need to train our elders and board members. We need to train our leaders who want to begin new ministries. We need to train our caregivers and our outreach teams and missions mobilizers. Part of the purpose of this training is to help us all see that we have the same priorities. We may be heading out in a hundred different directions, but we're all working together with one purpose.

Let's Look Inside

Now it's time to do that assessment of your own ministry programming in your church. You've been wrestling together over vision, value and purpose. You've been dreaming about a plan that will effectively bring life change to your own ministry. You realize the critical need to actually make disciples and not simply students or attenders. You've been thinking of some great ways to accomplish the goals that you've been dreaming of. So here are just a few of the questions we need to ask. How does all of this line up with what you're already doing? Are you on track? Are you moving in the right direction? Here's the really big question? Are you making disciples? And are you making disciples who make disciples? Do you have a clear vision of where you are going and where you want to be in five and then ten years? Do you have a plan? Have you developed a disciplemaking process? Do you have clear entry points that visitors can see and navigate? What's your plan to help visitors move from that entry point to being a multiplying disciple? Are you, as ministry leaders, working as a cohesive team, moving in the same direction? As you look at your individual arenas of ministry, have you developed a disciplemaking objective that drives your search for the right content for training and application? And have you either found or created that right content that accomplishes that objective? How about your delivery system? Are you finding that what you are doing is achieving your goals, or is there a better way? What is it? And what about your leaders? Do you have the right people doing the right jobs in your ministry? Do you have a system that helps your people discover the right place for ministry? Is it used throughout the church? Here's another tough question. Do you have the courage to bring about the necessary changes to reach these critical objectives? It's clearly of no value to read a book like this, discover ministry areas that need change and then do nothing. What a waste of time and energy! **Do Something!**

> We've lowered our standard to Christian Education rather than Life Transformation!

Becoming Disciplemakers!

God's ultimate design for our lives is for us to be part of a great movement of disciples who make disciples who make disciples. There's no doubt about it! That intentional focus is what Jesus called us all to in the first place. It's amazing that the North American church has drifted away and so completely missed the mark on this foundational call from God. We've lowered our standard to Christian Education rather than Life Transformation! That has to stop now or we'll lose the whole nation! We have to become Disciplemakers! And it has to start with you and me! It can happen, one person and one church at a time. Movements begin in the hearts and lives of people just like us. We repent and respond to the Spirit of God, we change and begin to impact others. It multiplies and watch what happens!

Notes

THOUGHTS ON CHANGE

Change is hard because people overestimate the value of what they have—and underestimate the value of what they may gain by giving that up.
James Belasco and Ralph Stayer
Flight of the Buffalo (1994)

God grant me the serenity to accept the things I cannot change, the courage to change the things I can, and the wisdom to know the difference.
Reinhold Niebuhr

Life belongs to the living, and he who lives must be prepared for changes.
Johann Wolfgang von Goethe

When you are through changing, you are through.
Bruce Barton

12. Outreach Plans- Partnering to Reach our Friends and Neighbors- Together!

We've traveled on a journey with our visitors, beginning with marketing, curb appeal and their arrival at our church. We've then moved with them through the process that will help them become authentic disciples who are focused on making more authentic disciples of others. But there's still been something missing. We can't assume that people will simply come to our church, even if we dial in all of the essential details. And even the best of non-personal marketing will only produce a slow stream of believers visiting your church. It all still comes back to the body of believers, your church family, young and old, newbies and regulars, mobilized to reach their friends, neighbors, coworkers, and everyone else in their sphere of influence. And, fortunately, this is not only God's will- this is **The Original Plan!** As we've walked through chapter after chapter, preparing for visitors to arrive, we've actually been setting this plan in motion. Most of our visitors need to be arriving with friends who attend our church. As a church community, we have to be ready for anyone coming through our doors. But, in reality, it's critical that most of those visitors are already deep in relationship with our church people who invited them, whatever the event. Imagine walking into a strange, new world, but with friends who seem to know everyone and everything. That makes all the difference in the world! Now, if that's going to happen, we have to revisit the heart of the issue. Let's go back one more time to the basics of a lifestyle of evangelism. It all starts there!

> As people see our character and actions, and then, as they hear the good news of His love for them, many will respond and will end up praising God alongside of us!

Everyday Living 101

God has called each of us to intentionally influence people toward their own saving encounter with our Lord and Savior, Jesus Christ. In Matthew 5, Jesus clarifies our role as disciples.

> *You are the salt of the earth. . . You are the light of the world. . . let your light shine before others, that they may see your good deeds and glorify your Father in heaven.*

This passage has stirred my heart and motivated me from my earliest days of knowing the great mission that God has placed before us. We are all to be salt and light in a dark and dying world. As people see our character and actions, and then, as they hear the good news of His love for them, many will respond and will end up praising God alongside of us. That's the beautiful and glorious picture that should drive all of us to live our faith out loud wherever we go!

As Jesus was preparing to leave His disciples, He shared His final words. These words were not grand suggestions. They were Great Commandments to be passed down for generations to you and me today. Christ's clear, unwavering intention and command was that we- every one of us- would obey and we would teach our new converts to also obey. Here's exactly what Jesus said in Matthew 28:

> *All authority in heaven and on earth has been given to me. **Therefore go and make disciples** of all nations, baptizing them in the name of the Father and of the Son and of the Holy Spirit, and teaching them to **obey everything** I have commanded you. And surely I am with you always, to the very end of the age.*

Do you hear what He was saying? Go and make disciples who go! There's nothing hidden about it. Then, in Acts 1, He added this incredible ending of vision, encouragement and direction before He left:

> *But you will receive **power** when the Holy Spirit comes on you; and **you will be my witnesses** in Jerusalem, and in all Judea and Samaria, and to the ends of the earth.*

Now, look at this. This is not optional! It's the life call for every believer, young or old, quiet or loud, shy or aggressive. There's no exception. We are all called to intentionally bring people to faith and then to maturity in their faith. Those are the two sides to making disciples. We make disciples as we bring them toward Christ. And we then make disciples as we help them grow up toward maturity in Christ. And we are all given supernatural power to do this. We are not on our own! He's with us, enabling us to do what He's called us to do. It's so hard to accomplish something that we're really not equipped to do. We've all experienced times like that in life. It would be difficult if God commanded us to do something that we just are not capable of doing.

Fortunately, He thought of that! He knew we would need special help to know how to tell people about Jesus and to walk with them to faith in Christ. So He gave us the Holy Spirit for so many reasons, including this important reason- to strengthen us, to help us think, to step into our circumstances and to guide us! In one passage, in Matthew 10, Jesus tells His disciple that the Holy Spirit even gives us the right words to say when we need His help. In the context of the passage, Jesus was saying, even if you are arrested, don't worry about what you will say or how to say it. Here's what He says:

> *At that time you will be given what to say, for it will not be you speaking,*

but the Spirit of your Father speaking through you.

Isn't that incredible! No wonder God felt comfortable commanding all of us to intentionally be involved in building relationships with pre-believers and sharing our faith with people around us. He knew we were covered. If we are filled with the Spirit and walking in His power, everyone of us will know what to say and how and when to say the things we're supposed to say to people who do not yet know God.

That's God's plan and His incredible provision. In fact, it all seems to work together. When we get close to God and are filled with His power, we automatically experience a greater heart for lost people. Love is one of the fruits of the Spirit. And when you get filled with God's love, you unavoidably receive a deeper, supernatural compassion for people who are lost! I've seen it over and over again and experienced it in my own journey. So God's command to go and make disciples is the natural response by believers when we are filled with God's Spirit. He gives us the desire, the compassion, and the wisdom. He walks before us and sets up our friendships. And He gives us the words to say when its time to begin sharing our faith! What a deal! Who could ask for anything more?

Now, there are radically different ways in which we share and point people toward God. Quiet people will do it quietly and gently. And louder people may be more aggressive and confrontational. God's made us just the way we are, and He doesn't expect us to move out of character. We'd look strange and rather scary! And some of us do when we try to share about Jesus in a way that doesn't match our personality.

As their pastor, many people always assumed that I would be better at doing lifestyle evangelism than they would. They were wrong! I had to deal

with my own insecurities and inadequacies, just like they did. Plus I was limited to the people in my circle of contacts and even more specifically, those who didn't mind my personality. All of that being said, I found great opportunities to make friends, and I eventually shared about Jesus with many people despite those limitations.

We all have limitations and great opportunities within those limitations. A quiet mechanic at a shop won't run up to strangers with the gospel, but he'll be the absolute best candidate to share the gospel with other quiet mechanics at his shop. He'll also be the best at getting to know other quieter neighbors. They'll trust him first and be more likely to listen to him when the time is right. An outgoing salesman, perhaps at the same shop, will easily make friendships with completely different people and will help them move toward faith. The quiet mechanic will never talk like the salesman and won't reach some of the people that the salesman will reach. But the loud salesman may never earn the respect and ear of those other mechanics at work. That's the way it is. And that's the way God planned it. We each have our personality, our mission, our mission field and the power of the Holy Spirit!

God wants an army of specialists going undercover everywhere, with the ability to love lost people right where they are. That's the plan! He's placed us in neighborhoods and careers and schools and sports and other arenas of influence. If we open our eyes, the fields are ready for harvest. People are hungry for something more in their lives. It's up to us to intentionally build friendships with the people who surround us. Quieter people are often better at reaching quieter people. And louder people often attract to each other and doors of friendship open wide. There are people who are easier for us to get to know and build a friendship just because of who we are. That's the way God made us and He wants to use us just the way we are!

Here are some secrets to sharing your faith with others in a responsible way.

1) Be filled with the Holy Spirit.
2) Learn how to share your faith and the Word. Be patient.
3) Be yourself.
4) Build a friendship first if you can.
5) Share your life with them, like an open book.
6) Walk them through the good news, a little at a time. Be patient.
7) Don't push- respect and treat them like you'd want to be treated.
8) Don't be afraid to ask if they're ready.
9) Introduce them to other Christians and church events.
10) Be patient! Did you get that?

Let's look one more time at the foundational words that summarize all of Christian living. In Mark 12, Jesus was asked by a teacher which of the commandments was most important. If we were asking Him today, what would He say? Is there is one thing, above all other things, that we can't afford to miss in our Christian walk? Jesus responded to the teacher and would tell us this today:

> *Love the Lord your God with all your heart and with all your soul and with all your mind and with all your strength. The second is this: Love your neighbor as yourself. There is no commandment greater than these.*

The religious teacher agreed with Jesus and recognized that these commands were even more important than burnt offerings and sacrifices. Jesus liked his response and said, "You are not far from the kingdom of God!"

This was an amazing dialogue. Everything in Jewish tradition pointed to outward rituals that demonstrated obedience and surrender through offerings and sacrifices. We might parallel that in our Christian tradition to our outward rituals of faithfulness through attendance and service and offerings or maybe even our "sacrifice" of "worldliness." But I'm afraid many of us put these things before the most important thing. This teacher recognized that sacrifice wasn't enough. There is something much deeper that God wants. He doesn't want our money. **He wants our everything!** He wants our whole heart. He is the Lord and we are but servants. But if we draw close to God, He gets our hearts and we become His friends. In James 4, we are told that as we draw close to God, God draws close to us. And it's true!

Our Solution

As we draw close to God, as we intentionally discipline our lives to love God and depend upon Him for everything, He changes everything. He fills us with love. And we love our neighbors like we never could have before. We love lost people like we never have before. He stirs our hearts and fills them with His very own passion and compassion. Obedience starts to become second nature to us. And we start looking more and more like Jesus. Isn't it amazing? Isn't it wonderful? That's the plan!

Here's my own story as a young man. I was a preacher's son, raised in the church. I was saved at an early age and made normal God–embracing decisions during the next 10-15 years. But at the age of 18, as I graduated from high school, I felt empty and powerless. I had seen friends who were on fire for God and filled with unnatural compassion for people. I knew I needed something more than what

I had experienced. So one day, I took my Bible and went out to meet with God. I cried out to Him for a change, determined that I would walk away if that change didn't happen. I wasn't disappointed!

I flipped my Bible open, put my finger down and began to read. I know that that can be dangerous, but God had mercy on me and spoke right to my heart. Here's what He said to me in II Timothy 1: 6-9:

> *This is why I remind you to fan into flames the spiritual gift God gave you when I laid my hands on you. For God has not given us a spirit of fear and timidity, but of power, love, and self-discipline. So you must never be ashamed to tell others about our Lord. And don't be ashamed of me, either, even though I'm in prison for Christ. With the strength God gives you, be ready to suffer with me for the proclamation of the Good News. It is God who saved us and chose us to live a holy life. He did this not because we deserved it, but because that was his plan long before the world began—to show his love and kindness to us through Christ Jesus.* [85]

God was talking directly to me! I knew it. It was exactly what I needed to hear. I repented, I responded with all my heart and He immediately transformed me. The changes were so radical that, for a while, I wondered if I had ever been saved. It took time for me to realize that I had been saved, with my child-like faith, and that this was a whole new step in my sanctifying process. Now, I was filled with the Spirit. His fresh, new control began to transform my life. As I drew close to God, my character and priorities automatically began to change. It was so natural. Love and patience and peace and kindness were showing up in my character out of nowhere. It was amazing. I shared about these changes with my Christian peers and their lives were significantly changed as well. God began to father a movement in me, and I wasn't even trying. I was 18! I didn't know better. I was simply doing what came naturally. God obviously was in control.

The greatest evidence of the Holy Spirit that appeared in my life was love! It was amazing! It was life-transforming. I had never had deep feelings like this for anything. I loved God with all my heart, I loved my Christian friends deeply and I really cared about my lost friends. I couldn't help it! My heart was broken over their lostness. I had to do something. I began to share Jesus with all of my friends. While some of them weren't ready, a number of my buddies gave their lives to Jesus that summer. It was incredible and unforgettable. My life has never been the same. Through the years, I have discovered that my character and priorities flow in direct relationship to my intimacy with God. When I'm close to God, I'm filled with the Spirit, and my character and my actions reflect His heart. And when I'm not as close to the Lord, when I'm too busy or too tired or distracted, everything changes. My character declines, my weaknesses get stronger and my priorities lose their focus. I see it and others do too! Just ask my wife. What a lesson on why we should get close and stay close to the Lord.

Let's look at the reality of our own lives and circumstances. So many of us have missed the mark. That's called sin! How do we turn our nation and our church around? Here's where it begins. It starts with YOU! You can make all the difference in the world right now by deciding to change. It can't start with that other guy, or the people in charge. You're reading the book. You're feeling that spirit of conviction. By the way, if you're in charge and God is speaking to you about this, you really need to change. Now, I won't assume that everyone reading this isn't living a Great Commandment / Great Commission lifestyle. But the truth is, so many of the pastors and church leaders that I talk to sadly admit that they aren't really living this life that I'm writing about. They've become so busy- with work, with family, with sports, and with church, that they've had little to no time left for the Lord or the lost.

Think about it! We try to function like Superheroes as Christians and especially as pastors and leaders, but we're not. Superheroes gain their power from themselves. They're made that way. They can't help it. But we gain our power from the One we serve. We need regular re-charging! We really can't authentically live this life without it. We can't. Craig Groeschel, in his book, *The Christian Atheist*, begins his book by saying, " Hi, my name is Craig and I'm a Christian atheist." [86] What in the world is he saying? He's saying, among many other things, that we, as believers and even as spiritual leaders, often function so adequately in our own strength that we get along fine without really depending upon God as our Source. We can become professional performers, attempting to life out the Christian life as our own source of power. I'm afraid some of us have become so good at it and so used to it that we don't even know what it would be like to live in His strength. We simply won't slow down enough to find out. And we don't want to think about it. It's too painful and difficult to deal with! I was moved as I read the list of leading pastors in America endorsing Craig's book and identi-fying with the crisis of self-sufficiency. And I too can identify with Craig's words! I personally find it so hard to slow down to spend the time with God that I need to truly re-charge and be filled with His Spirit. It so much easier to simply get enough rest to again run hard at a new day, serving Him. Isn't that true? A lot of the Mary and Martha issue, isn't it? Our unspoken prayer is, "Lord, Please give me a quick charge. I'm so busy! I **am** serving you! Got to go. Love ya!" But it doesn't work that way. I'm not just talking about putting in devotional time in His Word and in prayer and then jumping back in the race. I'm talking about the discipline of truly slowing down with God so we really fellowship with Him. Consistently. All the time. Like Jesus getting away from the boys. This is what God is trying to say to us in the midst of the storms swirling all around us. **"Be still and know that I am God!" It's so hard, it takes so much effort, but it's so critical. It does change everything!**

I've talked to hundreds of fellow pastors and Christian leaders who've admitted that they've become so overloaded and overwhelmed with the endless work of church ministry that they don't spend the time they ought to drawing close to God. Now, the fruit of drawing close and being filled is love. That's what flows naturally out of us when we are filled with the Spirit. We love! We love God, with all our heart. We love each other, with all of our flaws. And we love the lost. As I've already said, it just happens. We don't even have to try! That's what the fruit is. But when we're running in our own strength, it's all about effort. We have to really work at loving and obeying and caring and demonstrating. In reality, we don't even think about connecting with "outsiders." It doesn't come naturally. It's a lot of work. And, of course, we have no time. But how can that be? What in the world are we doing? What about that precious gospel that we hold so dear? Can we go on keeping it from those who need it most? It all comes back to the heart. And ultimately, it all comes back to that critical need to draw close to God.

Where do we start? There are three things we need to commit ourselves to:

1) **Repentance- The very first thing that we need to do is repent!** Repentance is acknowledging to God that we have not been obeying Him, making a complete turn in direction, and then obeying Him. It may come with great sorrow and conviction. But what God really cares about is obedience. We often feel bad but don't change. God looks for a repentance that leads to joy and great fruitfulness. Without genuine repentance, there is no hope for health in the church! It must be the starting point.

2) **Dependence- Next, we need to reaffirm our absolute need for God's strength in our daily lifestyle.** How in the world can we live this Christian life that we've been called to? How can we be victorious, demonstrating the consistent character and priorities of Christ? How can we model the life and love of God wherever we go? How can we influence and win our friends and

neighbors to Jesus? We can't, without the enabling power of the Holy Spirit! That's what He's here for. We've got to learn to let go of our own strength and train ourselves to depend more and more on the Lord for His daily power for living.

3) **Obedience- As we learn to rely on the Lord, He Himself will empower us to do His will.** "Draw close to Me and I **will** draw close to you!" What a great promise! Our struggles to obey and to find balance, motivation, and passion always diminish as we draw close and learn to trust Him. But what about all the times that we aren't motivated and don't feel like obeying? We do it anyway. We obey and do God's will because it's the right thing to do and not because we feel like it. And we use the evidence of our attitude to motivate us to repent and draw close to God. Will we stumble and fall? Of course, we will! It's a process and a journey. We obey. We succeed. We stumble. We repent. He lifts us back up to our feet, hugs us, and dusts us off. We learn. We depend again. We obey again!

Let's just stop- right here, right now. Can we take some moments with God to talk about all of this? **This is the main thing**! Let me share a story and a song to set up a time alone with God. Stephen Coffey was a youth minister serving Morningstar Ministries in the Carolinas. On November 1, 2002, during a church prayer meeting, Coffey prayed out loud, 'I'd give my life today if it would shake the youth of the nation.' That very night, he was in a multi-car accident and died of serious injuries. Meanwhile, John Mark McMillan, Stephen's best friend, was recording in a studio in Jacksonville when he received a call that two of his friends had been critically injured in a car accident. The next day, McMillan wrote *How He Loves* as a tribute to Coffey and out of a need "to have some sort of conversation with God" where he could speak to his frustrations and emotions over his best friend's death. He says, "This song isn't a celebration of weakness and anger. It's a celebration of a God who would want to hang with us through those things, who would want to be a part of our lives through those things, and, despite who we are, He would want to be a part of us, our community, and our family." [87]

How He Loves **is an amazing reflection of the heart of God, who is always there, even when we aren't.** As we are caught in the whirlwind of life, with it's momentary glory and it's alternating pain, He is there, loving us, waiting for us to slow down. He loves you! He wants to spend time with you. He wants to be your all in all and your only Source of strength, joy and life itself. I'm often deeply moved as I listen to Kim Walker singing this song of love. Read these words, or better yet, plug in your phone and listen. Let God speak to your heart.

He is jealous from me, loves like a hurricane,
I am a tree, Bending beneath the weight of His
wind and mercy
When all of a sudden, I am unaware of these
afflictions
Eclipsed by glory, and I realize just how beautiful
You are
And how great Your affections are for me

Oh, how He loves us so,
Oh, how He loves us, how He loves us so,

We are His portion and He is our prize,
Drawn to redemption by the grace in His eyes,
If His grace is an ocean, we're all sinking,
So heaven meets earth like an unforeseen kiss
And my heart turns violently inside of my chest,
I don't have time to maintain these regrets
When I think about the way,

He loves us,
Oh, how He loves us, Whoa, how He loves us, How
He loves
Yeah, He loves us, oh, how He loves us
Oh, how He loves us, oh how He loves,

*Yeah, He loves us, He loves us,
How He loves us, oh, how He loves!* [88]

**He's amazing, isn't He? He's right there, ready to pick
up where we last left off.**

Worship Him! Commit your time to Him! He deserves our All!

Let's summarize our thoughts before we move on to look at outreach. The solution to changing the direction of any church is always found in good leadership. And good leadership always models appropriate character and behavior before it asks it of others! So that's where you begin. You start by drawing close to God and allowing His Spirit to bring about a genuine heart change. Sit. Slow down. Wait. Rest. Listen. Draw. Let Him deepen your heart for Him. Let Him deepen your heart for people. That's what He wants to do! He'll do it if you let him. It's so easy to get re-visioned in an area of spiritual life and then simply use discipline and enthusiasm to jump in. There's nothing wrong with disciplining ourselves to do the right things in Kingdom living. But how sad if we keep using discipline and never truly experience the Spirit's life-changing power and strength in these areas. That's why we eventually burn out and drop out in areas like lifestyle evangelism. It's often not really coming from the heart and the overflow of the Spirit. Now, let's be honest. In the roller-coaster of life, there are times when we have to do what we know we should do even when we are fried and don't feel like it- like going to work or to church or smiling and treating people nicely even when we don't want to! But we don't want to live that way all the time. I know I don't!

> How sad if we keep using discipline and never truly experience the Spirit's life-changing power and strength in these areas.

Modeling this life of Christ is essential before we go after others and show them a better way. Think of all the times we've wanted to change everyone around us before we've given ourselves the time to demonstrate a track record of personal life transformation. We come home from a church service or a conference with a fresh conviction and desire to obey God in an area where we've not been doing well. But we're so excited that we tell everyone and want them to change too. The problem is, we have no track record. We haven't been modeling it. God has genuinely given us a fresh passion and excitement to obey Him. No wonder we want to tell everyone and get them going too. But let's do it first! Let's draw close to God for that daily strength to live for Him. Let's start making or deepening those intentional relationships with pre-believing neighbors and friends and fellow workers. Let's make it happen as a lifestyle. Let's have two or three actual friendships developing in our lives that we can point to before we start showing other believers how to do it. That's what modeling is all about.

When God saturates our hearts with love, it's actually a reflection of His very own heart. It's Big! In fact, John 3:16 tells us that. . . "God so loved the world that He gave His Son!" And Acts 1:8 again points to the different targets of God's compassion: "But you will receive power when the Holy Spirit comes on you; and you will be my witnesses in Jerusalem, and in all Judea and Samaria, and to the ends of the earth." In other words, God fills us with overwhelming love that begins overflowing on to the people we see all around us. But it doesn't stop there. If we are actually listening to God, we hear His burden for the people of our state or province and our nation. And it's so clear that He cares for dear, lost people all around the world, on every continent and in every tribe and nation. John Piper shares his thoughts as he introduces the book, *Finish the Mission*, a compilation by a number of writers, including Louie Giglio, David Platt and Ed Stetzer. "The contributors to this book are eager for us both to live 'on mission' among our native people and to preserve a place for the biblical category of reaching the unreached. The biblical theme is not merely that God reaches as many people as possible, but all the peoples. He intends to create worshipers of his Son from every tribe, tongue, and nation. The push for being missional captures something very important in the heart of God, but this is dangerous when it comes at the cost of something else essential in the heart of God: pursuing all the nations, not merely those who share our language and culture." [89] We can't ignore the world for our neighbors and we can't ignore our neighbors for the world. But we often do! We're limited in time, energy and resources, and we can't do everything. As leaders, it's critical that we help our people capture God's aggressive vision of reaching our communities and our world for Him. We are on a gigantic rescue mission. We need every one on board. Everyone! It's a lifetime mission. We all specialize in a great variety of ways, but, as a people, we can change the world.

Over one hundred and thirty years ago, a young pastor in his mid-thirties became deeply burdened for lost people everywhere. He became increasingly frustrated at the unwillingness of normal churchmen to join him in this growing compassion in his heart. As he moved through his own crisis experiences with God and also made several pastoral changes, A. B. Simpson finally abandoned the security and prestige that he had attained and started a simple missional ministry to reach the immigrants, the poor, prostitutes and the masses of New York City.

He eventually "established the Gospel Tabernacle, a church in the heart of the city, where all- the poor, homeless, sick, and displaced- would be welcome. Simpson's ministry to New York's immigrants caused him to wonder about the unreached masses throughout the world. It was then that he developed an insatiable burden for the worldwide evangelization of lost souls. Single-mindedly focused on this burden, Simpson began assembling like-minded people with a passion for taking the Gospel to the ends of the earth. He proceeded to hold evangelistic meetings on Sunday afternoons. These gatherings, which then grew to camp meetings and revivals in other locations along the east coast, were essentially the beginnings of The Christian and Missionary Alliance- a denomination fully devoted to experiencing the "deeper life" in Christ and completing the Great Commission." [90]

Simpson's driving burden was to reach "the neglected peoples of the world with the neglected resources of the church." WOW! Things haven't changed a lot in a hundred years. We've certainly impacted the world for Christ. But the need to reach our communities and to reach our world is as great and as neglected as it was in Simpson's day!

God, give us the same burden and vision that You gave to Simpson! Please keep that flame burning in our hearts!

We'll spend the rest of this chapter looking at how we, as a church family, can reach our own communities. Let's remember that, no matter how great the work at home, we can't neglect God's compassion for the world. It's part of the Mission that captures the hearts of our people and builds God's vision into their lives and minds.

Next Steps- Foundations for Outreach Ministries

The most effective way to reach people for Christ is through one-on-one relationships. People wander into all kinds of ministry events and church services out of curiosity and good marketing. But where are they one year later? The Billy Graham Association once acknowledged the fact that only two percent of crusade converts were attending church one year later. That's not a shot at crusade evangelism. It's an indictment on believers and communities inviting the lost with minimal friendship and follow-up! We can't succeed at evangelizing the lost and truly making disciples without believers committing themselves to making and maintaining genuine friendships with lost people. Then why do we do outreach ministries as a church? Because another key to effective evangelizing is partnering together with other believers in this great endeavor.

There are a number of reasons why partnering in evangelism can be so helpful and rewarding.

1) It's fun to do things together with our friends. Why not add the opportunity of influence and bring some pre-Christian friends along for the ride?

2) Events and activities can be created that are attractive to our pre-believing friends. They actually help us bring our friends toward Jesus! We might not be that creative ourselves, but we can enjoy the activities that are created by our church or ministry or small group.

3) Doing activities together can give some of us more courage to actually be involved in evangelistic relationships. As we see our church friends making friends with non-Christians and bringing them to events, it can motivate us to step out and do the same thing.

4) Our "Jesus glow" can rub off on pre-believers and draw them toward the Lord! Dann Spader talks about the 5.3 Principle. It often takes an introduction to and relationship with five or more believers before our friends will come to Christ. While this, obviously, is no rule, experience tells us that when our pre-believing friends encounter other genuine, spirit-filled believers and see Jesus in them, it moves them closer to their own encounter with God! It just works that way! [91]

You can see why outreach events can be so helpful to us as we build relationships with our friends. We often can do so much more to help our friends find Jesus by coming together than we can do alone. The impact of bringing our friends to be with other believers can be so powerful, even when it's simply having fun together. That's why we need to create a culture of evangelistic partnerships that goes far beyond the events and activities of the church. As believers partner up and take their non-Christian friends to dinner, to Starbucks, to the lake, park, movies, camping, hiking or whatever, friendships deepen and lives are touched, one day at a time. That partnering lifestyle is simply enhanced when it's complemented with great activities planned by the church.

Let's begin by looking at the church events and activities that are aimed at outreach. Some leaders today are convinced the church outreach activities and events simply don't and won't work in the 21st century. They feel that culture has changed and nonbelievers are hardened to anything more than a one–on–one relationship with an authentic believer. They've seen so many failures and fumbles that they believe that group efforts simply can't be done. They are wrong! Outreach activities and events are working everywhere, in every part of the continent, in every culture. They just have to be done right by believers who are in committed relationships with their pre-believing friends. The actual activities and events that will work change with every decade and with the shifting of culture. The problem is not that outreach can't work. The real problem is that there are much deeper, more embedded issues in the fiber of the church that need to change.

First of all, many churches do very few, if any, real outreach events in their calendar year. And secondly, most of those activities would never be attractive to non-believers. I've traveled extensively across North America, visiting churches, looking at monthly calendars and talking to both laymen and leaders alike. And this is what I've found. Most churches have become comfortable not doing many if any outreach events. The number one reason is that people don't bring their friends to the events. They may not have any non-believing friends. So non-believers rarely show up! Here's the question- why do events that don't succeed? They're a waste of time and energy and are emotionally defeating. Churches that have tried outreach in the past have given up over time or they've turned these activities into social opportunities for good fellowship. These churches will still occasionally tell their people to invite their friends to a special event, like a singing group or a valentine's banquet or a special Sunday event. But almost no one is inviting and almost no one is coming! What's wrong with that picture? Something **has** to change! Am I describing your church?

Let's talk about why non-believers aren't coming. We've already said that we have to have non-believing friends to invite them. That's the starting point! And we have to have a heart for lost people in the first place to have these friends. This **is** the base problem in our churches. But let's assume, for a moment, that some of our people actually have lost friends. Why haven't they brought them to our church events? My observation- what I've heard and what I've seen- is that most non-believers wouldn't want to come to many of the outreach events that I've heard about. And most of our believers would also feel embarrassed bringing their friends to those events. What am I talking about? I've discovered that lots of our churches are still living in the past when it comes to fun and activities that people really want to come to. There are events that worked in the 70's and 80's that won't work in this new century. A movie night or a singing group or a game night may have worked 30 years ago, but it may not be relevant today. And every community has a unique culture that needs to be reached in a relevant way. A Karaoke night might work in one community and one culture, but it might not work across town in a different culture.

Sometimes we'll take an event that we already have scheduled and we'll make it an outreach event. Now, that's usually unthoughtful at best and probably irresponsible as well. For example, I've discovered churches using missionary conferences and after-church potlucks as outreach events. Let's think about this. What's the attraction of an after-church potluck? Why would your people want to bring their friends to an after-church potluck? They'd have to bring them to church first or it wouldn't make any sense. But if there were no motivation to bring non-believing friends to church, no outsiders would ever show up at that potluck. That's exactly what was happening in one church that I consulted. And here's the second example. Why in the world would churchgoers bring their non-believing friends to a missionary conference? It's hard enough to get our own people to attend!

Most mission conferences are informing the body of our own worldwide mission and are calling for a higher level of commitment. They're generally not created for outsiders who don't have a clue and aren't even ready for the first level of commitment. Now, I'm not talking about a night with a dynamic missionary and an evangelistic message that's shaped and fine-tuned as a purposeful outreach event. That actually might work in the right settings with the right non-believers. I'm talking about doing outreach activities that most non-believers will never come to. Sometimes I wonder, what are we thinking? **Listen- irrelevance is a terrible curse and we don't need to keep living with it!**

> Often the process of outreach partnerships is backwards simply because the passion for outreach comes from the top down and not from the people themselves.

Here's another reason why many outreach activities aren't successful. Often the process of outreach partnerships is backwards simply because the passion for outreach comes from the top down and not from the people themselves. Church leaders plan outreach events and the people don't get involved because it's not their passion and vision. There's no lay-level ownership! On the one hand, leaders have to lead and are righteously motivated when they create these opportunities. They know that the events themselves will remind and encourage their people to be part of the mission. On the other hand, the only way for outreach events to really succeed is for the people themselves to see their value and to actually want them. Picture a church where the body is excited about their own outreach opportunities and I'll show you a church that's truly impacting its world! As leaders, how can we help that happen?

Purpose-Driven Planning- Keys to Change

There are several keys to turning a church in the right direction and creating a successful strategy for evangelistic outreach. All of them require purposeful thinking. We can't just go for it! **It** won't work. **It** will fail. It always has, so it will fail this time too! Going for it is trying to stir up evangelistic fervor without purposeful thinking and praying and planning. I've watched churches do it, and it always lasts for a season, until other priorities take over. And that's why the church is where it is today. So how do we do it right and on purpose?

A Commitment to Leadership Modeling

1) **First of all, we've already said that it takes leadership commitment to live it out, as a Spirit-filled and heart-felt response to God's call and command.** If the leaders won't live it, the sheep won't follow it! The first step of any great plan is called **Leaders First**. Leaders, draw close to God, let His love and presence saturate you through and through, and watch the overflow. Build those intentional relationships with three or four pre-believers. Pray for each other. Share your stories with each other. Help each other stay on track. Be accountable to each other. Make your spiritual journey and your evangelistic encounters a regular part of your sharing at board and leadership meetings. Wave the flag! This is critical! "This is the way of life for all of us as leaders in our church. There is no other way! It's Jesus' way or the highway!"

> Why in the world should someone be in leadership in any church if they're not modeling the mind, character and priorities of Christ?

I've encouraged church boards to make this lifestyle of Great Commandment / Great Commission living a requirement for leadership. Start with the board and then expand that commitment on to the rest of the leadership. I've told church boards to give themselves a two-year window of time so they as leaders can transform or transfer out of leadership. Now, as hard as that sounds, why in the world should someone be in leadership in any church if they're not modeling the mind, character and priorities of Christ? It just doesn't make sense! Yet that's disappeared from the job description for many pastors and most leaders in most churches. We've got to turn that around. We just have to! Will you do it? Will you have the courage to put God's priorities first in your leadership?

Leadership Lifestyle Training

2) **The second key to bringing appropriate change in your church is to get some training and then get going.** My experience tells me that most leaders don't know where to begin when it comes to making intentional friendships with non-believers. Let's talk about that. Find a good book to help you figure it out. There are so many of them! Bring in a training tool, like *The Great Commandment* by Sonlife Classic [92], to teach your leaders the basics of building friendships. Get together and talk about it and help each other. Share your stories with each other. Start partnering and doing some things together with your pre-Christian friends, like having a backyard barbecue or eating out and going to a movie together. As you pray and jump in, watch what God will begin to do! Get ready!

Sonlife Classic teaches us that building friendships is a process that doesn't need to be rushed. We're not in a hurry to get a prize. We're building relationships for the long run- as long as it takes to make a disciple-maker! Dann Spader helps us see that there are three phases in building friendships:

a) **Cultivating-** Building bridges of friendship with people. It's the skill of "breaking up hardened ground" to prepare it for the seed. That means hanging out with pre-Christians and becoming genuine friends.

b) **Planting-** Adding God to the conversation. It's the skill of sharing the seeds of God's truth at the right time, in the right way, and to the right depth. Planting may happen six weeks or six months into a friendship. Don't be in a hurry! Relax! Be sensitive and just let it happen naturally.

c) **Reaping-** Giving a clear presentation of the gospel with a call to respond. It's the joyous privilege of bringing in the harvest. This could happen soon, but it probably will take years, like everything else in life!

Some people are ready to meet God right away. Others have to be walked patiently through years of time spent together. I've had the opportunity to meet people and lead them to the Lord in a short period of time. What an excellent surprise! It's a wonderful and rewarding experience, but I've had very little to do with it. Others have put in all the hard work of praying, cultivating and preparing the soil for the seeds of the Gospel. I've just shown up at the right place and the right time to bring in the harvest.

Most pre-believers will need years of our cultivating a friendship and planting those seeds of truth until they are ready to step forward with that commitment to follow Christ. Love them and give them that time. Don't try to rush the journey. It seldom works! When they commit their lives to the Lord, it will be worth the wait. Then you get to help them move to the next level of growing up as a disciple and a disciple-maker. What a life!

I met Ralph as a young pastor looking for some large meeting rooms at a nearby hotel. He was the facility manager at the hotel. I liked him and decided to begin a friendship with him. I would drop by and visit Ralph every 3-6 months for years. As I cultivated a friendship, I learned all about his life, good times and bad times, and the journey that brought him to the Shasta Inn. It wasn't long before I asked Ralph if he was into church. He went all the way back to Junior High, told his horror story and why he couldn't trust pastors or Christians. I told him that I understood and that a lot of Christians had also done it to me! We began a conversation about the great difference between looking at people and looking to a God who loves us and can radically change our lives. Those seed-planting conversations lasted seven years. Ralph and his wife came to a concert, and it wasn't long before they both gave their lives to Jesus!

I immediately began to disciple Ralph, meeting with him weekly for lunch and spiritual conversations. Ralph and his wife were baptized and began to attend a small group. Three years later, Ralph began leading his own group. And a few years later, he began, on his own, an informal men's fellowship and prayer group that met every Saturday morning. I wish I could tell you the whole story. But I recently had lunch with Ralph, now 30 years later, and I'm so proud to see what God can do if we just open our eyes and get with the plan. Open your eyes!

Church-wide Lifestyle Training

3) **The third key to change is training and releasing the church family to live out this call that God has placed on their lives.** Now, that can't and won't happen all at once. As you as leaders learn to build friendships with non-believers, begin a process of multiplication in your church. Adopt someone and help that person learn to do it too. I encourage church leaders to go through their own process of training and

application before they go after others. That may take a year or two. Then have a plan for multiplication. For example, once 10 leaders are trained and living it, they can help 10 more to go through that same process, and then 20 more, and then 40 more. The goal can't be based on what percentages of our people have gone through training. The goal must be based on what percentage of our people are truly living and multiplying the life of Jesus. Everything must be designed around that goal!

If you want a majority of your people actively involved in life transformation, you'll have to start small, be focused and be accountable. Keep on it. Don't give up. Don't rush it. Take your time. DON'T GET DISTRACTED! This is so important. If you have a plan with a training process and strategy for continual multiplication, it won't take long before a large number of your people are living out this Great Commandment / Great Commission lifestyle. I've already said that small groups can also be an outstanding way to bring a lifestyle change throughout the church. Small group leaders can be part of a leadership commitment and transformation. And as these small group leaders get it and start living it, they can in turn train their groups and use their gatherings as a place for encouragement and accountability.

Remember- in all of this, don't take shortcuts. This isn't about moving as many people through a process as quickly as possible. It won't work. You will fail! And this isn't about getting everyone simply doing a religious practice that God wants us to do. That's not making disciples. That's making more Christians the American way. We don't need more of that. We want the real thing! And that means that we are discipling our people to live out a compassion for the lost that flows from a close, dependent relationship with God. That sort of change doesn't happen over night. It takes time, but it can last forever.

Outreach Planning

4) **The next key to changing this church paradigm starts with the process of assessing and creating great outreach events and activities.** Of course, the first step in that process is discovering what will work for your people and their friends in your community. How do you do that? You ask them! You make it your mission to find out what people are doing for fun. Now, there are things they may be doing that you won't want to do. That's the truth! So find the things that are fun, clean, current and relevant. Put together some teams of creative people who like to come up with things like fun activities and events. They can find all kinds of great ideas online. Subscribe to Outreach Magazine! There are also excellent books written to help us with outreach, like *Outreach in the 21st Century: The Encyclopedia of Practical Ideas.* [93] Find out what other churches are doing. Talk to other churches in your community. Visit churches in other communities. Why not? You have everything to learn and nothing to lose! Send a team to some of our great model churches for their training and seminars and learn what they are doing for outreach. It will excite you and motivate you. There are churches everywhere that have made this journey toward relevance. They've had to make mistakes along the way to discover what really works. And you will too. There's no doubt about it. But here's the question- why not learn from their journey? You don't have to make the same mistakes. Just remember that what works in one church and one community won't necessarily work in another church. Don't be afraid to try new things out. It's better to make mistakes trying than to not try anything at all. If something doesn't work, learn from it, but then move on and don't worry about it.

> It's better to make fewer mistakes, especially when we're trying to build consistency and earn trust from our people and their friends.

Everyone has to learn the hard way. Just remember, it's better to make fewer mistakes, especially when we're trying to build consistency and earn trust from our people and their friends. Our people will not be willing to experiment with the lives of their friends. The sooner you get it and start repeating it, the sooner you'll see the church family settling in to a pattern of partnering in outreach with you.

As you think about outreach, you have to remember that one size doesn't fit all. Our churches are filled with all kinds of people who will make all kinds of friends. That's why you will need a variety of outreach activities and events. We can't do everything, but we can easily break our church down categorically as we think of each of our segment groups. We have our special focus groups, like recovery. We have our age groups like children, youth, young married couples, singles and seniors, and our women's and men's groups. Within those segments, we have people with all kinds of special interests, like camping, hiking, shopping, house-boating, and that list goes on and on. And then there are things that we as adults and as church families can all do together, like picnics, movies, concerts and special Sunday events.

So we need to have year-round outreach plans for both the entire church and for each of our segment ministries. As I said in the beginning of this book, the events themselves need to be planned and calendared so they can be planned for and counted on by everyone in the church. We need to help our people get into the lifestyle of corporate outreach. Here are two balancing principles in planning.

> **a) We don't want to do too many events and activities or we'll burn our people out.** I've seen churches and ministries do too many things for their ability and they end up losing. Their worker bees quit and that's probably the end of those activities. Smaller churches need to do fewer things than larger churches. That just makes sense! But larger churches need to look carefully at all the things that they can do, and they need to decide which ones are truly being effective.

b) We don't want to do too few events and activities or our people will lose the vision and value of doing evangelism together. We are helping them get into a rhythm of bringing their friends to great activities. We don't want them waiting for a long time and losing the habit and passion.

Finding that balance takes good planning and some trial and error. Ministries need to team up and calendar together so they're not overlapping and overloading the very people that they're trying to serve.

Outreach Programming

Leadership

Let's look now at the details of programming for outreach. Outreach doesn't just happen. Someone has to take charge in each segment ministry or outreach will only happen when somebody gets around to it. And someone has to give oversight to all of your church outreach so ministry events are coordinated and not clashing. For example, you don't want a women's event at the same time as a men's event. This will raise issues, like who will take care of the children? And you don't want too many events happening too closely together. This will overwhelm your people and will defeat your efforts. So someone needs to be overseeing the big picture. That can be a volunteer, a ministry leader, a secretary, or a pastor in some churches. As churches become larger, they need more coordination and will create teams of leaders to work together in planning and coordinating. Who's responsible in your church to oversee outreach? And who's responsible for outreach in each of your segment ministries? Do you have an outreach strategy? What is it? Are you doing outreach in all of your segment ministries in your church? And do you have a coordinated plan for outreach throughout your church? Do you team up as leaders to dream, to plan and to calendar together? And is there regular planning and a yearlong timeline to help guide you and build consistency in your activities and events?

Quality and Effectiveness

Every church needs to evaluate the productivity of their outreach activities and events by measuring what they put into it and what they get out of it. Here are two thoughts as you look at what you are doing for outreach:

1) **The more you put into an event, the more you should get out of it.** We all know that. Some churches put little time, money and effort into their outreach and they get what they deserve! If you want good results, you've got to create a good product. I've watched too many churches procrastinate and throw events together at the last minute. There's been poor planning and organizing, late advertising and sloppy set-up. What would you expect to get out of an event like that? Why would anyone show up? And why would your people and the people you're trying to reach come back to something like that? Plan your events and get them well-organized so everyone can get onboard. Know yourself and then pace yourself so you can succeed and not feel the pressure of last-minute scrambling.

2) **If you keep putting good effort into any activity and getting limited results, you need to stop it and do something else.** All of us have tried a great idea and have discovered that it doesn't work. The only way you can know that a good idea works or doesn't work is to try it. Do your best! Plan well, organize well, recruit enough workers, do nice, attractive flyers and excellent advertising, promote the event and build enthusiasm. And watch and see what happens. People may not come. Sometimes it just works that way. We may like our idea, but others may not. Or we may have planned our event on the wrong day or week or month. As they say, timing is everything.

Here's a tip on trust and events. You will have to earn the trust of your people before they will bring their friends to your outreach activities. Count on it! People don't want to be embarrassed by bringing their friends to a mediocre event. They'd rather come alone than face the pain. Over many years of pastoring, I felt so defeated every time we started a new outreach ministry and our people didn't bring their friends. But I learned that our church family needed to test the waters first to check out both the quality and the temperature of the event. Why not? We could hope that they would trust us first, but this seems to be the way it often works.

As a developing church, we came up with the idea of doing a Hawaiian Luau out on our lawn in September as an outreach event. We worked so hard, planned everything out, and recruited a large team of workers to do hundreds of tasks. We had the sand, the lights, the tiki torches, fountains, loads of decorations, ocean sounds, Hawaiian music, appetizer and dessert stations and so much more. It was first class for a medium size church. Our program was fantastic- it was fun and entertaining, with just the right amount of worship and good news to stir hearts and draw people in. There was only one problem. The 150 people who came were mostly our own people. I was so discouraged and upset! What was wrong with them? We had worked so hard. This wasn't a social event. What I didn't realize was that our people were checking it out. They were seeing first if they liked our Luau and, if they liked it, then they would bring their friends. Well, they did! Every year after that, our Luaus got bigger and bigger. They were filled with pre-believing friends. Our people had taken ownership. It was their Luau now! They used it as one more opportunity to demonstrate that Christians can have fun and that the good news is relevant.

What all of this means is you can't see if an activity works until you try it. I'm assuming that everyone already believes that the activity is a good one and that it should work. And I'm assuming that you've looked for the right timing and don't have clashes with other events in the church or in the city. Try the activity. Get as many people to it as you can. See how it works. Test it like a dress rehearsal. Assess it and work out the bugs. Then do it again. Make it even better. Practice makes perfect! If people aren't bringing their friends, ask them why. Learn everything you can to make the event all that it can be. If you keep learning and keep trying and people, as a whole, won't bring their friends, there will be that time that you need to stop. It may be after three to six attempts, but it's just not working! Either the event isn't what your people want or your people aren't ready to do that kind of outreach event. Stop doing it! But don't take it as a defeat. Take it as a challenge. Don't give up! It's back to the drawing board. But please don't keep doing the event! At best, it's turned into a church social and it's using up time, energy and resources that were intended for outreach. It will give you, as a church and as a ministry, the illusion that you are doing outreach when you are not!

It's so essential that you stay focused and remain purpose-driven in your pursuit of genuine partnerships with your people in this critical area of ministry. Most of our people have been in the habit of **not** inviting friends to events for years. You may get excited about a new chapter for your church, but many of your people haven't gained that excitement yet. Be patient with them and bring them along. Live it, preach about it, teach on it, and begin to train your people how to also live it. But please don't move into the old pattern of accepting outreach events when there's no one attending from the outside.

Assessing Your Events

It's essential that you team up and assess your events and activities so you know if you are really being effective and achieving your goals. Don't try to do a fair assessment by yourself. We're all biased, whether we see it or not! There's great synergy that happens when we put the right people together brainstorming, assessing and working on solutions for greater performance and effectiveness. So bring that team together. Here are some of those questions that you need to ask. How well did we plan our event? Did we plan it early enough to organize, recruit, delegate and prepare properly? Did we do a good job of advertising and getting the word out on our event? What should we have done differently or better? Were we able to build quality into our event? Was it creative, relevant, and attractive? Did people have fun and enjoy themselves? Was it purposeful? What was our purpose and did we achieve it? Who was our target audience and did they come? Why or why not? How easy was it to invite people to this event? How could we improve that? How satisfied are we with the event? What would we change? Did our own people like the event? Did they bring their friends? Why or why not? Will they bring them next time? What percentage of our people attending brought friends? What percentage of attendees were friends? Did the friends seem to enjoy the event? Do we think they will come back? How can we increase the percentage of friends and outsiders coming to this event? Are our percentages increasing each time we do this event? Why or why not? I'm sure more questions will come as you team up and work to bring out your best.

I've already shared the story of a couple arriving at our church, and the wife having a great idea for a women's outreach ministry. As we released Jackie to do her dream, 40 women were recruited to do the bimonthly event and 150 women were showing up. Women found the Lord every time one of these events took place. It was wonderful. But here's the rest of the story. It was so great that women starting inviting their friends from other churches. And these women would pay for entire tables and would bring all of their church friends. Pretty soon, we were filling up with Christians. We

were exchanging our original purpose for a great Christian women's social club. Now, Jackie and I decided that that could not be. We had to return to our original purpose and intent or we would stop the whole thing. The next month, Jackie did the hard thing and told those dear women from other churches that we would help them start their own outreach ministries. At the same time, she invited them not to keep coming. It worked! They stopped coming and we were able to rescue our ministry and return it to its original intention. Think of all the ministries that have started out with purpose, have slowly drifted off course, and there has been no intervention. The sad truth is, our churches are filled with them!

Purpose-Driven Events

It's important to clarify the focus of each of your events. Different events should be created for different types of non-believers. We've seen how segment ministries will focus on their specific group for outreach. But we also need to realize that all non-believers fall into three different camps. Not every friend should be brought to every event. Some of them aren't ready to hear the gospel. But they won't be offended having fun with a group of Christians. Others may be ready to hear the gospel in a church setting, but they might not be open to an evangelistic appeal.

We've talked about a process of bringing people toward God that involves three phases- cultivating, planting and reaping. Dann Spader and Sonlife Classic talk about complementing these phases with ministry activities. [94] If we **are** in relationship with pre-believing friends, it would make sense that our partnering events with the church would also fit into these same three categories. We want:

1) **Cultivating activities and events**: to build bridges of friendship between a larger group of Christian and pre-Christian friends. These events are nonthreatening, fun, nonreligious opportunities to make friends and get past the weirdness that Christians and non-Christians often feel about each other! Christians will leave events like this feeling encouraged, with a greater confidence to move forward with their friends. Non-Christians will leave realizing that Christians aren't as strange as they thought they were and happy that they didn't get hammered with the gospel. The key to a cultivating event is that all the believers there know the purpose is to expose non-believing friends to Christians first and not to the gospel- yet. When everyone in a church or ministry understands this purpose, it brings great freedom. And as they learn to trust each other, these events can be very helpful bridges for everyone!

2) **Planting activities and events**: where we can bring our friends and know that activity will include some form of testimony or gospel presentation that my friends can hear. The goal isn't to see people get saved at the event. It's to share some component of Christian living and to help bring people one step closer to salvation! That's the total difference between a cultivating and a planting event. You can have the same ministry outreach picnic at the lake, and by adding a singer or testimony or speaker, you've changed a cultivating event into a planting event. Each of them serves a valuable purpose. By providing both cultivating and planting activities throughout the year, you allow your people to decide what is best for their friends at the stage that they are at. You can see how important it is to clarify your purpose and to then to make that clear to your people. Again, as they understand these differences and begin to use them with intentionality, it will give them great freedom as they build friendships and partner with other believers on the journey!

3) **Reaping activities and events:** where the purpose is to ultimately share a clear presentation of the gospel, asking the pre-believers in the audience to respond. All of us know that that presentation will happen, so we bring our friends, knowing they will hear the gospel and will be asked to respond. We've been talking a lot with our friends about Jesus and what it means to be a Christian. We feel it's the perfect time for them to hear it from someone else as well. Harvest and Luis Palau crusades are an example of reaping events. Easter and Christmas events, special Sundays and many other gatherings can be used as great reaping opportunities.

It is so good when we create cultivating, planting and reaping outreach activities and events throughout the year in our segment ministries as a church. All of our departments are then on the same page, working together with a matching focus and vision to reach friends for Christ. By doing that, we are providing our people, in every ministry, with the same pattern and opportunity to bring friends to just the right events that match their spiritual needs.

Outreach Events and Activities

Let's look at some of the things that churches are actually doing in the area of outreach. As you read through this section, you'll want to begin thinking about what you've been doing for outreach activities and events and what you think might work in your church culture and your community. As you look at each area, think about your church as a whole and about your own segment ministry. And think about how you would divide your events into cultivating, planting and reaping. You'll see that many activities naturally will fit into these categories, even if you haven't thought about it before. Start thinking about a year-long calendar filled with the right number of cultivating, planting and reaping activities for all of your church ministries.

Church-wide and Adult Outreach

There are all kinds of things that you can do as an entire church family. Most churches decide on about four to six events to do together each year and they often frame them around holidays and the four seasons. For example:

> **Spring-** Easter provides the perfect opportunity for special events and a great outreach Sunday. Churches will do pancake breakfasts, concerts, musicals, movies, sunrise services and amazing worship gatherings designed to celebrate the glory of the living Christ.

> **Summer-** This is our great church family time for outdoor adventures of all kinds. Churches will do picnics, concerts, fourth of July events, field trips to ballparks, lake and ocean camping and barbecues, to name a few.

> **Fall-** This kick-off season is just right for all kinds of thematic events, from great luaus, and outdoor festivals to harvest celebrations and hayride parties.

> **Winter-** Christmas again opens the door for a month of church-wide parties and events, including several great weekend gatherings.

Seize the Moment! Don't miss the opportunity to use the holidays and seasons to impact your community with the gospel. More visitors will come to church on Easter and Christmas than any other time of the year. They're still aware of the season and its religious overtones, despite Santa and the Bunny. If you have something great to invite them to, they will come with their friends. Great doesn't have to be big and spectacular. All the big churches started small and worked hard to do great outreach events. That's one significant reason why they grew. So you can too! Do your best at creating a quality event and watch what happens.

As a pastor, I always saw Easter and Christmas Sundays as great opportunities to tell lost people about Jesus. I had seen it as a pastor's son, so it was just logical to seize the moment and use them as outreach events. So we would create, plan, organize and present amazing services with worship, video, drama, music, lights and a mini-sermon, all clearly unfolding the gospel message with an opportunity to respond. Every inch of those services was designed to demonstrate the life of Jesus to seekers. We did it as a little church and we kept doing it as we became a large church. I lived for these Sundays! They were so exciting! We advertised and motivated our people to bring their friends. And did they bring their friends. We were packed out to the brim every Christmas and even more on Easter. Many, many non-believers were saved every year! Attendance always went up after those Sundays. And as we grew and kept building new buildings, the same thing happened over and over again.

Then, after 27 years of pastoring, I became a church health consultant. You can imagine my surprise and shock as I discovered that loads of churches didn't use those Sundays for outreach at all. I couldn't believe it! I found that many of my pastor friends had simply never thought about it. They saw Christmas and Easter as great celebration events for believers. Now, that's true. They are. But the whole reason for the seasons is to tell the whole world the good news of a Saviour! Why keep it in our churches and to ourselves- especially if we know that, if we invite them, they will come? There's a song about that. "Hide it under a bushel, No! I'm gonna let it shine!" You may be one of those churches that hasn't used Christmas and Easter as outreach opportunities. My goal isn't to "guilt and shame" you, but to stir you up and challenge you. Here's a ready-made, twice a year opportunity! Can you see the potential of what this change could mean to your church and to your people? It could change everything!

Have you noticed that these outreach activities are the same things that many churches are already doing, without the outreach, as normal church events. Here's my question. Why waste an event on ourselves when we could use it as an opportunity to reach our friends and neighbors? There's so much to do and so little time! With limited resources and the urgency of reaching people for Jesus, how can we afford to put on events just to make ourselves happy? If the same activity can be shaped to change lives and move people closer to salvation, then let's do it! It seems like a no-brainer. The only challenge is retraining our people to use the event for others and not for themselves. But with the leadership modeling this and influencing a growing circle of believers, it's just a matter of time before entire events can be reborn.

Segment Ministries Outreach Events and Activities

Now let's look at all the segment ministries of the church. These include children, youth, college, singles, single parents, women, men, seniors, other age and ethnic categories, special needs, small groups, recovery and more. Every segment ministry needs to look at outreach opportunities in the context of their own group and the people that their ministry can specifically reach. They can take advantage of the larger all-church outreach opportunities, but they'll also want to do their own thing. Each group will find a unique rhythm of their own on how many events they should do and what they should do. For example, many high school ministries do amazing outreach events on a monthly basis. And some youth groups will also invite friends to weekly outreach activities. Many children's ministries will also do weekly outreach ministries, like Awana, plus a monthly major event on a weekend. But that pace would kill most adult ministries. I've seen women's ministries comfortably planning and executing a bi-monthly outreach throughout the year. I've watched men's groups doing quarterly events with pre-believing friends.

Many segment ministries will do a series of major outreach events for everyone in their group. They'll then complement those with other activities that smaller groups of individuals will take part in. For example, the women's ministry may do a bi-monthly outreach brunch that a large group of ladies will attend. They may promote a Women of Faith Conference as a planting event with a completely different group attending and bringing their friends. They may also plan unique cultivating activities for small groups of women like a trip to an outlet mall or a day-trip to a ballgame.

It's important for each ministry to map out a set of cultivating, planting and reaping events in a calendar year. You will want to give enough variety that you provide good opportunities in each area for your people. You'll want some of them to be so easy to do that they take very little planning and organization. They're just simple and fun, like a day trip. Don't plan too many or you'll burn everyone out! Have fun as you dream together and plan your calendar. Make sure that your events don't clash with city and school activities or the other ministry plans in the church. That's why it's critical that you coordinate your plans together. Be flexible. You'll find that not everything that looks good on paper works out in reality. So try it, adjust it, perfect it and do it over and over again!

Here's an example of an adult ministry outreach calendar:

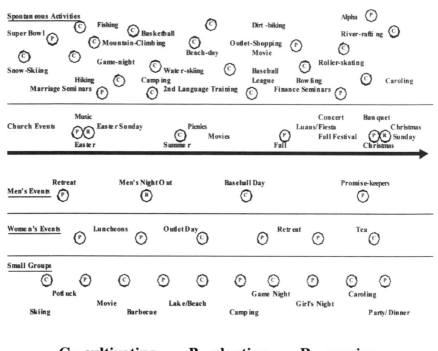

C= cultivating   P= planting   R= reaping

Spontaneous Outreach Activities

Outreach should be a lifestyle and not simply a response to a church program. We need to help our people build outreach into the regular patterns of their lives. The truth is, many of our people do all kinds of fun things, but they often do them with their Christian friends. I often hear of believers shopping, golfing, hiking, swimming, fishing, vacationing, eating or going to ballgames and movies together. So here's the question: Why aren't we inviting our non-believing friends to play with us? Why miss these opportunities of wonderful, spontaneous or somewhat pre-planned fun when we could be using them to build bridges of life? There is only so much time to go around. Most of us don't have the time to add many other events to our busy schedules. But we can use the activities that we are already involved in for a greater purpose! The fun and conversations probably won't change that much. We're not trying to look super-spiritual. We're trying to be real! I can't think of a better way to show Jesus off than to bring our friends along as we enjoy life together. Here are some of the things that so many of us do on a regular basis:

shopping	eating	camping	walking	picnics	soccer
skiing	fishing	eating	hiking	volleyball	sewing
swim-ming	biking	concerts	eating	basket-ball	football
baseball	clubs	exercise	games	eating	T.V.
kid events	karaoke	movies	climbing	bowling	eating

Eating out is a great example. Many of us eat out spontaneously. But with a couple of phone calls, we could invite some friends to come along. And then we could add some neighbors who are pre-believing friends. We'd have a great evening out, we'd still do exactly what we originally were going to do, but we've added purpose and mission to our plan. Planning to rent and watch a great movie? Why not invite a few friends over. Driving over to the outlet mall? Bring some friends along and have lunch together!

Let's train our people to broaden their thinking and their living. Have people in the church share examples of what they are doing and spread those ideas around. Some of our people are less creative than others. That's why it's helpful to get the word out on what types of activities people are doing. Mobilize your people! Help them to activate as individuals, without depending on the church to program all of this. Most of this sort of partnering around activities will and should happen spontaneously, between friends. But it's also great to open it up to others in the church who might want to join in on the fun. Some activities are weeks away and can be easily planned for.

Brief announcements can be posted in a bulletin or on Facebook so others can bring friends and come along. Here are examples:

Sat. / Nov 5- 9 a.m.- Trip to Outlet Mall- meet at Burger King on Madison

Sat. / Nov 12- 6 a.m.- Dirt Biking at Ruffen Hills Call Mike- 245-6785

Tues. Dec 4th- 6 p.m.- Chili's & a Movie-Rocky 15- Call Bill at 244-5631

Weds. Sept.7- 5 p.m. Giants game Call Sally- 234-7649

Remember, the goal is outreach and not simply one more way for us to socialize as believers in our church! It's great to hang out and to be with friends. But why not stay on mission? Why not grow friendships and help others move closer to a relationship with Jesus. That 5.3 principle is always at work. Let's take advantage of it and see what God will do!

Here's what this looks like in a church family. More and more of our people do their fun activities together, both spontaneously and with a plan. Outreach activities and events grow larger as more and more people begin to participate. More pre-believers begin to attend our small groups and church gatherings. More people get saved! So how do we get this started in our church? We already know that it all starts with a plan! Plan it. Team up. Start small. Spread the responsibility. Live it out as leaders first. Talk about it. Share success stories. Build a coalition of doers. Watch it spread!

Servant Evangelism

Jesus constantly modeled a lifestyle of servanthood in everything He said and did. He served in ways we can only imagine. Humility poured out of every word and deed. He loved deeply!

He demonstrated no air of superiority or condemnation. Imagine a leader washing the feet of his followers. Unfortunately, it's just not normal. Leaders are usually wired to give directions and not to serve. Some of us have to fight everything in our nature to stop leading and just be one of the peeps. Jesus had to wrestle with a pack of leaders just like many of us. He pressed them to completely change the way they were wired to think. In Mark 10:43, several of his men asked for an eventual place of rulership in the Kingdom. Jesus' response was amazing: "Whoever wants to become great among you must be your servant." "Guys, here are the rules. Learn to be a servant to all if you want a seat in My kingdom." The way to lead in the Kingdom is through serving. The way to win the hearts of others is through serving. It would only make sense that the way to win the hearts and minds of lost people would be to demonstrate God's love through serving them as well! Jesus went in verse 45 to say: ". . .for even the Son of Man did not come to be served, but to serve, and to give His life as a ransom for many." Reflect on this embodiment of servanthood woven into the very fiber of Jesus' being. And then add to this His heart for the lost!

Jesus modeled the perfection of servant evangelism because that was who He was. He was God in the flesh. He reflected the very heart of God, because He was God. And here's the bigger picture–". . .For God so loved the world, that He gave his only begotten Son, that whosoever believes in Him will not perish, but will have everlasting life." Jesus came as a servant to show us how to come to God. He died for us so we could live with him and for him. He showed us how to serve others so they too can be drawn to the One who died for them.

Let's paint a picture of what servant evangelism should look like today. Servant evangelism flows out of a lifestyle of lovingly and humbly serving people wherever we are. It's not a formal ministry, although it can be reflected in a ministry. It's the result of a close relationship with God that overflows and floods our hearts with love for people everywhere, including the lost and the least! That passion, that love for God and the lost, drives us to do something. We have to do Something! Can you think of a better way to attract people to Jesus than by serving them? We usually try to draw people to God by our meetings, messages and our many words. And they often run. They don't see Jesus. They see religion. But if our actions should be louder than our words, why aren't we doing more? One hundred years ago, liberal churches jumped at the opportunity to serve people with needs, largely because they had no gospel message. And we allowed them to do what we should have also been doing. Instead, we specialized in delivering the Word and often forgot about living out the Word. We supported good Para-Church ministries, like rescue missions, food kitchens and prison ministries. But, for years, so many in the evangelical community largely ignored the concept of actually living out a life of servanthood as a way to demonstrate the way of Christ. How could we have missed the point and the model that Jesus so clearly demonstrated?

Fortunately, it's become a new day for the church. It's happening everywhere. Churches are teaching their people to live out the gospel in their everyday lives. They're showing their people how to use their gifts and skills to make a difference in their own neighborhoods and communities. They're helping them see that if we are willing to give ourselves to the real needs of people around us, those people may begin to actually believe the goods news we also carry. So let's serve the lost. Let's serve our community. Let's learn to look like Jesus, as leaders, as believers and as churches. Let's model and then focus on a never-ending flow of generous living- with our time, energy, talents, resources and money. Imagine a congregation of disciples who are so filled with love that they are caught doing regular acts of kindness, living and giving, all the time, on purpose. I believe these would be the happiest people on earth!

What does servant evangelism look like? I see it everywhere! It's loving your neighbors and then discovering and meeting their needs. It's taking time to listen to your older or younger neighbor. It's taking a meal to a sick friend from work. It's pulling a neighbor's weeds when no one notices. It's paying for the utility bill of someone who has no other option. It's carrying groceries for an older woman or man. It's babysitting for a young couple. It's fixing a neighbor's porch or helping put in a new light bulb. It's going with a friend to bail out her son. It's sitting with that young, unmarried pregnant girl and showing her unconditional love! It's loving people at work, listening for opportunities to serve and then serving them. It's opening our eyes, seeing the needs all around us and targeting the ones that grab our hearts. God has made us on purpose, He's given us unique gifts and each a unique outlook on life. He's wired each of us so He can use us to serve Him and to touch lives in our own very special ways. As we draw close to God and listen carefully to His voice, He will use us to care and meet needs where so many others don't and won't.

Now, here's a question: Shouldn't we all be doing servant evangelism in the context of groups and ministries? Can't we serve others better together than we can individually? Yes and no! Yes, we should be doing things together to touch our communities for Christ. We can organize around our common concerns and accomplish so much as we impact others, working together. There are some things that we can do so much better when we have greater numbers of people. As smaller churches, we can join together and do things that we simply could not do on our own. So, yes, there are servant evangelistic ministries that we should do together. But no, we can't serve better together than we can individually! I've already talked about this in the context of ministries in the church, but I'll repeat myself again. Many people put in their two hours a week participating in a ministry or outreach, and they go home satisfied. Are you kidding? That's like going to church for two hours and feeling like you've done your God–thing for the week. The gathering is only the beginning. It's the refueling! It's one small part of a great week in the Kingdom. And that's the same thing when we're serving others. One or two ministry moments can't become a substitute for a life of serving generously–all week long! That type of thinking has created churches filled with watchers in the stands instead of players in the game.

God has called us all to get on the field and play ball. We need to make sure that we're developing a church-wide DNA that realizes that living out loud in the Kingdom is a seven day-a-week commitment. There is no day off in the Kingdom. There are no vacations from the Kingdom. Imagine God signing off for a day of rest or for a week of vacation. We'd be horrified! Imagine a great opportunity to serve someone or to even share with someone, on your vacation. Would God actually set that up? Of course He would! He does it all the time. And I'm just talking about my life. Let's create a culture of serving with all of our hearts, resting appropriately in the midst of our service, and seizing the moment when the opportunity stares us in the face. Don't you agree?

By the way, I love seeing the servant evangelism projects that are showing up in churches, all across this land. They vary like night and day because the issues and needs are so diverse and different in each community. Some churches do a few things, and they do them well. Other churches do lots of servant ministries, and they have the personnel to also do them well. Here's a church feeding the homeless on a regular basis. Look at all the churches teaching English as a second language to Chinese, to Southeast Asian, to Arab, to Spanish, and to Haitian adults, to name a few. There's a church near Hilton Head turning their entire church into a day spa for single moms. And they detail their cars while the ladies are being pampered. Here's a church in Paradise, California, feeding community families, repairing homes, and paying mortgages for needy residents. Their reputation has become so well known that the city officials will call them when they hear of local needs. That's amazing! There's a church ministry sharing with prostitutes and watching them get saved, one at a time. Here's a church in Kapahulu, Honolulu, focusing on after-school care for children, and parents are beginning to see the love. There's a church in Redding, California, raising support for and displaying the works of local artists and filmmakers at regular events. And they then take the proceeds from the tickets and buy supplies for local schools and shoes for local students. Here's an entire church family mobilized to use a Sunday morning to clean up a portion of a neighborhood in a poorer part of town. These are simply a few of thousands of examples of serving showing up everywhere. And I've seen many larger churches doing amazing things modeling this value. Miles McPherson's own heart shines brightly as a pastor in San Diego. He has an endless passion to mobilize people! He describes the critical journey that we all need to take to prepare our hearts for that adventure. In his book, entitled *Do Something*, Miles writes this:

> You were created to do something great. You want your life to count. . .But there's a step we all need to take first: you and I need to recognize that not only is the world broken, but we are broken also. . .Until you are in touch with your brokenness, you won't be able to relate to someone else's brokenness. Until you are able to express yourself through your pain, the cries of those we need to help will only sound like mumbling. . .keep in mind that our "DO Something" is all about allowing Him to do something through us. God has to first do something in you before He can do something through you. [95]

Isn't that true? One of Mile's church's websites, also titled *Do Something!* celebrates an extensive list of community ministries empowered to impact their city in overwhelming fashion. This church has earned an amazing reputation as they have raised hundreds of thousands of dollars to help the city. They've also sent an army of servant evangelists back into the darkness to love people into the light. I love it! No wonder so many of every age and stage of life are coming to Christ through these mobilized believers.

Are you getting the picture here?

Can you see what God is doing?

Are you beginning to see JESUS?

Let's love people wherever we can, just like Jesus he did!

Let's Feed the Hungry and Clothe the Poor,

Hold those Who need Comfort,

And Listen to those desperately wanting to be Heard.

Let's find needs and meet them!

Let's love- aggressively!

Let's sacrifice- generously!

Let's make them wonder Why we Do what we Do

And Why in the World we care!

Sooner or later, they're bound to ask.

And we'll be ready with the answer!

Notes

THOUGHTS ON CHANGE

You miss 100 percent of the shots you never take.
Wayne Gretzy

The best thing you can do is the right thing; the next best thing you can do is the wrong thing; the worst thing you can do is nothing.
Theodore Roosevelt

The dogmas of the quiet past, are inadequate to the stormy present. The occasion is piled high with difficulty, and we must rise -- with the occasion. As our case is new, so we must think anew, and act anew. We must disenthrall ourselves, and then we shall save our country.
Abraham Lincoln
December 1, 1862 in Message to Congress

13. Next Steps- Where Do We Begin?

Our greatest days of ministry are just around the corner. I'm sure of it! Why would God want you to waste all of the lessons and life experiences of your past ten or twenty or thirty or forty years. No matter what you've been through, good or bad, easy or difficult, the best is yet to come. But now the work begins! It's up to you to make the hard decisions to assess all of your ministries and activities, whatever the cost. Can you do that? We have looked at visitors, disciplemaking and our church ministries, from beginning to end. We've talked about all the attractors and distractors that can either draw them in and build them up or leave them out in the cold.

> . . .the original dream and vision can easily get shuffled into the back closet as the church and its programs become more about maintenance than about mission!

Now it's time to Do Something! Here are the tough questions. Can you see what you need to change to truly accomplish this mission that we are called to? What do you need to add? What do you need to faze out? What do you need to revitalize? If you could start over from scratch, would you? That's a tough question to ask, because many of you feel trapped in rigid systems that look impossible to change. And half of you created those systems! As I pastored a small church that became a large church, I watched, as many of the ministries that I helped create took on a life of their own! They grew–out of control! Ahhhh! That can be good or bad, depending on the outcome. An entire church can take a dramatic shift away from its original purposes as it develops and ages. In fact, the original dream and vision can easily get shuffled into the back closet as the church and its programs become more about maintenance than about mission. John Kotter, in his book, *Leading Change*, talks about the eight primary errors preventing necessary change. A big one is ". . .permitting obstacles to block new vision. . .Whenever smart and well-intentioned people avoid confronting obstacles, they disempower employees and undermine change." [96] We can't afford to go on avoiding the issues that need to be confronted if we want God's will for our church. We can't!

Some of you are feeling overwhelmed with the impossibilities of change that you know you face. Where do you begin? You begin at the beginning- with one step at a time. Change always comes one step at a time! Here are some of those steps.

1) Start with vision and value.
2) Let it grow into a conviction.
3) Meet together as leaders.
4) Work through the book and these concepts.
5) Become a team. Unify! Pray together. Assess together. Share the vision!
6) As you focus in on areas that need to change, begin to plan your action steps.
7) Develop that disciplemaking process if you don't have one.

Let's break down each of these concepts and talk about the steps we need to take to get to where we want to be.

1) **Start with Vision and Value.** Do you want to make real disciples? Do you want to reach lost people for Christ? Do you want to mobilize your people to be all that God wants them to be? Is this God's will for your church? These are the big questions! If you don't have that vision and these values, the changes that you attempt won't be worth it and will produce temporary results at best. Long-lasting, life-transforming change has to be driven by hearts that are captured by vision. And vision has to begin with you! Vision starts at the top. As leaders, you set the agenda for the church. Nothing will change if God doesn't get ahold of your hearts first! Leaders first! The starting point is remembering God's plan for your church. The starting posture is on our knees with open hearts.

God, we want to be all that You intend for us to be as a church and as leaders. Open our eyes to see Your will. Forgive us for our willingness to be less than what You called us to be! Lord, we want our church to be filled with devoted disciples who love You and love to serve You. We want to be filled with your Spirit. We want to be a people aggressively reaching our lost friends and neighbors and then making them into disciples. Help us as leaders to be First. Fill us with your Spirit! Break us of self-centered living! Fill us with a fresh love for You, our dear church family and the lost! Lord, please begin with us!

2) **Let this grow into a Conviction.** James tells us that if we draw close to God, He will draw close to us. Vision and values die quickly when they don't become the conviction of our hearts. We're so fickle! We can be deeply moved one evening and we can forget it completely by the next week. Isn't that true? That's why we need God's help. We can expect Him to build conviction in our hearts as we discipline ourselves to draw close to Him. It works that way. We draw closer and closer, and everything begins to change! If we want genuine change to take place in our churches, it has to begin with us. It can't be built on a great idea, a program or plan. It must be founded on the deep conviction of our heart that's actually transforming our own thinking and actions! People will listen when they see God's conviction firmly rooted in our souls.

3) **Meet together as leaders.** One leader can't change a church. A good leader will stand in front of the pack. But he can't possibly bring change by himself. It takes a team of leaders to bring about the type of change that we're talking about. Start with a few key leaders. Get the right people in the room! Build consensus.

Expand the group. Bring more on board. Make sure that you compensate for your weaknesses and the weaknesses of the group. It will take an entire team of leaders to effectively work through the concepts, the obstacles, the solutions and plans for real change. For example, a group of highly energized, creative visionary leaders must have someone in the room who can see the details, help organize the plan and help get it done.

Many years ago, I found a simple booklet that has helped me see leaders through a whole new perspective. The writer described the need for four types of leaders on every church board or leadership team. They were Visionary Leaders, Organizational Leaders, Analytical Leaders and Servant Leaders. We've all read of dozens of ways that we can look at people that work with us. But I've never forgotten this concept. These four perspectives will always help us to clearly see the best way to our end goals. We've got to surround ourselves with people who are different than us. Or we'll never get the job done! It may feel good to have a board or team filled with visionaries, but we'll never discover the problems in our plan until we do it and fail. A balanced leadership team with everyone committed to each other and to the same goals can achieve amazing things.

Now, analyzers can be dream-killers if they don't understand their role. I once had an analyzer on my board who was the negative voice on every decision we made. It was awful! I wanted him off the board so badly, after years of pain-filled meetings, until I realized the value of this concept. One day, he approached me to quit the board, tired of being the lone voice of reason and restraint. I told him that I actually needed him to be a part of our team, not as a negative dissenter but as our positive analyzer on the team. Can you believe it? I was out of my mind! I was taking a giant risk. But I told him that we needed him to help us trouble-shoot and accomplish the goals and not just shoot them down. He became one of my most valuable players on the team. He turned positive! He became a great supporter. It was amazing! I must add that I believe God led me to do that. Not every analyzer can handle visionary thinking. Get the right people in the room. I've shared all of this to again say that we need others in the process of change. And we need a balance of others so we're not just fortifying our own perspective. We all have far too many blind spots for that to work out well.

4) **Read the book first and work through its concepts.** I would recommend reading through this book individually and taking notes through each chapter as leaders. Underline or circle key areas for discussion later on. Then begin meeting as leadership teams, wrestling through major concepts first. Start with the big picture. For example, understanding why you must have a biblical End Product is so much more important than working on the details of your worship service. It will be tempting to skip the big picture to dial in the details. Watch out! If you aren't unified and speaking with one voice as a church-wide leadership team, you will lose! As you understand what you are doing, what changes need to take place will become so much clearer.

5) **Do the Assessment.** After you've read through the book, buy and do the assessment. Have your leaders do the assessment individually at first. It will serve your best interest to get as many people involved as possible. A broad representation of leaders will help you see more clearly and it will also help you sell changes more widely. The assessment will focus on the details of your church and your ministries. It will drive you to look at the hundreds of details that we often become blind to. Bring your leaders together as teams for evaluation, brainstorming and planning.

6) **Become a team. Unify! Pray together. Assess together. Share the vision.** Everyone in leadership needs to be on board. Everyone has something to offer. Everyone brings insight and perspective to the table. Every one brings influence, for the vision or against the vision. It's critical to take the time to walk through the vision, the values and then the changes, so that all of your leaders are in agreement. It may take months of talking together to gain a united vision. It will clearly be worth the wait in the end.

Thom Rainer and Eric Geiger have written an excellent book that I've already mentioned called "Simple Church." Here's their premise: "Many of our churches have become cluttered. So cluttered that people have a difficult time encountering the simple and powerful message of Christ. So cluttered that many people are busy doing church instead of being the church." [97] The book focuses us on four concepts that will help us think together and bring clarity of vision as leaders and as a church community. They are:

> **a) Clarity** is the singleness of purpose, stated in a single phrase.

> **b) Movement** is making sure there is a process of spiritual development that runs through the ministries of the church that fulfills the purpose.

> **c) Alignment** is the process of making sure that all the ministries of the church channel people through a similar movement to fulfill the purpose.

> **d) Focus** is the challenging process of saying "no" to everything that distracts the church from its purpose. [98]

> Buy the book! Applying these principles will help you gain that long-term perspective that we all need to build something that will last!

7) **As you focus in on areas that need to change, begin to plan your action steps. Take one step at a time.** Remember, you need to:

> **a) Rethink** the details of each particular subject,
> **b) Review** the way you are doing what you are doing and
> **c) Refocus** in those areas that you discover you need to change!

This process can be very overwhelming, depending on how many areas of change need to happen. I would recommend that you list your areas into categories, like the chapters of this book and the assessment. Decide which areas have the greatest priority for discussion and change. Write everything down. Put them on a big pad or board so everyone can see. It would be useful to walk through these ideas as a team:

a) What do we want this area to look like in the next year; five years; ten years? What is our preferred future? Is this our perspective or God's perspective? (Write individually. Talk about it as a group. Take your time! This is big thinking!)

b) What sort of changes will we need to make a) right now b) over the next few years in order for this to happen? Why?

c) What are our 2-3 areas of greatest strength that we can build on?

d) What are our 2-3 areas of greatest weakness to work on?

e) What 2-3 areas need to be changed completely?

f) What will this change cost us in the life of our church 1) if we don't do it? or 2) if we do it?

Write down each of the areas that need to be changed. Place them in an order of priority. What comes first? What specifically needs to be done? What will this change cost us- in time, resources, personnel and money? When can we afford to do this change? Place dates on each part of what needs to be done. What's the process? Who's responsible? Assign someone to be in charge of each responsibility. Make sure someone is the leader of change. Who will oversee the big picture to make sure the changes happen?

Here are some even more important questions. What needs to happen before we make any changes? Who do we need to prepare? How do we prepare the congregation? How do we prepare that segment ministry? How do we prepare other leaders? How will we know when the church is prepared enough for this change to happen? Some changes in our church facilities and programming can happen with no fanfare, but it's critical that we prepare the family for major change. Some changes will be far better received after a sermon series or a few family gatherings that help to pave the way. Pastors will jump ahead of their boards and wonder why they are upset. Then boards and leadership teams will jump ahead of the people and wonder why they are leaving or not giving. Slow it down. Get as many people on board for the ride!

Listen! It doesn't matter how long it takes to get this done. It just doesn't. Some of your church problems have developed over decades and decades. If it takes you several years to walk through this process to a place of great health and vitality, do it! I'll repeat myself here for your benefit. Don't rush the agenda to simply get done as quickly as possible. Don't do it! Scratching the surface only prolongs and increases the pain that will inevitably come. Let this process truly expose the issues that need to be addressed. Chip and Dan Heath, brothers and co-authors of *Switch: How to Change Things when Change is Hard,* say this: "Big problems are rarely solved with commensurately big solutions. Instead, they are most often solved by a sequence of small solutions, sometimes over weeks, sometimes over decades." [99] Even the pros have given us time to fix this one. So don't rush it. Fix it!

8) **Develop that disciplemaking process if you don't have one.** <u>This is the Goal!</u> Don't forget it! Change can become addictive and can sometimes become the end in itself. It can feel good to bring healthy change to a church. But if those changes don't get us to God's End Product, we're simply buying ourselves a few more years. Disciplemaking is God's key for the future of His church, until He returns. It will work in any structure, in any

nation, through any language. It will build any church, great or small. Try it! You'll like it!

The Warning

I've watched hundreds of fellow pastors and leaders go to conference after conference, attending seminars upon seminars. I've seen so many of us carrying home bundles of books and bushels of resources, year after year. And I've seen grand ideas and dreams and plans die within weeks, if not days after those events. How does this happen to us? Why can some people go to conferences, bring home the stuff and actually produce radical, church-shifting change, and so many others of us simply can't pull it off? Here's our problem- we can't be something that we're not. And we need to stop trying! We all have a unique and purposeful mix of spiritual gifts, talents and personalities. God has made us all just the way he wanted us. He didn't want one hundred, miniature Rick Warren's, Bill Hybel's, Chuck Smith's or Andy Stanley's. They're one-of-a-kind. Each of them has great strength and great weakness, just like you and me.

Will Mancini does a masterful job of unpacking the key issues of leadership that are critical in this new century. In his book, *Church Unique*, the subtitle describes his own vision for the book- how missional leaders cast vision, capture culture, and create movement. That's what we have to do! Or we will not succeed. Mancini ends his book with a provocative thought:

If you copy someone else's vision, who will accomplish yours? [100]

God has created you and me to be and to do exactly what He's designed us for. WOW! Think about that! We're all uniquely made in the eyes of God, on purpose for a great purpose. We need to learn all we can from each other. We must surround ourselves with those who complement our package of strengths and weaknesses. We need to soak in seminars and conferences and books. But then, we need to spend time with our real Boss, clarifying His vision and focus for our own personal ministry and then our church's ministry. We need to prayerfully sort out the issues and priorities that God helps us bring to the top of our list. Then we need to work the list, one or two things at a time. One step at a time. Don't get overwhelmed by the list–it may be really long. Change can't happen overnight. And it won't happen if you get overwhelmed. So just start and get going!

Once again- don't try to do this on your own. Don't be a lone ranger. It won't take long before it hurts someone- probably you! Working together with others in your leadership is so critical. God planned for most of us to be together in pairs. Solomon told us, in Ecclesiastes 4:9, that. . . "Two are better off than one, for they can help each other succeed." [101] God affirms and life confirms that we accomplish more when we work and think together with others. He created a plurality of priests then and elders now as leaders. In Ephesians 4, Paul wrote that God created and gifted a diverse group of leaders in the church, clarifying that we need each other! He also told the church that we, as a group, are gifts to them. Larger churches have the advantage of teams and staff to drive change in vision and values. But they all were small once upon a time. A handful of pastors and leaders in small settings can implement significant change, all by themselves. But most can't! Most of us need team. We need one or two or five or ten others to start with us, to dream with us, and influence with us. It's hard to stand alone. It's hard to bring change alone. That's why so many churches never change. Pastors try and then give up and give in. Don't do it! Don't try to be a one–man agent of change. It probably won't work. Find the right leaders to partner with for this fresh start. Find people who can dream with you and team together. Wrestle through the issues–together. Begin working the list–together. Hold your ground when difficulty comes–together. And celebrate as God breaks through in hearts and minds–together!

Final Thoughts

I want to leave you with two pictures in your mind as we come to an end. Let's start with the front porch. We began our journey visualizing the scene of a father, looking out across the horizon, patiently waiting on his front porch for the return of his prodigal son. We all know the story and it's message. It clearly portrays the heart of God toward the lost who surround all of us. And it's meant to stir us to compassion and personal action! In II Corinthians 5, Paul says:

> *This means that anyone who belongs to Christ has become a new person. The old life is gone; a new life has begun! And all of this is a gift from God, who brought us back to Himself through Christ. And God has given us this task of reconciling people to Him. For God was in Christ, reconciling the world to Himself, no longer counting people's sins against them. And He gave us this wonderful message of reconciliation. So we are Christ's ambassadors; God is making His appeal through us. We speak for Christ when we plead, 'Come back to God!'* [102]

We speak for God! Amazing! Humbling. Convicting. God is telling us that we all need to be on the front porch, leaning in, with compassion and in anticipation that our friends and neighbors will soon appear on the horizon. All of us! Every single person in our church. We need a big front porch. That's what we've got to build into our people. That's what we need to transform our churches into. That's God's heart and His vision for all of our churches! That's our Hope for tomorrow! That's your Mission, if you choose to take it. And it's your Mission Possible with the Enabling Power of God's own Spirit.

The second picture comes from an airport a few months ago. I was trapped, caught between cancelled flights and airline inefficiency. Tempers were rising as hundreds of people were being herded from gate to gate. As I sat, waiting for change, I noticed that the man beside me had no arms! He had an iPad and a notepad on the floor by his case. He was using his cell phone with his Bluetooth earpiece to patiently talk through flight changes so he could make it home to Canada by that evening. He was a clear-minded, excellent communicator, competently working toward his goal. Did I mention that he had no arms? His legs and feet had become his arms and hands. He quickly maneuvered using his pen and iPad, paper and cell like he had no disability at all. Several of us were watching with amazement and disbelief! In fact, a compassionate woman on the other side of me rushed over to help this guy when we heard that he was being given a phone number to write down. But she was too late. He had already entered it. Unbelievable! What an incredible example of living above the impossible circumstances of life.

Now, some of us feel handicapped! And some of us are handicapped. It may be the board, the building, the location, the people, the staff or even the pastor. Did I say the pastor? Just kidding! In reality, many of us feel handicapped by our own lack of talent or personality or gifting or anointing or intellect or. . . Heh! That's life! Join the club. Let's face it. We're all handicapped. God picked us that way. He even tells us that in the beginning of Romans. And He's placed us in a world of handicaps and difficulties. Now, here's the question. What are you going to do about it? Anyone can whine. But God picked you, called you and placed you because He believes that you can make a difference. You can overcome your handicaps, just like my neighbor in the airport. You can change your world! You can!

Let's summarize our thoughts. Change is critical. But change is hard. Change opens doors of great opportunity. Change can take away our comfort. Change makes life better for some people, but it's often at the expense of other people. That's the difficulty with change. You just can't please all of the people, ever. Never! So if you want to die with your church, don't change anything! But if you want God's great future for your church, you'll have to take risks and accept the pain that comes with change. Dave Ferguson calls crisis the birthplace of innovation. " It's in the middle of a crisis that we come to the realization that either the end is near or a new future is being born. On the verge of a crisis, we are also on the verge of our own greatest moment. It's at that moment that we must decide: innovate or die!" [103] God help us all to see the magnitude of our current crisis so we are humbled, dependent and willing to do whatever it takes to bring about God's Change!

We are in this together, with God! It's His church. It's His plan. We're His leaders. It's His mission. It's His heart. Lost people matter to God and He wants them Found! He's the one who commands us to be disciples who make disciples who Go. He's the one who is calling the church back to His original plan. He's beside us all the way. That's the promise. In fact, He's in front of us, leading, empowering, preparing, protecting, setting us up for His preferred future.

He has a great plan for us.

Let's find it and accomplish it.

We can do it! Let's go!

Change It Up!

Endnotes

Chapter 1

1 John Kotter, Leading Change, (Boston: Harvard Business School Press, 1996), 10-11

2 Clayton Christensen, Innovator's Dilemma, (Harvard Business Review, May 1, 1997)

3 George Barna, website

4 Tim Cook Interviewed by Brian Williams, NBC News, December 2, 2012

5 Wired Magazine, Clive Thompson, November, 2012

6 Jim Collins, Good to Great, (NY: HarperCollins Publishers, 2001), 11

7 Elmer Towns, Ed Stetzer and Warren Bird, 11 Innovations in the Local Church, (Ventura, CA: Regal Books, 2007), 17

8 Peter Drucker, Management Challenges of the 21st Century, (NY: HarperCollins, 1999)

9 Collins, Good to Great, 1

10 Robert E. Quinn, Deep Change, (San Francisco: Jossey-Bass, 1996, 140

11 Charles Snow, 5 Ministry Killers and How to Defeat Them, (Minneapolis: Bethany House, 2010), 13

12 Ed Stetzer, Outreach Magazine, May/June 2012

13 Collins, Good to Great, 65

14 Robert E. Logan, Beyond Church Growth, (Westwood, NJ: Fleming H. Revell, 1989), 74

15 Rick Warren, The Purpose-Driven Church, (Grand Rapids, MI: Zondervan, 1995), 81

16 Definition of Change, Wikipedia, the Wikimedia Foundation

17 Holy Bible, New Living Translation, copyright © 1996, 2004, 2007 by Tyndale House Foundation. Used by permission of Tyndale House Publishers Inc., Carol Stream, Illinois 60188. All rights reserved.

Chapter 2

18 John Kotter and Holger Rathgeber, Our Iceberg is Melting, (St. Martin's Press, 2006)

19 George Barna, website

20 David Kinnaman and Gabe Lyons, Un Christian, (Grand Rapids, MI: Baker Books, 2009), 24-26

21 David Olson, The American Church in Crisis, (Grand Rapids, MI: Zondervan, 2008), skewed poll numbers

22 Ed Stetzer, "Christianity isn't Dying", USA Today, 10/19/12, 10A

23 Dan Spader, Sonlife training content

24 Alan Hirsch & Dave Ferguson, On the Verge, (Grand Rapids, MI: Zondervan, 2011), 24

25 ibid, 13

26 Dale, Robert, To Dream Again, (Nashville: Broadman Press, 1981), 8

27 Robert Coleman, The Master Plan of Evangelism, (Westwood, NJ: Fleming Revell, 1963), 18

28 Kyle Idleman, Not a Fan, (Grand Rapids, MI: Zondervan, 2011), 18

29 Reggie McNealy, 27

30 Neil Cole. Organic Church, (San Francisco: Jossey-Bass), 2005, 50

31 Hugh Halter & Matt Smay, AND, (Grand Rapids, MI: Zondervan, 2010), 22

32 Alan Hirsch, The Forgotten Ways, (Grand Rapids, MI: Brazos Press, 2006), 55

33 Ibid, 517

34 Nelson Searcy, Ignite, (Grand Rapids, MI: Baker Books, 2009), 17,19

35 Ferguson and Hirsch, On the Verge, 289

36 ibid, 40

37 ibid, 41

38 Warren, The Purpose-Driven Church, 16-17

39 Evangelical Fellowship of Canada, Church and Faith Trends, August, December 2010

40 Lee Strobel, Inside the Mind of Unchurched Harry and Mary, (Grand Rapids, MI: Zondervan Publishing House, 1993), 15

41 Jim Henderson and Matt Casper, Jim and Casper Go to Church, (Barna/Tyndale, 2007), 147

Chapter 3

42 Aubrey Malphurs, Advanced Strategic Planning, (Grand Rapids, MI: Baker Books, 1999), 116

43 Mark Mittelberg, Becoming a Contagious Christian, (Grand Rapids, MI: Zondervan, 1994)

44 Dan Spader, Growing a Healthy Church, (Chicago: Moody Press, 1991)

Chapter 4

45 Mark L. Waltz, First Impressions, (Loveland, Group Publishing, 2005), 12, 41, 24

Chapter 7

46 Brian Orme, Outreach Magazine, May/June 2012

47 Ed Stetzer and Thom Rainer, Transformational Church, (Nashville: B & H Publishing, 2010,) 104.

Chapter 8

48 Stephen A. Macchia, Becoming a Healthy Church, (Grand Rapids: Baker Books, 2003), 44

49 Kem Meyer, Less Clutter Less Noise, (Camby, IN: Thirty: One Press, 2009), 17

50 Randy Alcorn, The Treasure Principle, (Multnomah Books, 2001), 8

51 John Maxwell, Thinking for a Change, (NY: Warner Books, 2003), 33

52 Andy Stanley, Communicating for a Change, (Colorado Springs, CO: Multnomah Books, 2006), 169-170

Chapter 9

53 Logan, Beyond Church Growth, 116

54 Andy Stanley and Bill Willits, Creating Community, (Colorado Springs, CO: Multnomah Books, 2004), 45

55 George Barna, Growing True Disciples, (Colorado Springs, CO: Waterbrook Press, 2001), 122

56 Nelson Searcy and Kerrick Thomas, Activate, (Ventura, CA: Regal, 2008), 15, 28

57 Stanley and Willits, Creating Community, 102-109

58 Nelson Searcy, Fusion, (Ventura, CA: Regal, 2007,) 27-28

59 Holy Bible, New Living Translation

60 Erik Rees, S.H.A.P.E., (Grand Rapids, MI: Zondervan), 2006 22, 24

61 ibid, 176

62 Gary McIntosh and Glen Martin, Finding Them, Keeping Them, (Nashville, TN: B & H Publishing Group, 1992), 91

Chapter 10 Facility and Programming

63 Thom Rainer and Eric Geiger, Simple Church, (Nashville, TN: B & H Publishing Group, 2006), 204

64 Collins, Good to Great, 11

Chapter 11

65 Dietrich Bonhoeffer, The Cost of Discipleship, (New York: Macmillan, 1937)

66 Dwight J. Pentecost, Design for Discipleship, (Grand Rapids, MI: Zondervan, 1971), 11

67 Francis Chan and Mark Beuving, Multiply, (David C Cook, 2012), 7

68 ibid, 26

69 Erwin McManus, An Unstoppable Force, (Loveland, CO: Group Publishing, 2001), 202-203

70 Bonhoeffer, The Cost of Discipleship, 64

71 Dan Spader, Live 2:6, Sonlife Classic, 2009

72 John Piper, Finish the Mission, (Wheaton, Il: Crossway, 2012), 20

73 Mike Breen, Building a Discipling Culture, (SC: 3D Ministries, 2011), 19-20

74 Gary McIntosh, Beyond the first Visit, (Grand Rapids: Baker Books, 2006), 132, 144

75 Hawkins, Greg and Parkinson, Cally, Reveal and Move, (Willow Creek/Zondervan, 2008, 2011)

76 Hawkins and Parkinson, Move, 22-25

77 Barna, Growing True Disciples, 107, 2

78 Neil Cole, Church 3.0, (San Francisco: Jossey-Bass, 2010), 186

79 Breen, Building a Discipling Culture, 212

80 Leroy Eims, The Lost Art of Disciple Making, (Grand Rapids, MI: Zondervan, 1978,) 51

81 Coleman, The Master Plan of Evangelism, 35

82 Barna, Growing True Disciples, 118

83 Chan and Beuving, Multiply, 15

84 Warren, The Purpose-Driven Church, 144

85 Holy Bible, New Living Translation

Chapter 12

86 Craig Groeschel, The Christian Atheist, (Grand Rapids, MI: Zondervan, 2010), 17

87 Wikipedia.org- How He Loves

88 John Mark McMillan, How He Loves, independent release from the album The Song Inside the Sounds of Breaking Down, 2005

89 Piper, Finish the Mission, 27

90 CMA Website

91 Dan Spader, The Great Commission, (Olathe, KS: Growing a Healthy Church)

92 Dan Spader, The Great Commandment, (Growing a Healthy Church, Olathe, KS)

93 Outreach in the 21st Century: The Encyclopedia of Practical Ideas, (Loveland, CO: Group Publishing, 2007)

94 Spader, The Great Commandment

95 Miles McPherson, Do Something, (Baker Books, 2009), 10-12

Chapter 13

96 Kotter, Leading Change, 10-11

97 Rainer and Eric, Simple Church, 19

98 ibid, 67-68

99 Chip Heath and Dan Heath, Switch- How to Change Things When Change is Hard, (NY: Broadway/Random House, 2010), 44

100 Will Mancini, Church Unique, (San Francisco: Jossey-Bass, 2008), 234

101 Holy Bible, New Living Translation

102 ibid

103 Ferguson and Hirsch, On the Verge, 311

Unless otherwise indicated, famous quotes have been found, at random, everywhere on the internet, at sites like famousquotes.com and quotes.com.

Your Next Step

Moving Forward as a Team!

This Companion Assessment Tool provides the opportunity to take your entire church leadership team on a significant journey toward transformation and change. Look at yourselves like perhaps you never have before. Discover where you are either distracting or attracting visitors. Examine hundreds of details throughout your ministry. Read the book. Go through this assessment first individually and then as a team. Then form action plans that will help you move to the next level of ministry and disciplemaking!

The Change It Up
Assessment

From the Outside Looking In

**Get Rid of those Roadblocks
To Healthy Church Disciplemaking
and Multiplication!**

Copyright © 2023 Change It Up Ministry   Pete H. Edwardson

For more information, to order the Assessment and to get more copies of Change It Up, go online and visit CHANGEITUP.COM

DATE DUE

CPSIA information can be obtained at www.ICGtesting.com
Printed in the USA
BVOW081308230513

321508BV00001B/1/P

9 781626 974234